The Hohokam–Akimel O'odham Continuum

Untitled painting by Amil Pedro of an Akimel O'odham archer using a recurved bow.

Gila River Indian Community
Anthropological Research Papers
Number 5

The Hohokam–Akimel O'odham Continuum

Sociocultural Dynamics and Projectile Point Design in the Phoenix Basin, Arizona

by
Chris Loendorf

Gila River Indian Community
Cultural Resource Management Program
Sacaton, Arizona

About the Author

CHRIS LOENDORF (Ph.D. 2010, Arizona State University) is a
Project Manager for the Gila River Indian Community Cultural
Resource Management Program and an Adjunct Faculty member
at the School of Human Evolution and Social Change at
Arizona State University.

Cover: Top background, map drawn by Kino of southern and
central Arizona (1701–1702). Bottom background, watercolor
painting of an Akimel O'odham village by Seth Eastman.
Front cover figure, Owl Ear with calendar stick (from Russell 1908).
Back cover figure, Pee Posh with bow and stone tipped arrows
circa 1875 (photograph by Elias A. Bonine).

Produced and Printed in the United States of
America, by Statistical Research, Inc.

ISBN 978-0-9723-3475-4

CONTENTS

Contents

LIST OF FIGURES

LIST OF TABLES

FOREWORD

This volume presents archaeological, ethnohistorical, and ethnographic evidence that shows remarkably long-term continuity in material cultural traditions in the Phoenix Basin. This is the fifth publication in the Gila River Indian Community (GRIC) Archaeological Research Papers (ARP) series, and the third that employs the extensive survey data that have been collected as part of the Pima-Maricopa Irrigation Project (P-MIP). Investigations undertaken during this project include survey of more than 58,000 hectares (144,000 acres) of the Community, where more than 1,300 archaeological sites have been recorded to date. Unlike much of the remainder of the Phoenix Basin, until the recent P-MIP work—and other tribal investments, including new home construction—were undertaken, the more than 150,000 hectares (371,000 acres) of the reservation remained underdeveloped. As a result, archaeological data from the area are comparatively pristine, and the GRIC data set is one of the most expansive and inclusive available for all of southern Arizona.

This research follows an earlier ARP publication by Loendorf and Rice (2004) on the nearly 1,000 projectile points that have been collected during P-MIP survey. Metric and attribute data, as well as images of all points analyzed in this volume are available in Loendorf and Rice (2004). The focus of the previous research was exclusively on the temporal associations of point types, and the following research explores broader social and cultural implications of the point data.

The GRIC encompasses the heartland of the Historic period Akimel O'odham (i.e., Pima) habitation area along the middle Gila River in the Phoenix Basin. The association between these people and the Classic period Hohokam who lived in the same area has been debated since Spaniards first visited in A.D. 1694. Despite centuries of speculation and discussion, the relationship between Prehistoric and Historic period populations remains unresolved among social scientists and historians. Data from the Protohistoric and early Historic periods are critical for assessing the Hohokam collapse as well as the continuum between the Prehistoric and Historic period populations. However, until the P-MIP investigations, comparatively little archaeological research had been completed within the GRIC, where Akimel O'odham archaeological data from this time largely occur.

Relationships among the Hohokam and contemporary groups are of considerable importance to the modern Akimel O'odham, and this issue continues to affect their lives in various ways, including matters of cultural patrimony and repatriation cases where their views are undervalued. Although the Akimel O'odham continue to maintain detailed and extensive social histories regarding their past, their perspective has been extensively ignored or misinterpreted. However, Loendorf devotes considerable attention to the Akimel O'odham views of prehistory, which suggest that prehistoric populations fluctuated dramatically over time. This possibility has important implications for understanding the patterning in the archaeological record that is explored in this volume. Ethnohistorical and ethnographic research is also used to generate expectations that are tested against the archaeological record.

This volume by Chris Loendorf is also the second publication in the ARP series to specifically address the Hohokam to Akimel O'odham continuum. The previous research by Wells (2006), which did consider projectile point data, focused mainly on site-based analyses of ceramic data. Due to the nature of archaeological data along the middle Gila River, multiple analytical issues exist if sites are used as the unit of analysis. Because of these limitations, Loendorf uses a non-site-based approach in which larger geographical areas are used to group artifacts, thus providing a different perspective on regional variation in the Phoenix Basin. Using this approach, Loendorf identifies robust patterns in the P-MIP survey data, which are consistent with other lines of evidence, including ethnohistorical and ethnographic observations of settlement patterns and other cultural practices.

In general, projectile point data previously have received comparatively little attention in the Hohokam region. Yet, as the following volume demonstrates, it is possible to use point data to address a wide range of research issues including facets of subsistence practices, settlement patterns, socioeconomic interactions, and inter-societal conflicts. Because stone points are commonly preserved and were produced throughout the archaeological sequence, point data can also be used to address issues of continuity or discontinuity in material culture between prehistory and history. This line of evidence has previously been largely ignored in the Hohokam continuum debate, and Loendorf presents substantial evidence for cultural continuity between the Prehistoric Hohokam and Historic period Akimel O'odham.

M. Kyle Woodson, Acting Director
Cultural Resource Management Program

PREFACE

In *The Hohokam–Akimel O'odham Continuum: Sociocultural Dynamics and Projectile Point Design in the Phoenix Basin, Arizona*, Chris Loendorf examines implications of changing projectile point forms in terms of stylistic, functional, and technological characteristics during the late pre-Hispanic era through the Historic period along the Gila River. Hohokam projectile points stand out in the Southwest, because they reflect the wide stylistic diversity and the greatest complexity in design of any regional subarea, and they appear to have been manufactured by craft specialists in many cases (Crabtree 1973). Because Hohokam flaked stone, even in this most elaborate form, has been given only cursory attention (for exceptions, see Hoffman 1997; Shackley 2005; Sliva 2010), the current study is a groundbreaking contribution to southern Arizona archaeology.

As Loendorf points out for the Akimel O'odham, ethnohistoric (e.g., Hallenbeck 1940; Winship 1896), ethnographic (e.g., Griffen 1969), and archaeological (e.g., Gladwin et al. 1937:95; Lambert and Ambler 1965; Wasley and Johnson 1965) observations across the expanse of the international four-corner borderlands of Chihuahua, Sonora, New Mexico, and Arizona similarly demonstrate that projectile points carry great symbolic and ritual significance as well as more-obvious technological and functional attributes. These combined characteristics make this artifact category particularly useful for the study of an array of anthropological problems. With a far-ranging and intensive review of relevant ethnohistoric, archaeological, and technological literature, the author establishes a comprehensive framework of questions and expectations for his analysis of projectile points in the Middle Gila River area. The summary and bibliography alone make the monograph a valuable resource for scholars conducting research on the topic.

Loendorf's research is one more illustration of the high level of scholarship produced by the Gila River Indian Community's (GRIC's) Cultural Resource Management Program (CRMP) and its commitment to professional contributions relevant to multiple constituencies. The backbone of the GRIC's research program has been a large-scale, full-coverage survey within community boundaries that is the source of the large numbers of projectile points analyzed in this study. U.S. Department of the Interior Bureau of Reclamation funding for the Pima-Maricopa Irrigation Project made possible systematic investigation of more than 58,000 hectares (144,000 acres) of dense pre-Hispanic era and later Akimel O'odham (Pima) and Pee Posh (Maricopa) settlements. Because the layout of new irrigation infrastructure was still in the planning stages during later portions of the field investigations, an extensive survey strategy permitted the subsequent cost-effective avoidance and preservation of many sites. Over time, this large database has been continuously expanded with management-related surveys from other parts of the community, which, in turn, has made available a site inventory that is even more useful as a planning tool for the Tribal Historic Preservation Office.

In addition to its management advantages, full-coverage survey produces more information relevant to a wider range of anthropological problems than any other category of field effort. The quality and strength of the present study would have been significantly different had it relied on sampling or reconnaissance survey or a limited number of excavations. Other investigative approaches would have provided a projectile point sample of limited size and spotty or fragmented spatial distributions that could have masked the significant Prehistoric to Historic period settlement change that Loendorf documents. In fact, given their highly clustered distribution, sites with late Protohistoric and Historic period points might have remained unsampled, or their presence simply unrecognized, if a less comprehensive methodology had been utilized. The interpretive power of full-coverage survey has been illustrated in a variety of other published instances, such as the changing configuration of settlement and irrigation (Woodson 2010), the response to evolving geomorphic landscapes (Waters and Ravesloot 2000, 2001, 2003), and the discrimination of nonresidential vs. residential locations through quantitative artifact measures (Wells, Rice, et al. 2004). The GRIC full-coverage-survey database will continue to provide a context for enriching much of the research that takes place within the community and will become an important point of comparison for the Hohokam region and beyond.

Interest in and documentation of continuity between past and present inhabitants of the GRIC is another programmatic theme evident in the volume. With neither monumental architecture nor an obtrusive archaeological record, contact period Akimel O'odham are often thought to provide few insights for interpreting Hohokam archaeology; some have even claimed that O'odham *rancherías* and the overall population were so dispersed that they might have escaped the devastating diseases of the Columbian exchange. In other words, at a time when many highly visible investigations in the southern deserts of Arizona emphasize cultural discontinuity and collapse before the transition to the Colonial period, GRIC research has provided alternative perspectives by underscoring continuities with present-day peoples that can provide information for the Phoenix Basin archaeological record. For example, post-contact Akimel O'odham settlement dynamics have been used to establish a baseline for understanding similar processes among the Hohokam (Darling et al. 2004), and O'odham song texts and archaeological trails provide the framework for articulating archaeological places and other aspects of the cultural and natural landscape into a ritual geography (Darling 2009; Darling and Lewis 2007). Chris Loendorf's projectile point analyses and interpretations provide another particularly good illustration of the importance of a perspective that highlights cultural continuity.

The Hohokam–Akimel O'odham Continuum: Sociocultural Dynamics and Projectile Point Design in the Phoenix Basin, Arizona, is based on Loendorf's Arizona State University Ph.D. dissertation research conducted as part of the Gila River Indian Community's ongoing cultural resource management studies. Educational outreach by the CRMP, however, is not limited to university-oriented student training and research. One of my first contacts with the CRIC's cultural resource efforts was through its Red Earth Program, an initiative in the 1990s to introduce community high-school students to archaeology, Akimel O'odham culture, and college life. Over a period of several years, we had the opportunity to host Red Earth participants at the Arizona State Museum and the University of Arizona for an entire week of the 6-week program, during which they worked with university archaeologists and Native American students, met with faculty, investigated university programs of future interest, gathered fruits at Stella Tucker's Tohono O'odham saguaro camp, and lived in college dormitories. At least two of these Red Earth program students are now professional archaeologists. The CRMP can truly be said to enhance and involve all parts of the local community, from pre-college to elders, but it also allows a wider appreciation of their connections to the Gila River area's previous inhabitants and the accomplishments by all communities.

Chris Loendorf's volume is the fifth contribution in the GRIC Anthropological Research Papers, and several more are in the pipeline. This monograph series represents one important pathway to fulfilling professional and scholarly obligations arising from the extensive and highly significant archaeological research conducted by the CRMP and supported by public funding. Along with the numerous and frequently cited academic journal and book publications of the sorts already mentioned, the quality of this series and its distribution by University of Arizona Press attests to the program's ongoing success.

Paul R. Fish
University of Arizona

ACKNOWLEDGMENTS

Information employed in this research was collected by the Gila River Indian Community, Cultural Resource Management Program (GRIC-CRMP) as part of the Pima-Maricopa Irrigation Project (P-MIP). This project is funded by the Department of the Interior, U.S. Bureau of Reclamation, under the Tribal Self-Governance Act of 1994 (P.L. 103-413), for the design and development of a water delivery system utilizing Central Arizona Project water. This study would not have been possible without this commitment to archaeological research and the efforts of the GRIC-CRMP staff who completed the over 10 years of field and laboratory work necessary for the P-MIP archaeological survey of the community.

Feedback and comments that were essential for developing this manuscript were provided by many people including Donald Bahr, J. Andrew Darling, B. Sunday Eiselt, David Jacobs, Keith Kintigh, Larry Loendorf, Ted Oliver, Glen E. Rice, Deni J. Seymour, Katherine Spielmann, Barbara Stark, E. Christian Wells, and M. Kyle Woodson.

Special thanks are due to Michael Barton, Geoffrey Clark, John Ravesloot, and Arleyn Simon for serving as members of my dissertation committee. Arleyn and Geoffrey were co-chairs, and I would not have been able to conduct this research without their support and encouragement.

This report was edited, produced, and printed by Statistical Research, Inc. I would like to thank their staff, including Beth Bishop, Linda Wooden, Andrew Saiz, Jacqueline Dominguez, and April Moles for their hard work, which was coordinated by Maria Molina. Many thanks to Tom Herrschaft for his overall oversight of the publishing process. Rob Ciaccio drafted several of the illustrations. This investigation would not have been possible without GIS analyses undertaken by Lynn Simon, who also created the maps and patiently and rapidly responded to the many revisions. Finally, my heartfelt thanks to Lorrie Lincoln-Babb, who helped me every step of the way through the long process of completing this book.

CHAPTER 1

Introduction

This investigation examines conflict and cooperation among Native American communities along the Middle Gila River in southern Arizona (Figure 1). The emphasis here is on analysis of the terminal portion of the flaked stone projectile point record, between roughly A.D. 1150 and A.D. 1880. Dramatic changes in material culture, social organization, and settlement patterns occurred during that time. Analyzing diachronic patterns in conflict and cooperation provides insight into broader issues regarding relationships between Prehistoric and Historic period populations as well as understanding of the nature and meaning of episodic changes that occurred in the material-cultural traditions of southern Arizona.

An etic design approach is employed in which analyses of tasks that stone projectile points were intended to perform are emphasized, and the role of performance in the reproduction of designs is considered (Nelson 1997; Odell 2003:192–193). Historical records for the study area and Native American traditions are also examined. People who lived along the Middle Gila River possessed few firearms until near the end of the nineteenth century, and stone points continued to be employed until the late 1800s (Ezell 1961:66, 1994:346; Hall 1907:420; Russell 1908:111). Thus, the situation along the Middle Gila River offers an important opportunity to compare patterning among stone projectile points with historically documented settlement patterns, socioeconomic interactions, societal conflicts, subsistence practices, and other observations.

This research further analyzes projectile point data recovered by the Gila River Indian Community Cultural Resource Management Program (GRIC-CRMP) as part of the Pima-Maricopa Irrigation Project (P-MIP), which is partially funded by the U.S. Department of the Interior (USDI) Bureau of Reclamation (BOR). With the prominent exception of the pre-Classic period Hohokam site of Snaketown (Haury 1976), archaeological data from the heart of the Akimel O'odham (i.e., Pima) Historic period settlement area were comparatively unknown until the P-MIP investigations (Ravesloot 2007:93). In particular, early Historic period Akimel O'odham data are critical for assessing issues related to the Hohokam collapse as well as the continuum of populations within the Phoenix Basin,

and these remains largely within the boundaries of the modern community. GRIC-CRMP has conducted full-coverage survey of more than 58,000 hectares (144,000 acres) of the GRIC, and this large and spatially expansive data set allows the investigation of a wide range of research issues (Darling et al. 2004; Wells 2006; Wells, Rice, et al. 2004; Ravesloot 2007).

Projectile points from the Sonoran Desert have previously received comparatively little attention from prehistorians; however, projectile point data are ideally suited for analyzing warfare and socioeconomic interactions among social groups. First, lithics are common, durable artifacts and are the most likely remains to be preserved, particularly in surface contexts, which form the primary data set for most regional analyses (Cotterell and Kamminga 1992:126). Second, stone tools were employed throughout the archaeological sequence from the Paleo-Indian period through the late Historic period. Third, projectile points in the Hohokam core area are commonly made from obsidian, which has properties that allow source locations to be objectively defined with a high degree of precision. Consequently, diachronic and synchronic obsidian-acquisition patterns can be employed to address socioeconomic interactions at different scales, from the local to the regional. Fourth, ethnographic research suggests that stone points were designed for use against other people or for hunting large game animals, and this investigation differentiates points designed for killing large quadrupeds from those made for warfare. Analyzing the density and distribution of points through both time and space thus provides evidence regarding conflict as well as subsistence data.

Although stone projectile points may seem to be small and insignificant pieces of material culture, their successful design has important consequences. Large-game hunting requires considerable energy investment but offers substantial economic rewards (Dean 2003:26–27; Shott 1996). Successful performance is of an even greater concern during human conflict, when point designs are directly competing with one another. The selection of effective designs and, more importantly, the negative consequences of ineffectual design combine to produce comparatively strict limits on variation (cf. Vanpool 2003).

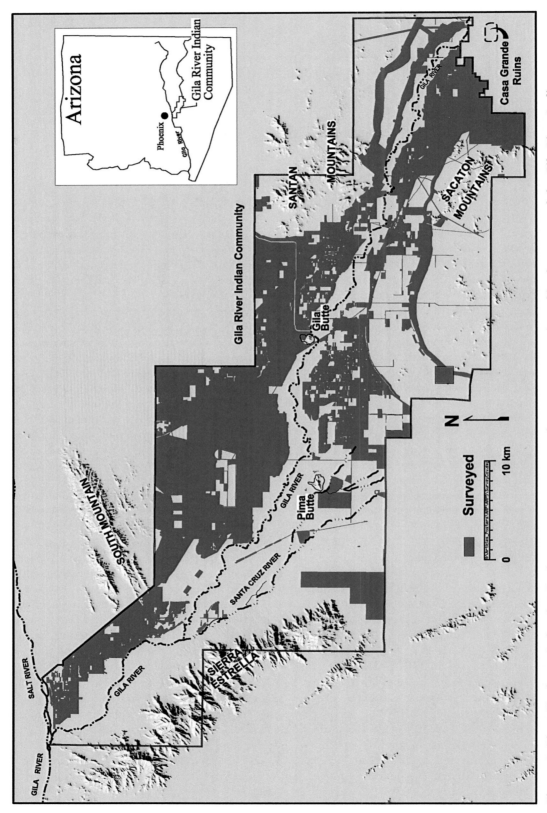

Figure 1. Pima-Maricopa Irrigation Project survey coverage, place names mentioned in the text, and the Gila River Indian Community study area.

Any analyses of these data, however, are complicated by the fact that morphologically similar projectile points were produced over a long period of time in southern Arizona. Artifacts with similar shapes have been found in Archaic through Historic period archaeological contexts (Figure 2). Some Hohokam archaeologists have even suggested that it is impossible to seriate projectile points that postdate the Archaic period (e.g., Peterson 1994). This investigation employs the hypothesis that flaked stone projectile points generally decreased in size over time; therefore, point weights are used to approximate age (cf. Mason 1894:653; Shott 1996).

As Shott concluded (1996:304), "if theory is developed more fully to link performance requirements to point size and form on the one hand, and economic and sociopolitical properties of aboriginal cultures on the other, then points can serve as more than simple time markers." The research presented here develops the former theory and, in part, employs obsidian data to address the latter. Although assigning age estimates to artifacts is not anthropologically interesting in and of itself, improving chronological associations for common remains, such as flaked stone points, allows investigation of a wide range of issues that are of importance to archaeologists.

Research questions that are considered here include the following: (1) Is there temporal variation in point design that is associated with patterns of hunting and/or warfare? (2) What does the spatial distribution of Classic and Historic period projectile points suggest regarding settlement patterns? (3) Did settlement locations change over time, and if so, what is the nature of this variation? (4) How does patterning in projectile point collections compare and contrast with other lines of evidence, including ceramics and architecture? (5) Is there patterning in point data that suggests that some types were introduced by immigrants? (6) Is there continuity in projectile point data (i.e., design, size, and obsidian source utilization) between the Classic and Historic periods, or are there discontinuities in these data associated with cultural-tradition disruptions? and (7) What do local and regional patterns of obsidian procurement suggest regarding synchronic and diachronic trends in economic cooperation and integration?

Studying materials that were transported to the Hohokam core area, such as obsidian, provides a complimentary perspective to the study of products that were produced locally (e.g., ceramics). In the past 30 years, obsidian analyses have become increasingly comprehensive, and consequently, broad regional and temporal patterns

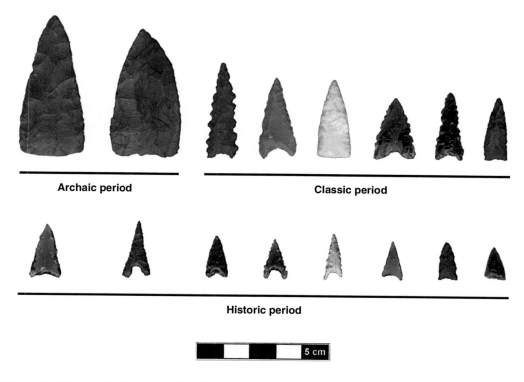

Archaic period

Classic period

Historic period

5 cm

Figure 2. Unnotched triangular flaked stone points and period assignments, Pima-Maricopa Irrigation Project collection. Archaic and Classic period assignments are following the Sliva (1997) typology. Historic period assignments are according to Loendorf and Rice (2004). The point on the bottom left is man-made glass.

have become apparent in these data (Shackley 1988, 1990, 1995, 2005). For Central Arizona populations, direction of the source has a greater effect than absolute distance on raw-material utilization (Rice et al. 1998). If people traveled directly to sources to obtain obsidian, then distance should be the primary barrier against acquisition; however, proportions for the most commonly utilized sources are only weakly correlated with distance. These observations suggest that Classic period people within the Hohokam core area in the Phoenix Basin maintained different trade relationships. Patterning in obsidian acquisition suggests that the strongest socioeconomic ties among communities were those between sites that were dependent on the same water sources. At the same time, variation in artifact data among geographical areas suggests that the Classic period Hohokam were not a politically centralized or economically integrated entity (Simon and Gosser 2001).

By the late Classic period, communities of sites received most of their obsidian from distant areas in different directions. Use of the closest source, Superior, decreased from the pre-Classic period to the Classic period, and Sauceda obsidian, which is located to the southwest of the core area, became the main supply by the late Classic period, and this pattern continued into the Historic period. This continuity of trends between the Classic and Historic periods is one example of the link between the Hohokam and the Akimel O'odham, who live in the area today.

Ethnographic descriptions and physical-performance constraints both indicate that warfare and hunting points were designed differently. This research suggests that stone points were employed to tip projectiles because they made the weapon more lethal than points made of organic materials (Figure 3). This, however, came at an expense in terms of durability, accuracy, raw materials, and manufacturing costs. For these and other reasons, stone points were designed only for hunting large animals and/ or for warfare.

This investigation defines point designs more precisely than previous analyses, and patterning in the collection considered here is consistent with expectations derived from this line of argument. Distinguishing projectile points that were associated with specific aspects of behavior (i.e., big-game hunting or warfare) provides additional evidence for assessing subsistence practices and provides data regarding conflict among social groups.

The relationship between the late Prehistoric period inhabitants of the Middle Gila River (i.e., Classic period Hohokam) and the Akimel O'odham has been debated since Spanish missionaries first arrived, in the late 1600s (Fewkes 1912:33; Russell 1908). Despite centuries of speculation and argument, this issue remains unresolved (Ezell 1983:149–150; Gilpin and Phillips 1998:28–43; Seymour 2011; Wells 2006), and some researchers have continued to argue that the Akimel O'odham are recent migrants to the Middle Gila River (e.g., Rea 2007a). One of the main limitations for understanding the relationship between the

Hohokam and the Akimel O'odham is that indigenously produced artifacts that are diagnostic of the Protohistoric and early Historic periods have remained poorly understood, and most absolute-dating techniques are of insufficient resolution to distinguish materials from that time span (Dean 1991; Wells 2006). Consequently, the identification of any distinctive artifacts associated with those periods is of considerable importance for understanding the past along the Middle Gila River, which is an issue that has modern sociopolitical ramifications in a region in which highly contested water rights are based on prior usage.

Recent research regarding the Classic period Hohokam collapse has focused on assessing the roles of socioeconomic interactions, conflict, and changes in subsistence practices over time (e.g., Abbott 2003; Clark 2001; Hegmon et al. 2008; Ravesloot et al. 2009; Redman 1999; Seymour 2011; Tainter 1988). It is possible to address each of these issues with projectile point data; however, comparatively little attention has been paid to this line of evidence. This investigation employs point data to assess settlement patterns and material-cultural evidence in an analysis of the Hohokam–Akimel O'odham continuum.

Data presented here indicate that the area between Gila and Pima Buttes on the south side of the Gila River—referred to hereafter as Casa Blanca—was a focal point for the coalescence of Protohistoric and Historic period groups that were decimated by intense conflict, repeated epidemics, and other changes visited upon them by external pressures. As populations declined, people who formerly lived throughout much of the Hohokam region in southern Arizona assembled along this short stretch of the Gila River. The population of the area then increased as the people gathered, and large areas of former occupation were left to others. Ethnohistorical and archaeological data both suggest that rather than "abandoning" areas such as the San Pedro River, sedentary agriculturalists were pushed from those regions by more-mobile hunter-gatherer populations that are difficult to identify in the archaeological record (Ferg and Tessman 1997; Herr et al. 2009; Seymour 2009:435–437, 2011; Vint 2005:3).

Small projectile points that lack notches or serration were employed by the people living in the Casa Blanca area during the Historic period. Groups coming from other locations tended to settle on the immediate margins of that area. Projectile points described here suggest corroborating evidence that one of those immigrations involved the San Pedro Sobaipuri. This pattern of population decline and subsequent aggregation appears to have been part of longer-term processes (Hill et al. 2004). The archaeologically and ethnohistorically documented coalescence of communities that happened during the Historic period began before the close of the Classic period, sometime around A.D. 1450, prior to the arrival of Europeans in the region (Hill et al. 2004). Akimel O'odham creation stories and episodic changes in archaeological data within southern Arizona both suggest that similar periods of collapse,

Figure 3. Akimel O'odham man using a self-bow for hunting small game with a wooden tipped *haapod* (arrow). Self-bows consist of a straight wooden stave with an attached string. (Photograph by Frank Russell, Negative 2691, National Anthropological Archives, Smithsonian Institution.)

aggregation, and reorganization occurred on a periodic basis in the region. These transitions appear to have resulted in substantial alterations to socioeconomic relationships and political organization in the Hohokam region.

Although the precise causes of these periodic fluctuations may have varied, it appears that climatic oscillations between warmer and colder periods may have alternately favored conditions for irrigation along the Salt and Gila Rivers in the Phoenix Basin that, in turn, affected variation in ideological, economic, and political relationships. The corporate-network conceptual model provides insight that is essential to an

understanding of the political responses that people developed to ameliorate these climatic oscillations (Feinman et al. 2000:453). The network strategy is associated with more-personalized forms of leadership; wealth is concentrated in the hands of certain individuals who use their network of connections to expand their personal power and authority. In contrast, within corporate organizations, economic resources are more dispersed, leadership is less personalized, and individual aggrandizement is uncommon.

It appears that pre-Classic period Hohokam social organization was characterized by an emphasis on corporate organizational strategies, as reflected in communal architecture designed for public gatherings, socioeconomic relationships that linked communities, and little differentiation in wealth. Reorganization in response to a down-cutting episode around A.D. 1070 (Waters and Ravesloot 2001) appears to have resulted in the emergence of more network-oriented political strategies with greater emphasis on individual aggrandizement, wealth accumulation, and differentiation in residential architecture. By the late Historic period, the inhabitants of the Hohokam core area (i.e., the Akimel O'odham and the Pee Posh) appear to have returned to a greater emphasis on corporate strategies, although vestiges of more-network-focused roles still persisted.

This investigation begins with a description of the study area and data set. Next, previous research in the Hohokam region of southern Arizona is presented, in Chapter 3. Chapter 4 discusses the methodological approach employed in this investigation and offers three middle-range hypotheses that are employed to link material culture and human behavior. The next chapter summarizes ethnohistorical data for the study area, which are used to generate expectations for patterning in the archaeological record. Chapter 6 presents analyses of projectile point data. The penultimate chapter explores broader implications of this research. Finally, conclusions are offered in Chapter 8.

CHAPTER 2

Study Region and Data Set

Study Region

Survey data employed in this research are from a physiographic region known as the Middle Gila Valley, which includes the southern portion of the Phoenix (Salt River–Gila River [Salt-Gila]) Basin (Figure 4). The Middle Gila River is conventionally described as encompassing a 120-km (72-mile) segment of the Gila River that begins at the North and South Buttes (collectively known as "The Buttes"), approximately 26 km east of Florence, Arizona, and continues downstream to the confluence of the Gila and Salt Rivers (Gregory and Huckleberry 1994; Waters and Ravesloot 2001). The Middle Gila River has ideal geomorphological conditions for irrigation agriculture. The valley is broad, ranging from 5 km (3.2 miles) to over 20 km (12.5 miles), and has a low gradient, descending only 176 km (579 feet) from The Buttes to the Salt-Gila confluence, an average of 1.4 m (4.6 feet) per kilometer.

The climate of the region is arid and hot (Sellers and Hill 1974; Sellers et al. 1985). The mean annual temperature is 21°C (70°F), with an average July high of 41°C (106°F) and a 1°C (34°F) minimum average in January (Camp 1986). The wettest months are typically July and August, when afternoon thunderstorms produce localized but generally heavy rainfall. A second period of precipitation occurs in the winter, when large storm systems from the Pacific Ocean enter the region. Rainfall associated with these storms is typically gentle and widespread. The spring months of April, May, and June are the driest. Occasionally, late-summer or early-autumn tropical storms pass through Arizona and may contribute considerable rainfall. Generally, however, the Middle Gila River is a water-deficient region, and evapo-transpiration usually exceeds precipitation (Waters 1996).

The valley contains three major landforms: the river channel, the terraces, and the *bajadas* (Waters 1996). An eolian sand sheet covers much of the upper (T-3) terrace, where Prehistoric and Historic period cultural remains are concentrated. Major tributaries to the Middle Gila River include the Salt River, the Santa Cruz River, and McClellan Wash.

The area falls in the Sonoran Desert subprovince of the Basin and Range physiographic zone (Brown 1994). Vegetation in the Middle Gila Valley is classified as part of both the Lower Colorado River Valley and the Arizona Upland subdivisions of the Sonoran Desertscrub biotic community. Local natural vegetation is generally sparse and includes creosotebush, mesquite, saltbush, palo verde, cholla, pricklypear, saguaro, ocotillo, and yucca as well as various desert grasses (Brown 1994; Brown and Lowe 1980).

The GRIC and the P-MIP Data Set

The GRIC borders Phoenix, Arizona, which is now one of the largest metropolitan areas in the United States. In contrast to most other Native American groups who lived close to major centers of Euroamerican settlement, the Akimel O'odham retained a comparatively large portion of their Historic period–territory core area. Consequently, this location encompasses a wealth of the archaeological data that are their heritage. Despite their location adjacent to affluent suburbs, community members continue to suffer from poverty that began as a result of the diversion of Gila River water by upstream settlers in the late 1860s (Dejong 2009; Dobyns 1989:49). Previously, people living in the area enjoyed considerable economic prosperity (Dejong 2009; Ezell 1994:359–366). Compared with the surrounding urban sprawl, the economic underdevelopment of the GRIC has kept its archaeological remains relatively untouched. Furthermore, because of community members' respect for their past, little intentional disturbance to cultural resources has occurred. This pattern differs from the surrounding state, federal, and private lands, where looters and development have extensively impacted archaeological sites.

As part of long-awaited economic redevelopment, the USDI BOR–funded P-MIP is being designed to bring water to the many long-dormant agricultural fields in the community. In 1993, planning was initiated for an irrigation system designed to serve 146,000 acres of land. As Ravesloot

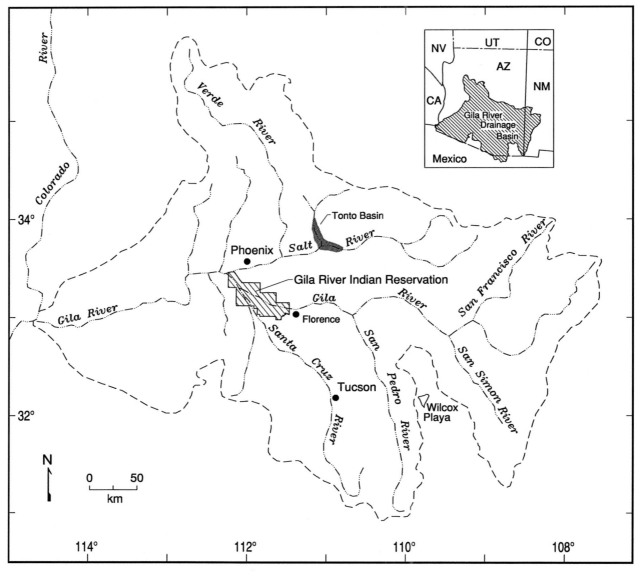

Figure 4. Map showing the Gila River Indian Community study area and the Gila River watershed (adapted from Waters and Ravesloot 2001).

et al. (2009:235) noted, "This project incorporates tribal social memory in the design and construction of a gravity-fed water-delivery system." The GRIC-CRMP was established as part of this project. In advance of construction, the GRIC-CRMP conducted full-coverage survey of over 525 km² of the community, and archaeological remains were identified in a range of geophysical settings, from the uplands to the lower river terraces (Figure 5) (Ravesloot 2007; Ravesloot and Waters 2004; Waters and Ravesloot 2000; Wells, Rice, et al. 2004).

This investigation further analyzes P-MIP survey data, which encompass much of the Middle Gila River portion of the Hohokam core area (Loendorf and Rice 2004).

Nearly 1,000 projectile points dating to the Early Archaic period (ca. 8000 B.P.) through the late A.D. 1800s have been collected. All metric data employed in this research and images of the points in the P-MIP survey collection are available in the study by Loendorf and Rice (2004). Excavation data from ongoing mitigation projects in the GRIC are also considered, where possible.

The surface collection also included nearly 10,000 pieces of obsidian (Darling 2000). To date, roughly 600 obsidian artifacts from the GRIC have been sourced, including both P-MIP survey data and artifacts from recent mitigation projects (Loendorf 2008). Obsidian data for over 1,000 additional artifacts are employed for comparison

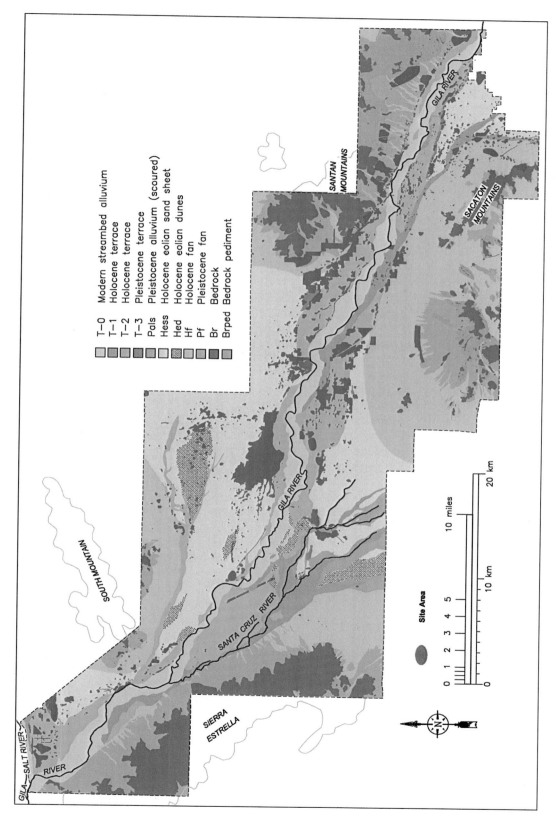

Figure 5. Map showing geomorphology and site areas within the Gila River Indian Community.

with the study area (Marshall 2002; Peterson et al. 1997; Rice et al. 1998; Shackley 2005; Shackley and Bayman 2001), from sites in the Salt, Tonto, and Tucson Basins of the Hohokam area.

Surface Data

When considering the projectile point sample used in this study, it is important to emphasize that the collection was derived almost exclusively (97 percent) from surface contexts. This has probably affected the sample in several ways (Barton et al. 1999:614–617; Redman and Watson 1970). First, because they are generally covered by deposition, artifacts in such contexts as pit-house floors or burial features are less likely to be exposed on the modern ground surface. Consequently, the sample may be skewed toward artifacts from trash mounds or other contexts that are less likely to be buried. Second, geomorphologic factors may affect the apparent frequency of artifacts of different ages. For example, recent artifacts are more likely to be exposed on the modern ground surface, because they have experienced a shorter period in which they may have been buried by substantial deposition or redeposited by erosion (Loendorf and Rice 2004:8–10). Third, during the survey, no artifacts were collected from areas with human bone; consequently, any points potentially associated with human remains were not sampled. Fourth, most of the archaeological sites in the study area have been occupied for considerable periods of time, and surface contexts include mixed deposits from different time periods. Consequently, temporal associations for nondiagnostic artifacts based only on recovery location are generally unclear. Fifth, extensive agricultural fields are present in the community, and both Prehistoric and Historic period farming may have disturbed cultural remains (Barton et al. 1999).

Geomorphology

Because the collection was recovered from surface contexts, which include landforms of differing ages, consideration of geomorphological processes that may alter the apparent distribution of projectile points is especially important. The effects of erosion and deposition condition the apparent spatial distributions of projectile points dating to different periods. Old landforms may have recent points, but younger landforms are less likely to have older points on the modern ground surface. Consequently, the apparent frequency and distribution of points with differing ages are affected (Loendorf and Rice 2004).

The main landforms within the study area include alluvial terraces along the Gila River and its tributaries, an extensive area of Holocene eolian sand-sheet and dune fields, and piedmonts (*bajadas*) that are either Holocene or Pleistocene in age. Ages for the terraces along the Gila River were estimated using the radiocarbon method, and other landforms that have not been dated are assigned only to general geological periods, such as early Holocene or Pleistocene, based on soil development and other factors (Waters 1996). The eolian sand-sheet and dune fields may have been deposited during the early Holocene, possibly ending around roughly 5000 B.C. The Pleistocene fans are more than 40,000 years old and predate human occupation of the New World. The greatest temporal range of projectile points will occur on the surfaces of the oldest geomorphic landforms. The younger landforms will generally have only more-recent archaeological remains. The current, active surface of the Gila River channel (T-0) will not contain projectile points, except possibly as secondary deposits derived from erosion of the upper terraces.

This investigation focuses on recent projectile points that postdate roughly A.D. 1150 and does not include remains from the modern floodplain. Consequently, geomorphological processes are less likely to have substantially altered the apparent distribution of the projectile points analyzed in the following research. The next section summarizes materials that were employed for projectile point manufacture in the study area and the effects of raw-material constraints on stone points.

Middle Gila River Lithic Raw Materials

The study area is located in the Basin and Range physiographic province of south-central Arizona, where northwest-southeast-trending mountain ranges rise abruptly from broad and flat basins filled with deep deposits of eroded sediments (Pierce 1985). These sedimentary basins contain thousands of feet of alluvial gravels, sands, and silts eroded from nearby mountain ranges. The mountains were formed by both the erosion of uplifted fault blocks and volcanic activity (Hendricks 1985). Although some ranges primarily consist of silicic- to basaltic-composition rocks (e.g., basalt, andesite, and rhyolite), most of the mountains are Precambrian granites, schists, and gneiss (Anderson 1992; Reynolds 1985; Wilson 1969).

The size, shape, and fracture toughness of available lithic raw materials constrain both the reduction techniques that can be employed and the character of the resulting artifacts (Andrefsky 1994; Binford 1979; Cotterell and Kamminga 1992:125–151; Parry and Kelly 1997). Consequently, it is necessary to consider the effects of raw-material constraints in any lithic analysis.

Fracture toughness is defined as the stress-intensity factor necessary to begin the propagation of a crack in the stone, and this factor is a fundamental characteristic of flaked stone raw materials (Cotterell and Kamminga 1987:678). Although oversimplified, a dichotomy can be drawn between fine- and coarse-grained stones. Fine-grained materials have a shiny or glass-like surface luster, whereas coarse-grained materials have a dull luster and visible grain. Coarse-grained materials usually have higher fracture toughness than fine-grained materials (Andrefsky 1994; Whittaker 1994). Consequently, prehistoric flint knappers appear generally to have employed fine-grained and coarse-grained materials for different tasks (Cotterell and Kamminga 1992:127–130).

Because of their lower fracture toughness, fine-grained materials are well suited for thinning and shaping into patterned tool types. In contrast, the high fracture toughness of most coarse-grained materials makes them extremely difficult (if not impossible) to retouch into patterned tools by pressure flaking. At the same time, high fracture toughness would have been advantageous for their use as expedient tools, because the working edges would have dulled less quickly than more-brittle fine-grained materials. As a result, fine-grained materials are closely associated with the production of patterned tools, whereas coarse-grained materials were generally used for the production of expedient flake tools (Cotterell and Kamminga 1992:129).

In general, fine-grained materials rarely naturally occur in the study area; most locally available materials are coarse-grained stones that have high fracture toughness. Consequently, the majority of the projectile points in the collection were made from nonlocal raw materials. These materials had to be obtained through trade or other means, and as a result, it is possible to consider socioeconomic interactions through analyses of projectile point raw-material utilization (Shackley 2005).

Fine-grained lithic resources have limited distributions throughout the Sonoran Desert (Anderson 1992; Shackley 1988). The few cryptocrystalline lithic materials that are present occur in two forms: as primary, concentrated deposits of lithic materials and as mixed, secondary geological deposits spread more diffusely across the landscape (Anderson 1992). Primary, concentrated deposits of fine-grained lithic materials are not common along the Middle Gila River. Larger deposits of low-fracture-toughness materials do occur in relatively nearby areas. Some of these resources include obsidian deposits associated with the volcanic fields of the Superior, Vulture, and Sauceda Mountains in south-central Arizona (Peterson 1994; Shackley 1988) as well as chert deposits in several nearby regions, including Windy Hill in the Tonto Basin (Rice et al. 1998). Extensive chert deposits also occur in the Payson area; however, these materials have numerous flaws and are of generally low quality for projectile point manufacture.

Course-grained materials that are better suited for ground stone artifacts and expedient lithic tools are more abundant locally. For example, primary, concentrated deposits of vesicular basalt were available at Lone Butte, the Santan Mountains, Picture Rocks, the Vaiva Hills, the McDowell Mountains, and the Gila Bend Mountains and at several locations in the New River drainage (Anderson 1992; Hoffman and Doyel 1985; Wilson 1969; Wilson et al. 1969).

The most widespread local sources of lithic raw materials were provided by secondary geological deposits, such as Pleistocene river gravels, *bajada* surfaces, and alluvial fans. These deposits contain a variety of igneous, metamorphic, and sedimentary gravels. Fine-grained cherts and chalcedonies occasionally occur in these deposits, but higher-fracture-toughness materials, such as quartzites, rhyolites, basalts, dacites, and other siliceous volcanics, are more common (Anderson 1992). These lithic materials are generally small and randomly dispersed at a low density across extensive areas.

P-MIP Projectile Point Raw Materials

Chert is the most common material in the P-MIP projectile point collection (Table 1). Nearly 40 percent of the recovered artifacts were identified as chert. Although obsidian does not naturally occur in the project area (Bayman and Shackley 1999), it is the next-most-common type, accounting for almost one-third of all projectile points. Basalt is the next-most-frequent material, with 19 percent of the survey collection. Finally, 6 percent of the artifacts are rhyolite. All other materials are uncommon, occurring in frequencies of less than 5 percent.

The points are separated by size. Large points are generally Archaic period atlatl tips, and small points are more likely to be arrow tips (Patterson 1985; Shott 1996:286–288; Thomas 1978). For example, Shott (1996:286–288) found that shoulder width was the most reliable characteristic for distinguishing between atlatl tips and arrow points. In the typological classification system, a shoulder width of 14 mm was used to separate these two types (Loendorf and Rice 2004). Raw-material choices differed for large and small projectile points. In general, fine-grained materials were preferred for the manufacture of small points. For example, less than 3 percent of the large points were made from obsidian, but obsidian is one of the most commonly identified materials for small points (36 percent of the collection). Basalt is substantially more common for large points, and these artifacts tend to be made of coarser-grained materials. Raw-material types also tend to vary among different types of projectile points (Table 2).

In general, varieties that were made at a given time were produced from similar raw-material types, and variation in material use is consequently apparent among time periods. For example, basalt is the most common material for Middle Archaic period projectile points. The use of basalt then declined until the Classic period, but it accounts for

Table 1. Material Type, by Point Size, for Projectile Points and Preforms

Material	Point Size							
	Indeterminate		Large		Small		Total	
	n	%	n	%	n	%	n	%
Chert	13	54	83	31	274	40	370	38
Obsidian	4	17	7	3	248	36	259	26
Basalt	3	13	97	36	88	13	188	19
Rhyolite	2	8	44	16	10	1	56	6
Chalcedony	1	4	3	1	45	7	49	5
Quartzite	—	—	13	5	4	1	17	2
Quartz	1	4	4	1	12	2	17	2
Meta-basalt	—	—	9	3	2	0.3	11	1
Glass	—	—	—	—	8	1	8	1
Siltstone	—	—	4	1	—	—	4	0.4
Welded tuff	—	—	2	1	—	—	2	0.2
Dacite	—	—	1	0.4	—	—	1	0.1
Tuff	—	—	1	0.4	—	—	1	0.1
Total	24		272		687		983	

Note: Adopted from Loendorf and Rice (2004). Percentages are of column totals.

Table 2. Projectile Point Raw Material, by Period

Period	n	Basalt (%)	Chalcedony (%)	Chert (%)	Obsidian (%)	Rhyolite (%)
Middle Archaic	95	56	1	30	2	11
Late Archaic	57	30	—	35	3	32
Pre-Classic	91	—	10	47	39	4
Classic	132	11	5	35	49	—
Historic	196	24	6	36	33	1

Note: Adopted from Loendorf and Rice (2004).

nearly one-quarter of the Historic period point collection. Chert was popular throughout the sequence. Chert use peaked during the pre-Classic period, composing nearly half of all the points from that time. Rhyolite was not commonly employed, but its use peaked during the Late Archaic period. Obsidian use in the study area was greatest during the Classic period, and other researchers have also suggested that obsidian use peaked during the Classic period (e.g., Bayman and Shackley 1999; Peterson 1994:103; Rice et al. 1998:110).

CHAPTER 3

Previous Research in Southern Arizona

Since the time Spaniards first came to the Middle Gila River in A.D. 1694, foreigners have questioned the relationship between the prehistoric (i.e., Hohokam) and Akimel O'odham populations (Fewkes 1912). Largely based on architectural differences between the Classic (ca. A.D. 1150–1450) and Historic (A.D. 1694–1950) periods, early observers simply assumed that the Akimel O'odham must be recent migrants from elsewhere (Russell 1908:26–29). Similarly, material-culture and settlement-pattern shifts that occurred between the pre-Classic (ca. A.D. 600–1150) and Classic periods were seen as evidence for the migration of an ethnic group termed the "Salado" (Gladwin and Gladwin 1930). Once again, material-cultural changes between the Archaic and pre-Classic periods were argued to have resulted from the migration of external ethnic populations (Haury 1976:351).

However, beginning with salvage archaeology in the 1960s and intensifying in the 1970s with the advent of contract archaeology, more data became available, and archaeologists began to increasingly dispute each of these migration models. Based on similarities between the archaeological record and ethnographic observations, researchers such as Ezell (1963) argued for cultural continuity from the Classic period to the Historic period. By the 1990s, the "Salado" were no longer regarded as an ethnic group that lived alongside the Hohokam, and ceramics that had been attributed to them were instead thought to be associated with a regional belief system (Crown 1994). Archaeologists have also increasingly developed a consensus favoring in situ development of the pre-Classic period Hohokam from an Archaic period base (e.g., Wallace 1997).

Although each of the migration models has been questioned, agreement does not exist regarding explanations for why these episodic changes in material culture occurred. This investigation compares projectile point patterning with other lines of evidence (e.g., ceramics and architecture) to improve our understanding of changing sociocultural dynamics between the Classic and Historic periods. This chapter begins with an overview of what is currently known regarding the culture history of the Middle Gila River region.

Culture-History Summary

This section briefly summarizes the culture history of the Middle Gila Valley and follows the background discussion that was developed to guide P-MIP research. More detailed overviews can be found in Bayman (2001), Berry and Marmaduke (1982), Bronitsky and Merritt (1986), Crown and Judge (1991), Fish (1989), Fish and Fish (2007), Noble (1991), and Gumerman (1991). Human utilization of southern Arizona spans the last 11,500 years. Nine main chronological periods are recognized, and each is characterized by different social and cultural attributes (Figure 6).

Paleo-Indian and Archaic Periods

Occupation in the study area during the Paleo-Indian (ca. 10,000–8,500 B.C.) and Early Archaic (ca. 8,500–5000 B.C.) periods remains poorly defined (Huckell 1984a, 1984b). The first definitive evidence of human habitation along the Middle Gila River dates to the Middle Archaic period. Recent work on the GRIC (Bubemyre et al. 1998; Neily et al. 1999; Woodson and Davis 2001) has documented Middle Archaic period sites, and surface finds of projectile points suggest widespread use of the Phoenix Basin during that time period (Loendorf and Rice 2004).

Beginning around 1500 B.C., the first agricultural villages appeared in the Sonoran Desert (Diehl 2003; Huckell 1995; Mabry 1998; Matson 1991; Sliva 2003). Pre-Ceramic semisedentary horticultural settlements have not as yet been identified in the Middle Gila Valley. It is likely, however, that any Early Agricultural period settlements within the study area were located along Holocene terraces with potential for floodwater agriculture, and these remains are therefore deeply buried in alluvium.

The succeeding early Ceramic (roughly A.D. 1–550) is characterized by small, seasonally occupied hamlets and the initial production of plain ware (around A.D. 1) and red

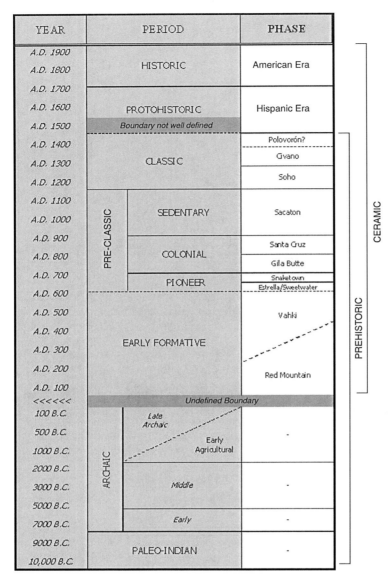

YEAR	PERIOD	PHASE
A.D. 1900	HISTORIC	American Era
A.D. 1800		
A.D. 1700	PROTOHISTORIC	Hispanic Era
A.D. 1600		
A.D. 1500	*Boundary not well defined*	
A.D. 1400	CLASSIC	Polovorón?
A.D. 1300		Civano
A.D. 1200		Soho
A.D. 1100	SEDENTARY	Sacaton
A.D. 1000		
A.D. 900	COLONIAL	Santa Cruz
A.D. 800		Gila Butte
A.D. 700	PIONEER	Snaketown
A.D. 600		Estrella/Sweetwater
A.D. 500	EARLY FORMATIVE	Vahki
A.D. 400		
A.D. 300		
A.D. 200		Red Mountain
A.D. 100		
<<<<<	*Undefined Boundary*	
100 B.C.	Late Archaic	
500 B.C.		Early Agricultural
1000 B.C.		
2000 B.C.		
3000 B.C.	Middle	
5000 B.C.		
7000 B.C.	Early	
9000 B.C.	PALEO-INDIAN	
10,000 B.C.		

Figure 6. Chronological periods and phases defined for the study area.

ware (around A.D. 450) ceramics (Doyel 1993; Mabry 1998; Wallace et al. 1995; Whittlesey and Ciolek-Torrello 1996). However, ceramics were not as widely used as they were at later Hohokam sites, and the range of types produced was comparatively limited (Whittlesey and Ciolek-Torrello 1996). Specialization in ceramic production began around A.D. 450, when potters in the eastern South Mountain vicinity fabricated most of the vessels used along the lower Salt River (Abbott 2009).

Hohokam Pre-Classic Period

Based on the many antecedents that have been identified, researchers have developed a consensus favoring

in situ development of the Hohokam from Archaic period populations (Bayman 2001; Cable and Doyel 1987; Doyel 1991; Wallace 1997; Wallace et al. 1995; Wilcox 1979). The Hohokam tradition initially appeared in the Phoenix Basin and was characterized by the development of large-scale irrigation agriculture, red-on-buff pottery, a distinctive iconography, exotic ornaments and artifacts, a cremation mortuary complex, and larger and more-complex settlements (Fish 1989; Howard 2006). The Pioneer period of the Hohokam sequence traditionally included the Vahki, Estrella, Sweetwater, and Snaketown phases (Gladwin et al. 1937; Haury 1976). However, researchers now agree that the Vahki phase is more consistent with Early Formative period developments in southern Arizona, and they place the beginning of the Pioneer period around A.D. 550/650, with the introduction of decorated ceramics in the Estrella phase (Ciolek-Torrello 1995; Mabry 1998; Wallace et al. 1995; Whittlesey 1995). For the next 5 centuries, residents of the lower Salt River appear to have received most of their decorated ceramics from the Middle Gila River (Abbott 2009:552).

During the Colonial period (ca. a.d. 700–900), village structure became more formalized, and groups of houses were arranged around central courtyards, where a variety of extramural activities were undertaken (Howard 2000; Wilcox et al. 1981). Villages were composed of several courtyard groups organized around a large central plaza, which was a place for communal gatherings and frequently included a cemetery (Abbott and Foster 2003:25; Fish 1989:20; Howard 2006; Wilcox et al. 1981). The geographic range of the Hohokam expanded during this period, and ball courts appeared (Bayman 2001; Wilcox and Sternberg 1983). Agricultural intensification occurred in the subsequent Sedentary period, a time when marketplaces may have emerged and the ball-court system reached its maximum extent, with over 230 courts spread across much of central and southern Arizona (Abbott 2009; Abbott et al. 2007; Bayman 2001; Dean 2003; Howard 2006; Marshall 2001a).

Hohokam Classic Period

The transition between the pre-Classic and Classic periods was marked by many dramatic changes in Hohokam society (Bayman 2001; Doyel et al. 2000:222). During this interval, between roughly A.D. 1100 and 1200, the

Hohokam regional system appears to have weakened (Abbott et al. 2007). Transitions in Hohokam cultural traditions that occurred at that time included a shift in burial practices from cremation to inhumation, replacement of semisubterranean pit houses with surface structures, enclosure of courtyard groups inside compound walls, reduction in red-on-buff manufacture, increase in red-ware-pottery production, and extensive alterations in regional exchange networks (Abbott 2009; Abbott et al. 2007; Bayman 2001; Crown 1991; Doyel 1980, 1991). The Classic period has been divided into the Soho (around A.D. 1150/1200–1300) and Civano (around A.D. 1300–1450) phases. The Soho phase saw the construction of platform mounds, a type of communal architecture that replaced the ball-court system, which fell from use near the end of the Sedentary period (Abbott 2003; Abbott et al. 2007; Bayman 2001; Elson 1998).

The end of the Classic period, around A.D. 1450, was marked by the collapse of the platform-mound system and the abandonment of Hohokam sites along the lower Salt River and in the Tonto Basin (Hegmon et al. 2008; Ravesloot et al. 2009). Considerable debate exists regarding the cause or causes of this population decline as well as the relationship between the Hohokam and subsequent people (i.e., the Akimel O'odham) who lived in the area (Bayman 2001; Hegmon et al. 2008; Ravesloot et al. 2009; Reid and Whittlesey 1997). Researchers have generally agreed that sedentary agriculturalists no longer inhabited the lower Salt River by A.D. 1450.

Prehistorians have offered many explanations for why this occurred, including salinization of fields, the introduction of European diseases, overpopulation and resulting environmental impacts, conflict with the Apache, warfare within Hohokam society, rigidity traps, and various aspects of climatic conditions, such as flooding or drought (Abbott 2003; Bayman 2001; Dean 2000; Ezell 1983; Graybill et al. 2006; Grebinger 1976; Haury 1976; Hegmon et al. 2008; Ingram 2010; Meegan 2009; Mindeleff 1897:13; Ravesloot et al. 2009; Redman 1999; Reid and Whittlesey 1997; Tainter 1988:46–47; Weaver 1972). These explanations are not mutually exclusive, and as will be further explored in the following research, it appears that a combination of factors led to the dramatic changes that occurred between the Classic and early Historic periods.

Hohokam–Akimel O'odham Continuum

The relationship between the Classic period Hohokam and the Akimel O'odham has been contested since the first written descriptions of the Middle Gila River area were completed in the late 1600s (Fewkes 1912). Based on the assumption that Classic period adobe structures, such as Casa Grande, were superior to the brush houses that the

Akimel O'odham built, the early Spanish observers concluded that the Akimel O'odham were recent migrants.

The subject of who constructed Casa Grande has continued to interest travelers since these first descriptions. For example, Cozzens (1874:194–195), who visited in 1859, wrote:

What race of people dwelt here? By whom were these decaying walls erected? Who constructed the many thousand miles of acequias [canals]? How did they live, and where are they now? are [*sic*] questions that suggest themselves at every step; and as yet they have never been satisfactorily answered. It seems to me that our government ought to take some measures towards solving this great mystery, as well as preserving these monuments of an extinct people.

Until recently, almost all outside observers who speculated on the relationship between the builders of Casa Grande and the Akimel O'odham have focused on the differences between Historic period construction techniques and Classic period architectural styles, which are, themselves, a departure from the long-standing structural forms of the Hohokam pre-Classic period. Similar changes in construction styles, settlement patterns, subsistence techniques, and material culture also occurred earlier in time along the Middle Gila River, and few researchers have considered the possibility that these periodic fluctuations are part of broader patterns of cultural change.

Most early observers also focused almost exclusively on the differences in architecture, and they ignored the many other similarities in material culture between the Classic and Historic periods. However, Emory, who was one of the first people from the United States to visit the O'odham villages along the Middle Gila River, was an exception (Figure 7). Emory (1848:133–134) wrote:

Wherever the mountains did not impinge too close to the river and shut out the valley, they [ruins] were seen in great abundance, enough, I should think, to indicate a former population of at least one hundred thousand.

Based on what he observed along the Middle Gila River, Emory (1848:133) wrote:

My own impression, and it is stated so in my journal, is that the many ruins we saw on the Gila might well be attributed to Indians of the races we saw in New Mexico, and on the Gila itself. I mean by the last, the Pimos [Akimel O'odham], who might easily have lost the art of building adobe and mud houses. In all respects, except their dwellings, they appeared to be of the same race as the builders of the numberless houses now level with the ground of the Gila River.

Figure 7. Watercolor painting of an Akimel O'odham village (by Seth Eastman).

At the time, this conclusion was almost universally rejected, and it wasn't until the 1960s that the possibility of a Hohokam and Akimel O'odham continuum gained favor. Ezell (1963, 1983) examined material-cultural traits and found both similarities and differences between the Prehistoric and Historic period people who lived along the Middle Gila River. For example, he argued that although Akimel O'odham architecture and settlement patterns differed from those of the Classic period, the Historic period patterns were more similar to those of the pre-Classic period (Ezell 1963:62). Based on his analysis of the data available at the time, Ezell (1963:65) concluded that the Akimel O'odham could provisionally be considered to be related to the Hohokam.

By the 1990s, a measure of consensus that the Akimel O'odham are related to the Hohokam was reached among archaeologists. For example, Gilpin and Phillips (1998:117) suggested:

> The Hohokam and Saladoan archaeological cultures were transformed into historic Piman culture, involving a shift from irrigation-based, centralized communities . . . to dispersed rancheria settlements, with concomitant changes in subsistence, social organization, architecture, and other aspects of material culture, although the timing, causes, and specifics of these changes are poorly understood.

However, some researchers have continued to argue that the Akimel O'odham are recent migrants to the Middle Gila River and completely or partially replaced the Hohokam populations. Rea (2007a), for example, maintained that older members of the GRIC do not believe that they are related to the Hohokam; however, Rea did not begin his work until the 1960s, and many other observers have argued that the Akimel O'odham recognize descent from the Hohokam. For example, George Webb (1959:53), an Akimel O'odham from Gila Crossing who was born in 1893, said, "I think, as all Papagos and Pimas, that we are their [the Hohokam] descendents." Furthermore, prehistoric sites play a prominent role in Akimel O'odham traditions, and close similarities between the prehistoric record and these stories are unlikely to have occurred by coincidence (Lewis and Rice 2009; Teague 1993). The following research further explores this debate and introduces previously underutilized lines of evidence in this discussion.

The Protohistoric Period

The Protohistoric period (ca. A.D. 1500–1700) is generally defined as the time between the end of the Hohokam Classic period and Spanish contact (Doelle 1984; Wells 2006; Whittlesey et al. 1997:185). In contrast to the Prehistoric periods and phases, the Protohistoric period is defined based on an external event (the arrival of Europeans in the New World) rather than changes in the material culture of the region. As a result, the Protohistoric period remains poorly defined throughout southern Arizona. Furthermore, there is a small sample of excavated material and poor chronometric control, and a cohesive interpretive framework does not exist for these remains (Ravesloot and Whittlesey 1987; Wells 2006; Wilson forthcoming). Therefore, the Protohistoric period is not discussed as a distinct period in the following research.

Akimel O'odham Historic Period

The Historic period is traditionally defined to encompass the time between A.D. 1694 and 1950 for which written records exist. The first definitive European contact in the Phoenix Basin occurred in A.D. 1694, when Father Kino visited the Akimel O'odham villages along the Middle Gila River (Darling et al. 2004; Ezell 1961, 1983; Russell 1908; Wilson forthcoming). The Akimel O'odham did not experience intensive colonial contact during the Hispanic era (A.D. 1694–1853); instead, exchanges were limited to parties traveling through the territory or community members visiting settlements to the south. Nevertheless, the Akimel O'odham were affected by introduced European elements, such as new cultigens (e.g., wheat), religious practices, livestock, metal, and especially disease (Ezell 1961, 1983; Shaw 1994; Wells 2006).

The American era (A.D. 1853–1950) began in 1853 with the Gadsden Purchase, when southern Arizona became part of the United States (cf. Ezell 1983). Euroamerican contacts with the Akimel O'odham in the Middle Gila Valley increased after 1846 as a result of the Mexican-American War (Dejong 2009). New markets were developed to supply grain to the military and to immigrants heading for California, and the Akimel O'odham experienced a period of prosperity (Dejong 2009; Doelle 1981; Ezell 1983; Hackenberg 1983; Russell 1908). Thereafter, interaction between Native American groups and Euroamerican settlers became increasingly tense, and the U.S. Government adopted a policy of pacification and reservation confinement of Native Americans (Spicer 1962). The GRIC was established in 1859.

The following years saw the arrival of large numbers of Euroamerican migrants to upstream locations along the Gila and lower Salt Rivers (Dejong 2009). Uncertainty and variable crop yields led to major settlement reorganization, including the movement of some Akimel O'odham and Pee Posh to the lower Salt River (Webb 1959:45–46). The establishment of agency headquarters, churches and schools, and trading posts at Casa Blanca and Sacaton during the 1870s and 1880s led to the growth of these towns as administrative and commercial centers, at the expense of others (Webb 1959:49–52; Wilson forthcoming). By 1898, agriculture had nearly ceased within the GRIC, and although some Akimel O'odham drew rations, woodcutting was the principal livelihood (Shaw 1994:122). The first allotments within the GRIC were established in 1914. Each male who was the head of a household was assigned a 10-acre parcel of potentially irrigable land located within districts watered by the Santan, Agency, Blackwater, or Casa Blanca projects on the eastern half of the reservation. In 1917, the allotment size was doubled to include a secondary, usually noncontiguous 10-acre tract of grazing land.

The most ambitious attempt to rectify the economic plight of the Akimel O'odham in the early 1900s was the San Carlos Project Act, which authorized the construction of a water-storage dam on the Gila River (Pfaff 1994, 1996). However, the San Carlos Project failed to revitalize the O'odham farming economy and never provided sufficient water to the community (Hackenberg 1983). Over the years, the U.S. Government placed severe acculturative pressures on the Akimel O'odham that caused changes in nearly every aspect of their lives. Since World War II, however, the Akimel O'odham have experienced a resurgence of interest in tribal sovereignty and economic development. The community has now become a self-governing entity, has developed several profitable enterprises in such fields as telecommunications, and has built several casinos. The tribe has also worked to revitalize its farming economy by constructing a water-delivery system across the reservation (Ravesloot et al. 2009).

The researchers who have developed this culture history have paid comparatively little attention to projectile points from the Sonoran Desert, especially those made after the appearance of decorated ceramics, sometime around A.D. 600. Stone projectile point data, however, provide essential insight for reconstructing patterns of social conflict and cooperation in the study area during late prehistory. The following discussion considers analytical approaches that have been previously applied to projectile points.

Projectile Point Analysis

Archaeologists have offered many explanations for why flaked stone projectile points varied over time and space (Shott 1996). Suggested sources of apparent synchronic or diachronic variation include differences among cultural or social groups; raw-material constraints; use wear or reworking after breakage; variation in motor skills of the makers; low standards of conformity to ideals; random drift as a function of time or space; measurement or classification error by researchers; variation in propulsion technology (e.g., atlatl vs. bow); toy point variants (Bonnichsen and Keyser 1982); pragmatic modifications to facilitate hafting

(Flenniken and Raymond 1986:606); change in mechanical-stress factors (Shott 1996:281); point types made for ritual or mundane purposes (Haury 1976:297); durability concerns (Cheshier and Kelly 2006); variation in cultural-transmission modes (Mesoudi and O'Brien 2008); differences related to functional requirements, such as hunting or warfare (Ahler 1992); and change in ballistic-performance requirements (Shott 1996).

These mechanisms for differentiation and change are not mutually exclusive. Instead, more than one of them must have affected variation among stone points. Until recently, however, archaeologists have largely analyzed points with the often-tacit assumption that patterns they could measure were essentially direct reflections of differences in cultural groups (Mason 1894:655; Whittaker 1987, 1994:260–268). Comparatively little attention was paid to the functional aspects of projectile point technology and the role that performance played in technological change.

Style and Function

Researchers have long debated the meaning of the term "style," and most lithic analysts now recognize style as something that is conceptually separate from function (Brantingham 2007; Carr 1995; G. A. Clark 1989; Hoffman 1997:42–65; Kooyman 2000:7; Whittaker 1994:270). As G. A. Clark (1989:32) has noted, "Style can be conceptualized as an axis of variability (or causal vector) free to vary independently of function, raw material and other factors." Further, lithic-artifact style can be a passive and unintentional reflection of culture, or it can be a deliberate expression that has an invested symbolic component (Kooyman 2000:96).

There are also two main aspects of how function has been implicitly or explicitly defined. First, the "function" of a tool can be operationalized as the task or tasks that the tool was designed to perform. This definition emphasizes the intent of the maker rather than realized uses of the object, whereas the second characterization focuses on the task or tasks for which a specific tool was actually employed. Design theory is focused on understanding function in the former sense, whereas use-wear and residue analyses are generally employed to address lithic use in the latter sense (Odell 2003:135–173).

In general, archaeologists have concentrated their research on cultural aspects other than functional variation, and as a consequence, they have tended to focus on the identification of style rather than facets perceived to be functional traits. In practice, however, it may be impossible to separate stylistic and functional aspects of artifacts, and understanding diachronic morphological variation requires consideration of both function and style (Brantingham 2007; Carr 1995). For example, changes through time in the appearance of projectile points may have occurred as a result of variation in the frequency of the tasks that

points were designed to perform. Stone projectile points were often designed differently for hunting and for warfare (Ellis 1997:45; Justice 2002:38–44). Those intended for the former activity have aspects of design that facilitated secure hafting (e.g., notches), whereas those designed for the latter activity lack notches or have thick stems that were intended to split the shaft on impact (Keeley 1996:52). Thus, diachronic patterns in the frequency of unnotched projectile points could be related to temporal variation in the intensity of conflict. Seen from this perspective, the increasing incidence of unnotched projectile points over time at Ventana Cave (Haury 1950:268) would suggest a general diachronic trend in the intensity of warfare in southern Arizona.

At the same time, other aspects of projectile point morphology that may change over time are more closely related to stylistic variation, in the sense that these differences are unrelated to variation in function (either intended or actual). Unintentional flake-scar patterns on points caused by habits of manufacture, for example, have been shown to be effective for distinguishing the work of individual knappers, and these differences are less likely to have functional aspects (Whittaker 1994:292–298). Synchronic variation in serration data among points from the Hohokam region also suggests that this practice may have been more closely related to stylistic expressions than to functional aspects (Hoffman 1997).

Sackett (1982, 1985, 1986, 1990) used the terms "isochrestic" and "iconological" to distinguish, respectively, between unintentional and intentional expressions of style. He defined isochrestic style as choice among functionally equivalent alternatives, which is generally an unintentional expression of cultural identity that results primarily from passive enculturation and interaction among groups of artisans. He argued that isochrestic style is embedded within functional variation, because this type of style is created by specific production strategies and manufacturing techniques for achieving functional ends. He used the term "iconological style" to refer to intentional expressions of cultural identity, and he argued that such media as lithic artifacts were unlikely to generally be used to convey such messages.

Following the work of Wobst (1977), Wiessner (1983, 1985, 1990) defined two different types of style in which artifacts are consciously employed to communicate information (i.e., iconological style). She used the term "emblemic style" to refer to intentionally codified cultural information and "assertive style" to refer to personal expressions of identity created by the artisan who made the artifact. Wiessner (1983) studied San arrows from the Kalahari and argued that this medium was well suited for communicating cultural information, because arrows had social, economic, and symbolic importance in San society. Emblemic and assertive stylistic expressions most commonly occurred on the shaft of an arrow, which is the most visible portion.

criteria, on a project-by-project basis. Consequently, little consistency exists among previous typologies for Hohokam projectile tips.

Most studies of stone points from the study region have tended to focus on only a few attributes (e.g., the presence or absence of notching) within collections. Sayles (Gladwin et al. 1937) was one of the first researchers to classify Hohokam points recovered from the initial excavations at Snaketown. His system defined seven classes based on differences in morphology as well as perceived temporal associations. Subsequent researchers did not systematically employ the types he suggested. Crabtree (1973) completed the first detailed technological analysis of Hohokam points. The intent of his research was the identification of specific manufacturing techniques and consideration of the craftsmanship quality. He argued that the skill necessary to produce certain styles suggests specialization by individuals in the production of projectile points (see also Sliva 2010). Subsequent researchers also failed to adopt the classification system proposed by Crabtree.

Subsequent typologies of Hohokam projectile points have been largely descriptive (e.g., Bernard-Shaw 1988; Hoffman 1988; Montero 1993; Peterson 1994; Rozen 1984), and the functional as well as temporal systematics of Hohokam points have received less attention (but see Craig 1992; Justice 2002; Marshall 2001b; Sliva 1997). Peterson (1994:103) observed that "many studies have dealt with relatively small collections from single-component sites." This factor, when combined with the availability of better age estimates from other lines of evidence (particularly ceramics), probably accounts for the general lack of emphasis placed on the temporal sequencing of Hohokam points. Furthermore, the Hohokam produced more than one point shape at a given time, which also complicates the identification of temporally relevant types.

A factor that has further complicated comparisons of the various samples considered by previous Hohokam researchers is that those collections were generally derived from a variety of archaeological contexts, whereas the present study is focused on surface data. In particular, previous analyses of large Hohokam collections have included substantial numbers of points from mortuary assemblages, whereas mortuary contexts are underrepresented in the collection considered here. Points associated with burials frequently differ markedly from those recovered in other contexts, and individual interments may be associated with large numbers of highly similar projectile points (see Peterson 1994; Vint 2005; Whittaker 1984). This variation has been variously interpreted (e.g., the points from mortuary contexts are sometimes assumed to be too large or fragile for use), but whatever its source, failure to control for recovery context affects comparisons across time and space to the extent that sampled contexts are not uniformly distributed across these dimensions.

For example, the typology developed by Hoffman (1997) was based largely on points recovered from mortuary contexts from three geographical areas: the Middle Gila River (i.e., the Snaketown collections), the lower Salt River, and the Gila Bend area. Furthermore, his study focused on pre-Classic period Hohokam points and thus is of limited relevance for the present analysis. In addition, he was primarily concerned with synchronic rather than diachronic variation among Hohokam projectile points. His intent was to "address questions about the ethnic and/or linguistic diversity of regional Hohokam populations, and their potential organization into one or more alliances" (Hoffman 1997:iii). Hoffman identified quantitative variation among these three geographical areas that he interpreted as evidence for social variation among them.

More recently, Justice (2002) reviewed southwestern archaeological research and defined projectile point types based on both regional and temporal variation. He identified three type "clusters" that occurred on the Middle Gila River during the Ceramic period, including the "Western Triangular Cluster," the "Snaketown Cluster," and the "Pueblo Side Notched Cluster" (Justice 2002). However, examples of many small point styles he defined for the southwestern region are present among the collection considered here, and at the same time, several styles he suggested as typifying the Hohokam are rare in the P-MIP survey data (Loendorf and Rice 2004). In addition, styles in his typology were not systematically differentiated, and he did not employ a taxonomic classification system, which complicates comparison of these types.

Most recently, Sliva (2006:38) attempted to define temporal variation in a projectile point collection from northern Arizona and concluded that "the primary differences in projectile point style appear to be related more to culture than to temporal variation." She examined data from Anasazi, Hohokam, Mogollon, Cohonina, and Sinagua sites in order to better define both regional and temporal variation among projectile points. She found that simultaneous shifts occurred in projectile point types across much of Arizona during the Ceramic period (Sliva 2006:63). She argued that greater variability existed in point types from A.D. 950–1150 and that increased homogeneity occurred across Arizona during the A.D. 1150–1350 interval. She suggested that this patterning "may be related to increasing levels of population movement and conflict that have been postulated for the region during this time" (Sliva 2006:63).

Lithic Raw-Material Studies

Identification of source locations for materials at archaeological sites provides data that allow evaluation of many aspects of prehistoric societies. Lithic-material studies have been employed to infer mobility patterns and interregional contacts, including migration and trade or exchange networks (Kooyman 2000:136–149; Odell 2003:89–90). Much of the work on lithic diversity has been directed toward research questions associated with settlement strategies, especially the degree of sedentism. As Andrefsky (1998:219–220) noted, "some researchers believe that nonlocal raw materials are more likely to be found on shorter-duration sites than on longer-duration sites," and lithic raw-material diversity is also similarly suggested to be associated with occupation length.

Colin Renfrew (1977:72–78) suggested the "Law of Monotonic Decrement" to describe the negative correlation he observed between distance from the source and quantity of material, and lithic researchers generally expect that stone abundance should decrease with distance from the source. In addition to a decrease in quantity, studies have demonstrated a relationship between source distance and cortex percentages on artifacts and a general tendency for greater reduction of stone from distant locations (Odell 2003:196). Some researchers have used perceived distance-decay-relationship deviations to infer territorial areas for mobile groups. For example, Goodyear (1989) observed that many Paleo-Indian sites have substantial quantities of nonlocal lithic material from up to 200 km away, and he argued that the distance to these sources indicated the size of the band territory. It is sometimes argued that variations from expected distance relationships indicate that a raw material had a special ritual or social significance (Kooyman 2000:147).

For many reasons, much of the lithic-analysis literature has focused on research issues associated with mobile hunter-gatherers, and lithic studies of sedentary agricultural societies have received less attention (Odell 2003:202; Whittaker 1994:291). The "neutral model" for lithic acquisition developed by Brantingham (2003), for example, is based on assumptions that are not applicable to sedentary populations. The model assumes random and complete mobility with a limited amount of material that can be transported. Sedentary populations, in contrast, have a fixed location in space where materials can be accumulated, and logistical forays or other mechanisms were required to bring items to that location (Binford 1979). Research by Barton (1998) suggested that the effective local lithic abundance is controlled as much by human land-use patterns as it is by absolute raw-material distributions and that mobility patterns consequently affect both the density of artifact accumulations and the intensity of lithic reduction. Patterning observed by Riel-Salvatore and Barton (2004) suggested the importance of controlling for raw-material variation in order to better distinguish technological patterns.

In situations in which a fully sedentary settlement pattern is apparent from additional lines of evidence (e.g., substantial and persistent architecture), archaeologists have often simply assumed that raw materials from distant sources (e.g., those farther than a day's travel) arrived at sites as the result of trade relationships. In order to demonstrate that trade or exchange occurred, however, researchers must address three primary issues (Odell 2003:209). First, it is necessary to reliably establish the source of raw materials. Second, the manufacturing location for the product must be identified. Third, the mechanism for material displacement must be established.

Although analyses of the first two factors have often produced widely agreed-upon results, demonstrating the third aspect has proven more difficult and controversial. For example, some researchers have argued that the presence of unworked exotic raw materials indicates direct access, whereas finished goods of nonlocal materials at a site that lacks manufacturing debris are evidence for trade (Bayman and Shackley 1999:842). Although the latter may be possible evidence for trade, the former does not necessarily indicate direct access to sources, because raw materials as well as finished products can be exchanged (Peterson et al. 1997:236).

Examination of distance-decay relationships is one method archaeologists have employed to suggest different mechanisms for material transport (Kooyman 2000:136–140). Within the supply zone, for example, "direct access should result in a slightly curved, almost linear, decline in quantity with distance," and in contrast, "[d]own-the-line reciprocal exchange should be similar in shape, since distance and number of exchanges in the chain are really the only factors affecting the exchange, but the decline with distance from the source should be much more rapid and so the slope of the line will be steeper" (Kooyman 2000:139). Although the slopes of the lines are expected to vary, exchange relations should distribute materials over a larger area, whereas with direct access, material densities rapidly fall to zero after the limit of the supply zone.

Analytical problems exist when comparing archaeological data with hypothetical distance-decay relationships; some major issues include the following. First, this approach requires data from many sites, but archaeologists rarely have information from contemporaneous components that are also spread uniformly across the landscape at evenly varying distances from a given source. More often, data from just a few sites or even one site are available, site data may cluster in groups at similar distances, and/or sites at varying distances are from different time periods. Second, different raw-material-acquisition mechanisms are not necessarily mutually exclusive, and multiple approaches may have been taken, even at a given moment in time. Third, the slopes of distance-decay-correlation lines are related to many variables, including such things as transport costs (i.e., transporting goods over land vs. water or with human porters vs. pack animals) and the nature of trade or exchange interactions.

Another factor demonstrated by Brantingham's (2003) simulation is the effect of raw-material density and distribution in the environment on both material diversity at sites and distance-decay relationships. Despite these limitations, examination of the relationship between material quantities

and distance to the source provides useful information regarding the movement of goods on the landscape. The following discussion explores obsidian source characterizations, tool-manufacturing locations, and transport mechanisms in the Hohokam region of southern Arizona.

Southwestern Obsidian Source Identification

Obsidian is well suited for the study of socioeconomic-interaction patterns in central Arizona because (1) obsidian is a desirable, but not ubiquitous, material for small-point manufacture (Figure 8); (2) obsidian sources are generally localized deposits that are also abundant; (3) obsidian does not naturally occur in the study area, but sources are present to the north, south, east, and west; and (4) obsidian has physical properties that allow source areas to be objectively defined with a high degree of precision. Because of these characteristics, diachronic and synchronic patterning in obsidian acquisition has been employed to address economic, political, and ideological aspects of Hohokam society.

Source geochemical characterization is the initial step in the reconstruction of patterns of human obsidian exploitation. In the last 3 decades, Shackley (1988, 1990, 1995, 2005) has identified sources of both calc-alkaline and peralkaline obsidian in western New Mexico, Arizona, Nevada, California, Baja California, and Sonora (Figure 9). These relate to silicic volcanism that occurred during two periods: the middle to late Tertiary and the Quaternary. Both the geologic ages and the locations of sources are

important factors in raw-material utilization for projectile point manufacture.

In general, older sources tend to be composed of small, remnant obsidian nodules, known as marekanites or "Apache Tears," located in primary and secondary deposits mixed with devitrified, perlitic obsidian that appears mainly at the primary deposit or in volcaniclastic sediments. Perlite is unsuitable for tool production. Marekanites, however, are a common source of volcanic glass. Marekenites are small, residual obsidian fragments that occur both at the source and in streambeds or alluvial deposits away from the flow zone. Obsidian in this form typically has low fracture toughness, but because of the small nodule size, tool size is limited, and reduction is generally bipolar (Shackley 1990, 1992, 2005).

Middle to late Tertiary sources in Arizona included Antelope Wells, Burro Creek, Bull Creek, Cow Canyon, Vulture, Sauceda Mountain, Superior, Los Vidrios, and Tank Mountain. Somewhat more-recent marekanite sources farther to the east include Mule Creek and Red Hill in western New Mexico. Secondary sources or alluvial deposits of obsidian gravels may occur many kilometers from the primary deposits, in major drainage systems that flow away from primary deposits located at higher elevations.

More-recent, Quaternary sources include nodules as much as 30 cm in diameter that allow larger tools to be produced (Shackley 1990). Obsidian sources of this period include the San Francisco Volcanic Fields in northern Arizona (Government Mountain) and the Rio Grande Rift zone, including Jemez (including Valles Caldera) and Taos Plateau Volcanic Field in central and northern New Mexico.

Figure 8. Examples of obsidian flakes, marekanites, and projectile points.

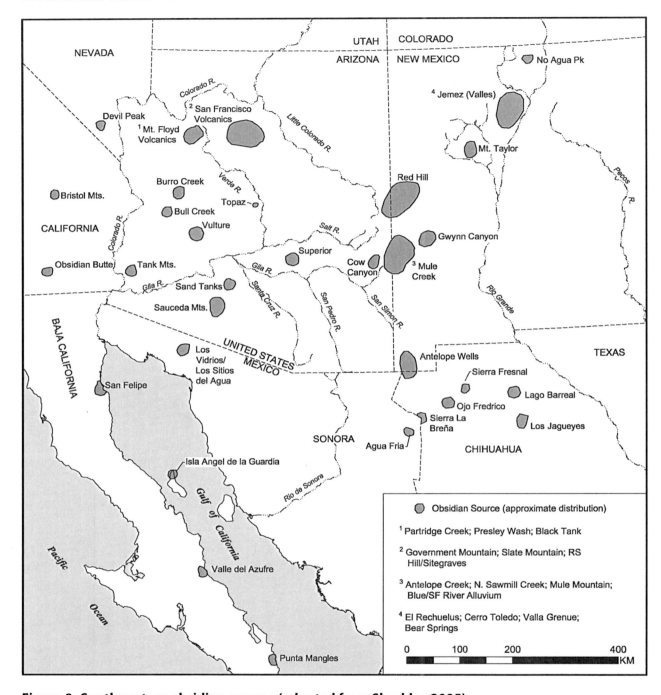

Figure 9. Southwestern obsidian sources (adopted from Shackley 2005).

Exchange, Social Interaction, and Material Transport

Although it is a relatively straightforward process to identify source locations for obsidian found at archaeological sites, understanding how that material arrived is more complicated. As noted by Bayman and Shackley (1999:842),

"[i]dentifying the precise behavioral mechanisms behind Hohokam, indeed any form of obsidian circulation, is extremely difficult given that multiple processes could account for its movement." Although obsidian acquisition may have been a complicated process that currently lacks a single universal explanation, it is still possible to evaluate different explanations for obsidian movement. Moreover, analyses of multiple lines of evidence for prehistoric interactions (e.g., ceramic-manufacturing locations and ceramic distribution) provide ways to more rigorously assess different models for transport (Simon and Gosser 2001:220).

Models proposed by Hohokam researchers for obsidian acquisition during the Classic period can be grouped into three general categories: direct-access, elite-control, and social-exchange models (Peterson et al. 1997). Ceramic studies add a fourth context for pre-Classic period remains: some researchers have argued that the exchange of commodities occurred in markets associated with activities at ball courts (Abbott et al. 2007; Shackley 2005:169). By the Classic period, however, the ball-court system was no longer in use, and associated marketplace transactions are thought to have ended (Abbott et al. 2007). Recent research has demonstrated that the elite-redistribution models do not apply to either obsidian (Peterson et al. 1997; Rice et al. 1998) or ceramic (Abbott 2000) exchange, and currently, most researchers argue for direct-access or social-exchange models. The following discussion considers each of the models through an examination of previous archaeological research.

Direct-Access Models

Models in this category assume that the end user of the obsidian personally traveled to the source to collect the material. This acquisition pattern is generally assumed to have been the primary or exclusive means of obsidian transport during the Archaic period in the Southwest (Bayham et al. 1986). Peterson et al. (1997:237–238) referred to this category as the Opportunistic Model, in part because some researchers have argued that obsidian-procurement strategies were embedded within the acquisition of other goods. For example, researchers have suggested that the Hohokam obtained Sauceda obsidian during shell-collection trips to the Gulf of California (Bayman and Shackley 1999). It is assumed that obsidian was a comparatively low-value item that was obtained, when possible, in the context of other activities. This model holds that distance to the source should be a primary factor that determines obsidian frequencies at sites, and deviations from this patterning are generally thought to be related to the embedded acquisition of other goods, variation in raw-material quality, or sampling errors.

Although direct obsidian procurement must have occurred in some regions and time periods, a number of observations have suggested that it is not the most parsimonious explanation for Classic period obsidian-acquisition patterns in the Hohokam core area. First, the incidence of obsidian at sites increases throughout the region for the Classic period (Loendorf et al. 2004; Marshall 2002:127–132; Peterson et al. 1997:234–235; Rice et al. 1998:109), indicating that greater effort was expended to acquire obsidian and suggesting that the material was more highly valued at that time. Second, Classic period obsidian frequencies are generally only weakly correlated

to distance to the source (Bayman and Shackley 1999; Marshall 2002; Rice et al. 1998). This contrasts with pre-Classic period obsidian-procurement patterns in which stronger distance-decay relationships appear to have been present (Bayman and Shackley 1999; Loendorf et al. 2004; Marshall 2002:129). Third, steep falloff curves for lithic raw materials are inconsistent with direct procurement (Kooyman 2000:139).

Chert from Windy Hill, which is the one of the few substantial and localized sources of fine-grained materials in the Hohokam region, provides an example of rapid raw-material falloff during the Classic period (Rice et al. 1998). Sites in close proximity to Windy Hill had comparatively high proportions of chert, and sites only slightly farther away were nearly devoid of chert and, instead, had higher proportions of other fine-grained materials (including obsidian) that could not have been from the source. Rice et al. (1998:129) concluded:

All settlements in the excavated sample could have satisfied their requirements for fine-grained lithic materials by directly procuring chert from the Windy Hill quarry. However, even settlements that lay 20 kilometers from Windy Hill had sufficient difficulty in procuring Windy Hill chert that they found it feasible to make up the balance by substituting fine-grained lithics from sources that lay hundreds of kilometers away.

These observations and others presented in the following research suggest that direct procurement was not the primary mechanism for obtaining obsidian within the core area during the Classic period. Historic period data also are not consistent with direct procurement, and sources located in close proximity to the core area were no longer extensively used at that time (Loendorf et al. 2004).

Elite-Control Models

These models posit that Classic period obsidian acquisition was part of complex organizational networks that controlled raw-material distribution (see Teague 1984). Researchers have suggested that platform mounds were centers for managing economic interactions and have argued that elite members of society controlled access to exotic materials, such as obsidian. Teague (1984), for example, argued that obsidian was a highly valued resource that was exchanged in a prestige sphere of interaction. Other researchers have posited that the elite members of societies who resided at the mounds were responsible for controlling redistribution of exotic materials, including obsidian. As another example, Bayman (1995) argued that elites provided obsidian to residents during "give-away" ceremonies at mound events and that this material was then further distributed throughout the wider community through reciprocal exchange.

In one of the most detailed and comprehensive studies to date, Rice (1998a) evaluated the elite-redistribution model through analyses of multiple exotic items, including obsidian. Rice (1998a:141) found that although platform mounds did have greater quantities of some goods, including obsidian, the levels of exotic materials were well below those expected for centralized managerial-control systems. Further, materials that were more abundant at mounds consisted of items associated with ceremony and ritual, and other exotic items had roughly similar distributions within communities.

Throughout the Hohokam core area, debitage- and finished-tool-source proportions for most types are similar, suggesting that obsidian was not usually transported as completed tools and that core reduction commonly occurred at sites (Bayman and Shackley 1999; Loendorf et al. 2004; Marshall 2002; Peterson et al. 1997:243). Rather than stockpiles of cores or large flakes, as would be expected with redistribution, obsidian at Tonto Basin platform mounds occurred largely as manufacturing debris, and other sites in the community had similar evidence for on-site obsidian-tool manufacture. Based on his analyses, Rice (1998a:150) concluded that elites at platform mounds "did not exercise managerial control over long-distance exchange or the production of craft items." Peterson et al. (1997) examined raw-material diversity, tool-manufacturing locations, and intrasite as well as intersite variation in obsidian at Classic period sites in the Salt Basin and along the Middle Gila River. They similarly concluded that there was little evidence to support elite-distribution models for obsidian (Peterson et al. 1997:255).

Social-Exchange Models

This class includes models that suggest that Classic period populations in southern Arizona predominantly acquired obsidian through exchange interactions. Researchers differ in their characterizations of the bases for these associations, but these differences are largely a matter of emphasis, and the various explanations are not mutually exclusive. Peterson et al. (1997:255), for example, suggested that exchange networks were "based on family and simple reciprocal ties." Other researchers have argued that trade networks were established by the arrival of immigrants from different regions (Simon et al. 1998). Some analysts have considered the possibility that itinerate traders moved obsidian among areas (Di Peso 1974; McGuire 1980). Based on the distribution of imported goods, Rice et al. (1998) argued that the ability to produce agricultural surpluses was an important factor that determined involvement in trade networks. As a final example, Seymour (2011:293) argued that intergroup marriage both facilitated and benefited trade systems.

Diachronic and synchronic patterning in obsidian acquisition provides evidence for Classic period socioeconomic-

interaction networks. For example, in their analyses of Tonto Basin materials, including obsidian, Simon and Gosser (2001:236) found evidence that the sites on the Tonto and Salt River portions of the basin were integrated into distinct polities that maintained separate trade relationships. They also found that the division among communities within the basin started in the early Classic period and that the two polities became increasingly polarized over time.

In some respects, Tonto Basin is a microcosm of the Hohokam core area, and similar economic distinctions developed and intensified throughout the area during the Classic period. For example, sites in the Salt and Tonto Basins both generally have higher proportions of obsidian from the sources in northern Arizona than do sites along the Middle Gila River, where this obsidian composed only 4 percent of the collection (Shackley and Daehnke 2004). Northern Arizona obsidian accounted for 49 percent of the pre-Classic period collection and 24 percent of the Classic period collection from the Salt Basin (Marshall 2002:132–133). This diachronic trend was reversed in the Tonto Basin, where Government Mountain obsidian was less than 10 percent of early Classic period assemblages but was the most common obsidian, at roughly 35 percent, for both the Tonto and Salt River portions of the basin in the late Classic period (Simon and Gosser 2001:227). The northern Arizona sources are approximately 265 km from the Middle Gila River, a distance that far exceeds the roughly 30 km between the Salt River and Gila River sites. Diachronic patterning in the Salt Basin suggests that ties to the north decreased over time, whereas interaction to the north increased in the Tonto Basin and at Casa Grande (Bayman and Shackley 1999:841; Rice et al. 1998:120).

Chapter Summary

This chapter has provided background information for the investigations that follow, including a summary of current knowledge concerning the culture history of the study area. Although consensus exists regarding the general outline of events that occurred during prehistory, there is not similar agreement regarding why changes in material-culture traditions occurred over time. Although such alterations have long been recognized and are still used to define periods and phases in the archaeological record, until comparatively recently, most seemingly abrupt changes in material culture were simply assumed to have resulted from the migration of outside groups.

Compared to ceramics, projectile point data have previously received little attention in debates regarding cultural variation in the study area. It is suggested here that stone-point data can be employed to provide a different perspective on cultural-historical events, which may help to elucidate such issues as the Hohokam-continuum debate.

Much of the previous research regarding projectile point variation has revolved around debating the meaning of the term "style," which is now generally agreed to be something separate from function. Style can be a passive and unintentional expression that results from habits of manufacture, or it can be consciously communicated information regarding social identity. In addition, there are two different ways that function can be defined: (1) as the use or uses an artifact was designed to perform or (2) as the use or uses that the artifact was actually employed to perform. The failure to explicitly recognize these and other distinctions has been the source of considerable disagreement over the meanings of the terms "style" and "function." As will be presented in the next chapter, this study focuses on point function rather than style, and a design approach is employed that attempts to define the tasks that points were intended to perform.

Addressing the use-life of projectile points is essential for any analysis of variation in point shape and size. Although some previous researchers have argued that wear and subsequent reworking commonly resulted in substantial alterations to the size and appearance of projectile points, P-MIP survey collection data suggest that this practice only rarely occurred in the study area, especially for the small arrow points considered in this analysis. As will be discussed further in the following research, it appears that performance characteristics and differences in the intended use of a weapon had a more substantial effect on the size and shape of stone points.

Little consensus exists among previously proposed classification schemes for arrow points from the Hohokam region. Instead, most researchers employ ad hoc types on a project-by-project basis. Rather than following this pattern, types employed in this study were developed following those defined by Sliva (1997). Type classifications, metric data, and images of all P-MIP survey points employed in the following analyses are available in the study by Loendorf and Rice (2004).

Fine-grained raw materials that were preferred for the manufacture of stone points rarely occur in the study area. Consequently, most of the materials had to be brought in from elsewhere, and projectile point raw-material source studies are therefore well suited for the consideration of regional socioeconomic-interaction patterns. After nearly 30 years of research, regional patterns in obsidian procurement have become apparent. Three models have been proposed for obsidian transport in the Hohokam region. The first of these models (elite control) has been rejected because extensive excavation projects completed during the 1990s failed to identify supporting evidence. Most Hohokam researchers now argue for direct-access or social-exchange models. Both synchronic and diachronic patterns in obsidian acquisition are inconsistent with direct access, and it appears that the most parsimonious explanation is that the Hohokam of central Arizona obtained most of their obsidian through social mechanisms. This suggestion is stated as a hypothesis in the following chapter and is subsequently tested using P-MIP survey and excavation data in Chapter 6.

CHAPTER 4

Research Methods

The following discussion considers point variation from an etic design perspective, which holds that highly shaped artifacts, such as projectile points, were produced with the intent of performing one or more specific tasks. The design process is limited by available materials and known manufacturing techniques, and the performance of projectiles is constrained by the laws of physics (Cotterell and Kamminga 1992; Klopsteg 1993; Kooi 1983). These laws are employed in the subsequent discussion to suggest cross-cultural constraints on the point design process.

This research employs both an attribute-based approach and analyses of projectile points based on previously defined types (Loendorf and Rice 2004; Sliva 1997). Quantitative variation in Classic and Historic period projectile point metric attributes, including weight and notching characteristics, are evaluated through the use of Exploratory Data Analysis (EDA). The EDA approach emphasizes visual displays of the data rather than summary statistics derived from the assemblage (Shennan 1990:22). This technique is well suited for archaeological data that may not conform to assumptions that underlie many summary statistics. Bivariate analyses are subsequently employed to test the statistical significance of distributions identified in the EDA. Multivariate analyses are used to examine variation in obsidian data. Obsidian source areas were determined through X-ray fluorescence (XRF) elemental analyses.

This chapter presents three middle-range hypotheses that are employed to link patterning in archaeological data to past human behavior. The first hypothesis is employed to seriate point collections. The second hypothesis defines the tasks that stone points were designed to perform. The third hypothesis is based on considerable previous research, and it postulates that obsidian distribution patterns can be used as proxy measures for socioeconomic interactions among communities. Survey methodological issues are addressed prior to discussion of the hypotheses.

Survey Methods

During the P-MIP survey, crewmembers walked parallel transects spaced 20 m apart. The Arizona State Museum

(ASM) definition of an archaeological site, provided in the ASM site-recording manual (Fish and Fish 1993), was used to determine those areas that had site-level artifact density. These guidelines define a site as having 30 or more artifacts of a single artifact type within a 15-m area, 20 or more artifacts of at least two artifact types within a 15-m area, one or more features in temporal association with artifacts, or two or more temporally associated features with no artifacts. Areas that met these criteria and were separated by 100 m or more were recorded as separate sites. Locations that met these criteria and were less than 100 m apart were recorded as separate loci of the same site.

Each site was assigned a Gila River (GR) site number, and a datum with an identification tag was established. All datum locations were recorded using a real-time differential Global Positioning System unit. Sites were delineated by marking artifacts and features with pin flags. This enabled visual determination of the site boundaries and any internal fluctuations in artifact density. AutoCAD mapping software was employed to calculate site and survey areas based on recorded boundaries.

An ASM site form was completed for each site, and photographs were taken. Each artifact collection included at least one quantitative unit and a sample of diagnostic artifacts. Quantitative units consisted of 2-m-diameter circles from which all artifacts were collected. A sample of diagnostic artifacts (including obsidian, decorated ceramics, undecorated nonbody sherds, and projectile points) was collected. Rough estimates for the total counts of nondiagnostic artifacts were noted in the ASM site-description form. In addition, a GRIC-CRMP Artifact Diversity Form was completed; this form includes estimates for the counts of nondiagnostic artifacts of different materials and presence/absence data for various artifact types.

Isolated occurrences (IOs) were defined as individual artifacts or features or dispersed nonsite scatters that did not meet the site-definition criteria stipulated in ASM guidelines (Fish and Fish 1993). IOs were numbered consecutively by township, range, and section. Each IO was described and plotted on the appropriate U.S. Geological Survey (USGS) 7.5-minute topographic map. Generally, these artifacts were not collected for analysis.

Discussion

For several reasons, site size varies widely within the study area. First, dispersed *ranchería*-style habitations are common in the area, and the locations of these settlements have tended to drift over time (Darling 2011; Darling et al. 2004; Ezell 1961:110; Spier 1933:22). As noted by Spier (1933:22), "[b]ecause of this, practically every inch of the valley from Sacate to Gila Crossing had at one time or another been the site of dwellings." As a result, essentially continuous scatters of artifacts occur in some locations, and following the ASM guidelines leads to the creation of expansive sites. Second, comparatively little topographic relief exists in many locations, and few natural features are present to delineate site boundaries. Consequently, site and loci limits were often arbitrarily based on modern features, such as roads or agricultural-field boundaries. In areas with little modern development, site boundaries were extended until roads or other recent features were reached—in some instances, for many kilometers. Third, because of the arid environment, comparatively little deposition and erosion has occurred in most locations. Pleistocene deposits are exposed on the ground surface in some places, and less than 50 cm of sediment has accumulated during the Holocene in many areas. Consequently, the entire Holocene record is exposed at or near the surface throughout much of the study area (Wells, Rice, et al. 2004:632). Rather than being covered by deposition or eroded and thus dispersed at a lower density, very-high-density surface-artifact concentrations occur in some areas (Wells, Rice, et al. 2004). Fourth, vegetation is sparse, and ground visibility is generally high in the study area, which facilitates the identification of surface artifacts.

Sites recorded during the P-MIP survey range from small scatters of less than 1,000 m² to extensive and dense deposits that cover more than 15,000,000 m². In areas with few modern features, even the loci defined at sites range to over 700,000 m². Surface-artifact densities at sites also have a large range of variation, from lower than two artifacts per square meter to over 200 (Wells, Rice, et al. 2004:635).

Because provenience control for most artifacts was defined based on archaeological site and locus, the exponential variation in site and loci size created sampling issues. First, the sampling fraction of collection units differed by many orders of magnitude. This was complicated by the fact that artifacts are unlikely to be evenly distributed across sites or loci. Second, the generally low depositional rates and spatially expansive habitation areas that tend to drift resulted in a situation in which cultural remains from a long time frame were mixed together on the modern ground surface. This problem was exacerbated by the large size of sites and even loci within sites, which were the only levels of provenience control available for most of the projectile points collected. Thus, dating nondiagnostic artifacts based on nearby diagnostic artifacts was problematic. Third, the extensive Prehistoric and Historic period agricultural fields in the community have mixed and dispersed remains in some locations, whereas other expansive areas have not been similarly disturbed.

One solution to address some of these analytical limitations is to only consider the data that were collected from the small quantitative units (Wells, Rice, et al. 2004). More-precise provenience information is available for these units, and all artifacts were collected, rather than just a sample of diagnostic remains. However, each quantitative unit encompassed just 3.14 m², which represents a minor fraction of site areas. As a result of the small sampling area, projectile points were never found in the units, and the only provenience data for points were at the site level and sometimes the locus level.

In this analysis, artifact provenience and temporal-control limitations are addressed in several ways. First, instead of comparing site data, much larger areas of roughly similar size are employed as sampling units. Second, the total survey area is used to standardize the data (i.e., densities were calculated by dividing point counts by the area surveyed in each unit). Third, temporal estimates for the points themselves are used, rather than ages for other diagnostic artifacts in the sampled contexts.

P-MIP Survey Data

Figure 10 shows the 13 units used as sampling areas in the analysis of point data. Unit boundaries are based on the locations of topographic features and streams. Because of the provenience limitations, it was necessary to jog unit boundaries around site borders in some locations (e.g., between Units 4 and 7 on the map). All units are separated by the Gila River, and adjacent boundaries are divided along the modern floodplain.

Table 5 shows sampling-unit hectares, survey hectares, and site-area hectares for the P-MIP survey data in 2002. Data are available for relatively large proportions of most areas except Blackwater, the Sacaton Mountains, and Santa Cruz, where sampling error was a concern. Site densities are also reported.

The high site densities in the Blackwater and Santan units resulted from the presence of extensive nonirrigation agricultural fields along the Santan Mountains *bajada*, where site areas were defined on the basis of features rather than artifact densities. With the exception of these two areas, site density was highest in the Snaketown and Casa Blanca areas, and the overall site densities on the northern and southern sides of the river were similar. Despite extensive survey coverage, no projectile points were collected from the Santan or Sacaton Mountains units; these areas are therefore not included in the following analyses of point data. No survey data are available for Unit 13 on the map, which therefore is also not included in this study.

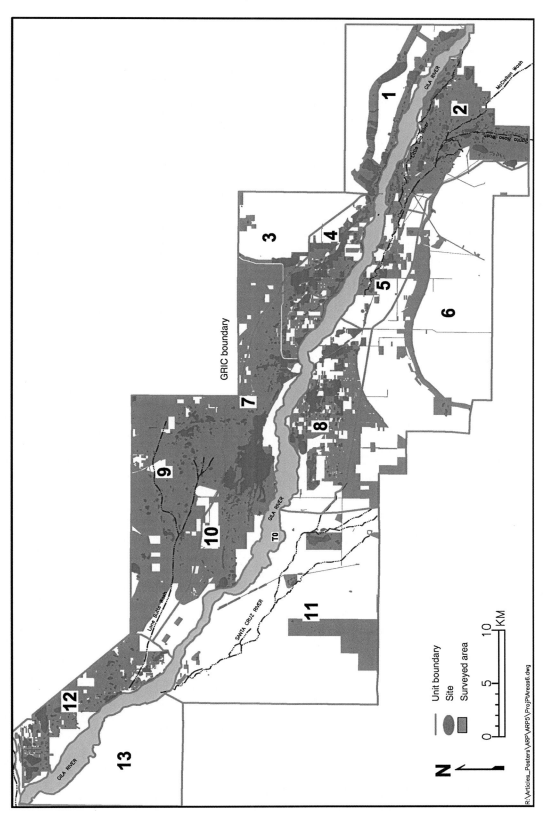

Figure 10. Survey coverage, site areas, and study units employed in the analyses.

R:\Articles_Posters\ARP\ARP5\ProjAreas6.dwg

Table 5. Survey Coverage and Site Size, by Study Unit within the Gila River Indian Community

Site Group	Map No.	Unit Area (ha)	Survey Area (ha)	Survey Proportion (%)	Site Area (ha)	Site Proportion (%)
Northern side						
Maricopa	12	7,273	5,223	71.8	791	15.1
Santan Mountains	3	7,990	3,096	38.7	224	7.2
Borderlands	9	15,109	13,752	91.0	582	4.2
Blackwater	1	9,748	1,778	18.2	1,036	58.3
Santan	4	3,989	3,052	76.5	1,238	40.6
Lone Butte	10	5,752	3,432	59.7	245	7.1
Snaketown	7	9,434	8,267	87.6	2,327	28.1
Total, northern side		59,295	38,600	65.1	6,443	16.7
Southern side						
Sacaton	5	4,083	1,535	37.6	267	17.4
Santa Rosa	2	8,883	5,449	61.3	931	17.1
Sacaton Mountains	6	25,592	4,404	17.2	167	3.8
Santa Cruz	11	25,107	3,047	12.1	250	8.2
Casa Blanca	8	8,651	5,325	61.5	1,448	27.2
Total, southern side		72,316	19,760	27.3	3,063	15.5
Total		131,611	58,360	44.3	9,506	16.3

Historic and Classic Period Projectile Point Types

This section summarizes metric data that were collected and a typological classification system that was designed to seriate Classic and Historic period points from the study area (Loendorf and Rice 2004). Although the term "style" is commonly employed to refer to the categories in point-classification schemes, the use of this word introduces confusion, because both stylistic and functional variations appear to be associated with the morphological traits on which the types are based. Therefore, the following discussion eschews use of the term "style" in favor of "type" or "variety" when referring to categories in the classification system.

Previous research in southern Arizona has attributed small, unnotched points to the Historic period (Figure 11k–m). Traditionally, two types were recognized, one associated with the O'odham (Pima or Papago) and the other suggested to have been made by the "Sobaipuri," a designation, derived from early Spanish sources, for people who lived along the San Pedro and Gila Rivers (Bronitsky 1985; Canouts et al. 1972; Di Peso 1953; Doyel 1977; Gilpin and Phillips 1998; Haury 1950; Justice 2002; Loendorf and Rice 2004; Masse 1981; Ravesloot and Whittlesey 1987; Rosenthal et al. 1978; Seymour 1993, 2009, 2011; Vint 2005).

Points that fit these two categories are common in surface contexts in the study area, and in total, 205 examples are present in the P-MIP collection (Loendorf and Rice 2004). It appears, however, that this dichotomy is an oversimplification of variation present among Historic period projectile points (Seymour 2011:90–95). Morphologically similar points were produced during the Classic period, and attribution of individual artifacts to either type or even to the Historic period, itself, has remained uncertain (Justice 2002:273; Ravesloot and Whittlesey 1987:96; Seymour 2011; Vint 2005:41).

Stone projectile points attributed to the Akimel O'odham include small, triangular forms that lack notches or serration (see Figure 11k) (see Brew and Huckell 1987:171; Gilpin and Phillips 1998; Haury 1950; Rosenthal et al. 1978). Haury (1950:268), for example, suggested a pattern at Ventana Cave in which unnotched points occurred only sporadically prior to the appearance of ceramics but were common afterward, until intensive use of the cave stopped. He described point collections from several "known historic Papago village sites" and concluded that small, generally unnotched points typify these sites and the most-recent material from Ventana Cave (Haury 1950:274). Points fitting this description were classified as "Straight Base Triangular" by Loendorf and Rice (2004).

The second variety that has been associated with recent assemblages from southern Arizona includes small, triangular points with U-shaped, concave bases (see Figure 11l) (see Gilpin and Phillips 1998:89–91; Justice 2002:272–274;

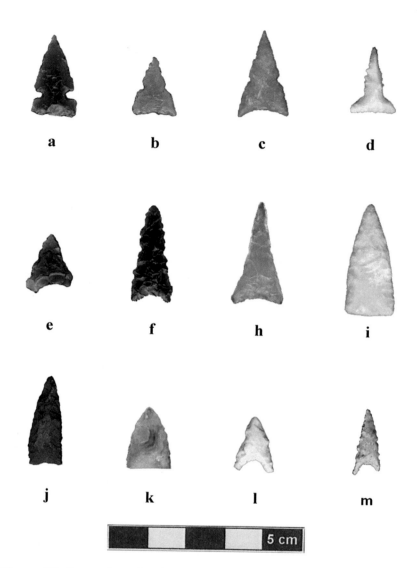

Figure 11. Examples of point types from the Classic and Historic Periods: (*a*) intermediate-side-notched; (*b*) upper-side-notched; (*c*) middle-side-notched; (*d*) flanged; (*e*) bulbous base; (*f*) straight-blade serrated; (*h*) concave-base triangular; (*i*) thin triangular; (*j*) long triangular; (*k*) straight-base triangular; (*l*) U-shaped base triangular; (*m*) Huachuca (adapted from Loendorf and Rice 2004).

Seymour 2009, 2011; Vint 2005). These points were classified as "U-shaped Base Triangular" by Loendorf and Rice (2004). Previous researchers have classified these artifacts as "Sobaipuri" points, based, in part, on Pfefferkorn's (1989) description of points from southern Arizona. When describing "Sonoran" points from the mid-1700s, Pfefferkorn (1989:202) stated, "this [a triangular, pointed flint] is about one inch long, not quite an inch wide, and as thick in the middle as the back of a strong knife. The edges, however, are filed as thin as a single card and are armed all along with sharp saw teeth."

Serrated points with deeply concave bases are common at late sites along the San Pedro River (Di Peso 1951, 1953; Justice 2002:272–274; Masse 1981; Seymour 2011; Vint 2005:40). As will be discussed further in Chapter 5, this is the location generally associated with the "Sobaipuri." These definitions of "Sobaipuri" points, however, are different from that employed for U-shaped Base Triangular points and are restricted to serrated points with U-shaped, concave bases and straight blade margins that lack notches (Seymour 2011:92). Points judged to be most similar to this definition of the "Sobaipuri" type are therefore reclassified here as a subcategory of the U-shaped Base Triangular (see Figure 11m), hereafter referred to as the Huachuca variety, following arguments presented by Seymour (2011:92).

Based on a recent analysis of Historic period projectile points from southern Arizona, Vint (2005:41) concluded:

> Throughout this paper, I have referred to the points from sites discussed as "Sobaipuri" or "Piman" points. In part this is forced by convention to clarify the social contexts of the sites: the Spanish clearly identified the people living along the San Pedro River and in the Santa Cruz Valley as Sobaipuri, and so sites known to date to the early historical period (as identified by sites with Spanish artifacts), and sites that share similar material culture (architecture, tool types), are defined as Sobaipuri. This is done even though in the discussion above I assert that assigning ethnic significance to variation in point shape is tenuous at best. However, in contrast to the very murky definition of "Soto" points, the association of triangular, concaved-based points with Piman people—specifically Sobaipuri—in southern Arizona seems legitimate.

Sliva (1997) defined nine projectile point types that have been recovered from Classic period archaeological contexts in the Sonoran Desert (see Figure 11a–j). These include both side-notched and unnotched forms. Sliva (1997) defined three types of side-notched points, based on the placement of notches along the blade margins. One variety consists of points with notches in the lower one-third of the blade (see Figure 11a); the taxonomic definition of this type overlaps with a pre-Classic period category she defined, and the two types were therefore combined by Loendorf and Rice (2004). The second side-notched-point type has notches near the middle of the blade (see Figure 11c), and the final type has notches closer to the upper one-third of the blade (see Figure 11b).

Although notched points have not previously been associated with the Historic period in southern Arizona, highly similar unnotched flaked stone points have occurred in both Classic and Historic period contexts, which has complicated the identification of temporally relevant point shapes (Justice 2002:273; Ravesloot and Whittlesey 1987:96; Vint 2005:41). Sliva (1997) defined six Classic period varieties that lack notches. One category (Classic Flanged) has wide, flaring bases and long, parallel-sided blades (see Figure 11d). Classic Long Triangular points are narrow, bifacially retouched artifacts with length-to-width ratios of 3:1 or more (see Figure 11j). Another type is based on the presence of serration and straight blade margins (see Figure 11f). The fourth type is defined based on the presence of crescent-shaped, concave bases (see Figure 11h). She defined the fifth type "on the basis of their uniform thinness" (Sliva 1997:54) (see Figure 11i). The sixth and final unnotched type is rare in the P-MIP collection, and these points have irregular, bulbous bases (see Figure 11e).

Figure 12 shows measurement locations and the terms used to refer to aspects of the points in the following

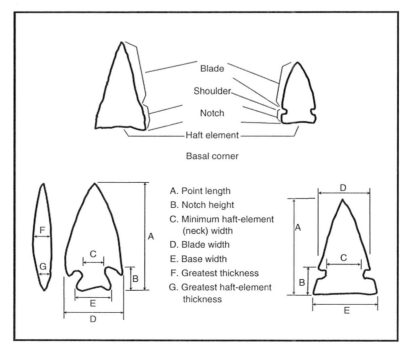

A. Point length
B. Notch height
C. Minimum haft-element (neck) width
D. Blade width
E. Base width
F. Greatest thickness
G. Greatest haft-element thickness

Figure 12. Measurement locations and point terminology employed in the analysis.

research. Table 6 lists attributes that were recorded for each artifact. Where possible, these data were collected from all projectile points or point preforms in the collection.

Projectile Point Design Theory

Performance constraints do not determine the appearance of points but merely set limits for effective design within which there is room for cultural expression and individual variation (Nelson 1997:372). Deviations beyond theoretically optimal design parameters also certainly occurred for myriad reasons, but if these are indeed exceptions, they cannot invalidate generalizations regarding projectile-performance design constraints. Most importantly, designs are subject to modification through chance, trial and error, emulation, and inspired innovation. Simply put, although humans are constrained by this world, our practices are not determined by these limits.

Flaked stone projectile points are small portions of composite weapons, the remainders of which are rarely preserved in archaeological contexts. Although points are seemingly small elements, their design is constrained by forces involved in successfully launching an elongated projectile and having it penetrate an intended target at range (Cotterell and Kamminga 1992; Klopsteg 1993; Kooi 1983; Vanpool 2003). No single ideal design exists for projectiles, because these weapons were used for a variety of purposes, and optimization of one design aspect usually results in the compromising of others (Knecht 1997:200). Effective projectile design is therefore the result of compromise, the exact nature of which is largely dependent on the intended use of the weapon (Knecht 1997).

Projectile performance requirements are not static and, instead, vary based on a number of variables (Knecht 1997). A partial list of these factors includes target size, target range, target type (human or other animal), target location (air, land, or water), whether the intent is to wound or to kill, and general vegetation density and type in the environment. Some of the factors that affect the performance of the projectile itself include kinetic energy, momentum, spine (resistance to bending), durability, maintainability, sectional density, and point geometry, including edge sharpness and haft design (Vanpool 2003:116–165). In order to consider design constraints of projectile points, it is therefore necessary to address the range of uses for which these artifacts may have been intended and the technological responses that were possible.

Contrary to a common assumption, a stone projectile tip is not necessary to "balance" the shaft. Ethnographic observations and unusually well-preserved Prehistoric period artifacts suggest that projectiles commonly lacked stone points (Figure 13). Instead, organic tips, such as those made of bone, antler, or wood, were frequently employed. In a cross-cultural study of over 100 preindustrial societies, Ellis (1997) observed that different types of projectile tips were employed for separate purposes. Stone points were closely associated with hunting large (>40 kg) game animals and/or with warfare, whereas organic tips were far more commonly employed in hunting small (<40 kg) game. "In fact, this pattern is so strong that in prehistoric cases one can almost always assume that stone points were used in large animal hunting [or warfare]" (Ellis 1997:63). The main reason that stone points were employed was to make the projectiles more lethal, and contrary to a common assumption, almost no indications were found that stone-point size was correlated to the size of the animal hunted (Ellis 1997:45–46). These data suggest that stone points were used for a subset of all projectile tasks (i.e., large-game hunting or warfare), and the following discussion focuses on physical constraints that are common to both practices.

Many reasons why stone points were not designed for small-game hunting exist. First, it is possible to have a larger blunt striking area using organic materials (Ellis 1997:47). These large tips made it easier to hit a target and were less likely to damage the thin skin of small animals. Second, stone points would too easily pass through a small animal, so the game could run away unimpeded. Third, stone points were seen as a liability in waterfowl and small-aquatic-mammal hunting, because the weight of the stone would cause rapid sinking of the arrow (Ellis 1997:47). Fourth, the weight of the point would decrease the speed of the projectile (Cotterell and Kamminga 1992; Klopsteg 1993); benefits of higher projectile velocities are discussed further below. Fifth, the broad, flat surface of the point affects the aerodynamic performance of an arrow, making it less accurate (Klopsteg 1993; Vanpool 2003:162). Sixth, the additional manufacturing costs of procuring raw materials and producing and attaching a stone point (which is likely to break with use) would not be warranted, given the limited return from small game (Dean 2003). Finally, stone points are simply not necessary to effectively kill small animals (Ellis 1997).

Christenson (1997) argued that penetration (i.e., depth) and wound size (i.e., diameter) are the two most critical aspects of stone projectile point performance (see also Vanpool 2003:123). He maintained that wound size is principally related to point width. Penetration, however, is more important than wound width, because the victim of a large but shallow wound is more likely to survive than one who receives even a minute wound to a critical internal organ, especially the heart (Bill 1862:385). The most efficient and rapid way to kill any large animal with a projectile is to completely penetrate both lungs and the heart; even a puncture to a single lung is likely to cause death through suffocation. This area is a larger target than the head or neck and is encased by less bone, although

Table 6. Attribute Definitions Employed in the Projectile Point Analysis

<u>**Point Shape**</u>

Teardrop: convex blade margins taper asymmetrically from the base to the tip

Lanceolate: lower blade margins are parallel and taper in a curve to the tip

Triangular: straight blade margins with the maximum width at the base

Diamond: trapezoidal shape with shoulders (maximum blade width) near the midpoint of the blade

<u>**Haft Treatment**</u>

Notch: depressions in the blade margin that are at least as deep as wide (Holmer 1986)

Side notched: notches are approximately perpendicular to the long axis of the point, and the base width is equal to or greater than the shoulder width

Corner notched: notches are at an angle of less than 90° to the long axis of the point, and the base width is less than the shoulder width

Corner/side notched: notches are perpendicular to the long axis of the point, and the base width is less than the shoulder width

Stemmed: hafted portion is separated from the blade by a shoulder

Unnotched: lacks notching and stem; the haft element is not differentiated from the blade by either a shoulder or a notch

<u>**Stem Shape**</u>

Expanding: base width is greater than the minimum haft-element width

Straight: base width is approximately equal to the minimum haft-element width

Contracting: base width is the minimum haft-element width

<u>**Base Shape**</u>

Concave: basal corners are lower than the center of the base

Convex: basal corners are higher than the center of the base

Straight: basal corners and central portion of the base form an approximately straight line (as straight as possible given the irregularities of flake scars)

Pointed: basal corners meet

<u>**Shoulder Shape**</u>

Obtuse angle: junction of the blade and the haft element is greater than a right angle

Abrupt: junction of the blade and the haft element forms a right angle

Barbed: junction of the blade and the haft element forms an acute angle

<u>**Proportionate Criteria**</u>

Haft-element width: see Figure 12 for location of measurement

Shoulder width: see Figure 12 for location of measurement

Base width: see Figure 12 for location of measurement

<u>**Serrated Edge**</u>

Present: blade has adjacent small notches forming teeth along the edge

Absent: blade edge is not serrated

<u>**Blade-Margin Shape**</u>

Straight: blade margins define straight lines between the basal corners and the tip

Concave: blade margins define concave lines between the basal corners and the tip

Convex: blade margins define convex lines between the basal corners and the tip

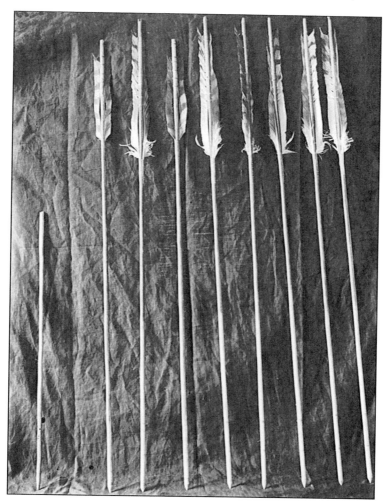

Figure 13. Akimel O'odham small-game-hunting *haapod* (arrows) with wooden points collected from the Gila River Indian Community (photograph by De Lancey Gill, Negative 2678 A, National Anthropological Archives, Smithsonian Institution, Washington, D.C.).

it is still protected by the rib cage, a potentially effective barrier, and the shot requires passing through or between ribs (Stevens 1870:564). Flaked points must necessarily be made from brittle stone that readily fractures on impact (this is how points are shaped), and wider points are more likely to hit the ribs and shatter, resulting in a wide but shallow and non-life-threatening wound on the exterior of the rib cage (Bill 1882:104).

These two performance characteristics (wound width and penetration depth) are also inversely related, such that all else being equal, projectiles with larger cutting diameters will not penetrate as deeply (Nelson 1997:377; Pope 2000:43). Because of the greater importance of penetration, it is likely that the cutting diameter was compromised in favor of penetration for stone projectile tips. The nature of

this relationship, however, differs for projectile points made from metal, the performance characteristics of which are different from those of stone.

Penetration is the product of kinetic energy (i.e., impact force), sectional density (i.e., point cross section), and projectile geometry, including edge sharpness (cf. Christenson 1997:137; Kooi 1983:24; Vanpool 2003). Kinetic energy is a fundamental factor, because without sufficient force, a projectile will not penetrate, regardless of how sharp it is or the nature of the cross section. The kinetic energy of a projectile is a function of its mass and velocity. Using a bow of a fixed propulsive energy, heavier arrows have greater force, because as Newton's laws of motion inform us, for every action there is an equal and opposite reaction; consequently, more energy is transferred to heavier projectiles during launch (Adams 2000:81; Baker 2001:107; Cotterell and Kamminga 1992:33–35; Klopsteg 1993; Kooi 1983:28; Vanpool 2003:162). Not only does a heavier arrow have more kinetic energy when launched, it also decelerates at a slower rate (Kooi 1983:69; Vanpool 2003:122). Therefore, a heavier arrow begins with more kinetic energy, and it retains a higher percentage of its impact force downrange. On the other hand, because they have lower inertia, lighter projectiles will leave the launching mechanism at higher velocities than will heavier projectiles (Baker 2001:107; Cotterell and Kamminga 1992; Kooi 1983:28; Vanpool 2003:122).

Increasing the velocity of projectiles has many important performance advantages. First, higher velocities allow greater range (Klopsteg 1993; Ratzat 1999; Vanpool 2003:119). Excluding friction, this is because projectiles begin to fall, accelerated by gravity at the same rate, as soon as they leave the launching mechanism, regardless of their speed. Consequently, the greater the velocity, the longer the forward distance a projectile will travel before hitting the ground. Second, higher velocities allow greater accuracy; because it is possible to aim more directly at targets, this is colloquially referred to as "flat-shooting" (Cotterell and Kamminga 1992; Klopsteg 1993:14; Kooi 1983:24). The lower the velocity, the greater the necessity to aim above a target at a given range (the maximum distance occurs at an approximately 45° angle above the target) (Cotterell and Kamminga 1992:162–163). For the same reason, low-velocity projectiles also require greater accuracy in the target-distance estimation and control over projectile speed to determine precisely how far above the target to aim (Klopsteg 1993:24). Third, the higher the velocity, the shorter the time lapse between launching the projectile and its impact with the target. This makes hitting moving targets easier and allows less time for an intended target to avoid the projectile. Fourth, higher velocities allow the use of smaller projectiles while maintaining the same impact force; therefore, it is possible to carry more individual projectiles, which allows for more shots without having to retrieve fired projectiles.

At the same time, the mass of stone tips attached to elongated projectiles is also constrained by the acceleration method employed to launch the missile. Hand-thrown spears are held closer to the center of mass (i.e., the balance point) during launch, whereas both atlatl darts and arrows are launched by accelerating the distal ends, which creates different constraints on the distribution of mass for these projectiles. For example, when an arrow is launched from a bow, the nock (i.e., the notch for the bowstring) is accelerated before the tip. The greater velocity of the nock, when combined with the inertia of a tip of higher density than the shaft and on its opposite end, tends to spin the distal portion of the projectile forward (Ratzat 1999:201). A heavy point also increases stresses that occur in the shaft when rapidly accelerated from the opposite end, which can result in "porpoising" of the projectile or

even shatter of the shaft, if severe (Blyth 1980; Klopsteg 1993:22; Ratzat 1999:200). Fletching (e.g., feathers) near the nock slows this end of the shaft and helps counteract these forces (Ratzat 1999:201). Fletching, however, is the primary source of drag that slows the projectile after launch (Klopsteg 1993:23), which would result in unacceptable performance even if large fletching and a massive shaft were used in an attempt to compensate for a heavy arrow or atlatl tip (Klopsteg 1993:22; Ratzat 1999).

Diachronic changes in launching technology also suggest that the range of acceptable variation among projectile tips became increasingly constrained through time. The thrower receives feedback during launching both spears and atlatl darts that, within certain limits, allows compensation for differences in the masses of individual projectiles. In contrast, once an arrow is released, it is not possible to alter the rate of acceleration, and projectiles of varying mass will have different points of impact (Klopsteg 1993:11–22; Mason 1894:660). Consequently, reworking broken points is less likely to have occurred for arrow tips but may more commonly have happened with atlatl-dart and especially spear points (Hoffman 1985; Flenniken and Raymond 1986). In addition, the comparatively small sizes of the arrow points considered here limit the extent to which fragmented portions could have been maintained or reused for other tasks.

Furthermore, any energy savings accrued by reworking arrow points would have been offset by variance in the performance of projectile tips of different sizes. Instead, other explanations—including reworking at a later date, when smaller points were produced—may generally account for the reworked points in the collection. Creating an arrow point requires less than 10 minutes (Cushing 1895:318–319), whereas reworking might take perhaps 5 minutes, resulting in a savings of no more than 5 minutes. In contrast, successfully stalking within range of a deer or other large game animal can require hours or even days of effort, and it is unlikely that any hunter would commonly use less-than-optimal designs for such a minor energy savings.

Finally, the suggestion that arrow weight was a carefully controlled variable is supported by ethnographic observation (Mason 1894:660):

The same tribe used arrows of about one length and weight, as correct shooting, like good penmanship, is a balancing of a hundred sensibilities. Every good archer drew his bow to the arrow-head [sic] every shot, for near or for far. If one's bow be drawn always to the arrow-head, and one's arrows be always of the same length, whether from his own quiver or from another's, the elements of variability are much reduced. It must be from some such cause that the arrows of each tribe agree so nearly in length. . . . It is not here affirmed that the arrows of a tribe are exactly of a length. The variations are within certain narrow limits. The author has measured a large number of quiver contents. The arrows of one quiver agree absolutely. The arrows of a tribe agree within a narrow margin.

Similarly, Coues (1866:351) suggested the Apache stone points that he removed from soldiers he operated on were "quite uniform in size and shape. I think I never saw one much over the dimensions stated."

Temporal Variation in Stone-Point Weight: Why Size Matters

Because of the performance advantages of velocity, it is expected that projectile mass was minimized in order to maximize velocity within the performance limits of a given propulsive design. Developments in the technology for launching projectiles (e.g., spear, atlatl, bow, and firearms) that occurred over time and alterations within mechanism designs (e.g., atlatl length, weight, and flexibility) can increase the maximum attainable projectile velocity (Cotterell and Kamminga 1992:166–175; Cushing 1895:329–349; Ratzat 1999). Such technological changes are expected to be associated with decreases in projectile point weight (Mason 1894:653; Owens et al. 2000; Shott 1996; Vanpool 2003:162–163). Developments of the latter type should result in incremental modification to points, whereas changes of the former type must be associated with substantial alterations. Hypothetically, these changes may produce a kind of "punctuated equilibrium" in point design in which long periods of gradual weight decrease are interspersed with comparatively short periods of more-dramatic change (cf. Shott 1996:295).

Although the appearance of the atlatl in the region is poorly dated, Sliva (1999) argued that experimentation with the bow and arrow occurred in the southern Southwest as early as 800 b.c., and Justice (2002:44–46) suggested a date of a.d. 500, based on an extensive literature review. A more rapid decrease in stone-point weight is expected to be associated with the advent of bow technology. Similarly, Shott (1996:295), in his analysis of points from the American Bottom, identified a gap in the distribution of metric attributes that was possibly associated with the introduction of the bow and arrow.

Modifications within technologies can also increase the maximum attainable projectile velocity (Cotterell and Kamminga 1992:185; Klopsteg 1993; Kooi 1983:56; Vanpool 2003). For example, many aspects of bow design can be altered to incrementally or more substantially increase potential arrow velocity (Baker 2001; Cotterell and Kamminga 1992:180–186; Hamm 1991; Heath 2001; Laubin and Laubin 1980; LeBlanc 1999; Klopsteg 1993; Kooi 1983; Vanpool 2003:151–162). Such changes in bow design are expected to be associated with concurrent decreases in flaked stone projectile point weight (Vanpool

2003:162–163). The more rapidly a bow springs back to shape when the string is released, the faster the arrow will be propelled (Baker 2001; Klopsteg 1993). The speed at which the bow snaps back is related to the draw weight (i.e., how much energy is required to deform the bow from its resting state), the characteristics of the bow limbs, the nature of the string, and other factors (Heath 2001; Klopsteg 1993).

Bow design changes to increase recovery speed can occur within as well as between bow types (e.g., self-bow, recurved bow, or composite bow). For example, the limbs of self-bows can be tapered to decrease the mass at the tips and thereby reduce their inertia and increase bow performance (Baker 2001:109). The species of wood and/or other materials the bow is made from (e.g., bone, horn, or sinew), the portion of the tree used (e.g., heartwood and/or sapwood), the diameter of the tree the bow is cut from, the length-to-width ratio of the bow, the cross-section shape of the bow stave, the string material (e.g., plant fiber or sinew), and additional factors can all be modified to increase recovery speeds (Baker 2001; Cotterell and Kamminga 1992:185–187; Heath 2001; Klopsteg 1993). More dramatic changes to bow design include recurving the limbs such that the handle is "set-back" (Hamm 1991:37), thereby raising arrow velocities by increasing the draw length of the weapon (Baker 2001; Hamm 1991). Consequently, as will be discussed further in Chapter 6, the advent of the recurved bow (Figure 14) in the Southwest is one example of a change in bow construction that is expected to have resulted in a more substantial decrease in arrow-point weight.

To summarize, changes in the technology for launching projectiles, from spear to atlatl to self-bow to recurved bow, are expected to select against larger projectile tips over time. These transitions in technology may or may not be associated with changes in point shape. As will be considered further in the following section, differences in shape are more likely to be related to variation in the intensity of tasks that stone points were designed to perform (i.e., big-game hunting and warfare) or with societal changes. These observations led to the formulation of the first hypothesis employed in this research.

Hypothesis 1: The average size of stone projectile points declined progressively over time.

- Implication 1.1: Because technological changes (e.g., the introduction of recurved bow designs) increased the recovery speed of bows and thereby the velocity of arrows, there should be a general decline in the weight of stone projectile points from a.d. 1150 (Hohokam Classic period) to a.d. 1880 (Akimel O'odham Historic period).

- Implication 1.2: Projectile point weight patterns among large artifact assemblages are such that relative age assessments can be made with these data.

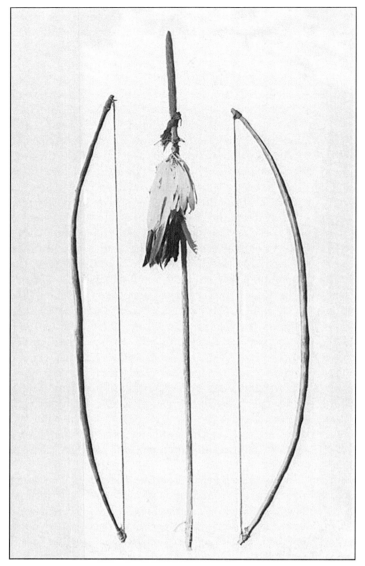

Figure 14. Akimel O'odham recurved bow designed for warfare (*left*) and self-bow used for hunting small game (*right*). A recurved bow consists of a piece of wood that has been reshaped so that it forms a double arch. (Photograph by De Lancey Gill, Negative 2678 D, National Anthropological Archives, Smithsonian Institution, Washington, D.C.)

Warfare- and Big-Game-Projectile-Point Designs

The terms "warfare points" and "hunting points" are used for convenience in this discussion; however, the suggestion here is only that certain projectile point designs may have been intended for use against humans whereas other point types may have been designed for killing other animals. In practice, points designed for "warfare" may actually have been used in altercations between individuals, raiding, small-scale intergroup conflicts, and/or larger-scale battles. Differentiating among these possibilities is not relevant to this discussion and is therefore not attempted. This section begins with a review of ethnographic research that

indicates that projectile points were often designed differently for hunting and for warfare.

Ethnographic Descriptions of Warfare- and Hunting-Point Designs

The following discussion summarizes ethnographic research that describes cross-cultural variation among warfare and hunting projectiles; observations regarding Akimel O'odham practices and those concerning other Historic period groups from the Middle Gila River region are presented in the following chapter. This body of research shows that warfare projectile points from around the world were commonly designed differently from points intended for big-game hunting. These descriptions suggest characteristics that may be used to distinguish warfare points from large-game-hunting points.

The extensive review of the North American ethnographic literature by Ellis (1997) found that stone points were by far the most common tip type for warfare arrows. Stone points were employed on warfare projectiles in 57 instances (83 percent) of the 69 cases he considered. In 10 examples (14 percent), materials other than stone (horn, bone, or wood) were sometimes employed to tip war arrows. In only 2 cases (3 percent) were materials other than stone exclusively employed. Ellis (1997:45) noted, "It is of some interest that the stone points used for warfare could differ in size and shape, and often in the presence or absence of barbs, from those used on large game." When discussing preindustrial warfare around the world, Keeley (1996:52) also observed that "[p]oints of war projectiles were commonly weakened or hafted in such a way that when the shaft was extracted, the point or some part of it would remain in the wound."

The description of Plains arrow technology given by Catlin (1975:109) in 1832 is an example of the most common distinction described for warfare and hunting arrows recorded in the literature:

The one [arrow type] to be drawn upon an enemy is generally poisoned, with long flukes or barbs. They are designed to hang in the wound after the shaft is withdrawn. The other [arrow type] is used for their game, with the blade firmly fastened to the shaft and the flukes inverted so that it may easily be drawn from the wound and used on a future occasion.

This distinction and other morphological characteristics of warfare projectile points were described by Mails (1995:425) for Plains arrow technology in general:

The war arrowhead can easily be distinguished from the hunting point. If one looks at the design of the head and sees that it would resist being pulled back out of the wound, it's a war point. . . . A war arrowhead could not be extracted by pulling it back out. To remove the war arrowhead, the victim had to suffer the excruciating pain of having the head either cut out or pushed on through his body.

When summarizing North American bows and arrows in general, Stevens (1870:564) noted the following:

The Indians of the West [western North America] use two kinds of arrows, the one for hunting and the other for war. The hunting arrow is armed with a leaf-shaped or triangular head, sometimes with a stemmed head, but never with one possessing barbs. The war arrow has invariably a barbed head; this is very slightly

attached to the shaft, so that, if the arrow enters the body of the enemy, it cannot be withdrawn without the head being left in the wound.

Pfefferkorn (1989) also made similar observations regarding hunting and warfare points of "Sonoran" arrows in the mid-1750s:

[T]he arrow is divided into two pieces. If one tries to pull out the arrow, the front shorter part inevitably remains stuck and cannot be removed except by horribly cutting and enlarging the wound and thus placing the wounded person in danger of becoming a cripple or of losing his life (Pfefferkorn 1989:202–203).

Pfefferkorn (1989:203) also said that hunting arrows differed from war arrows in that they were made from a single piece of wood and lacked stone points.

Figure 15 shows examples of hunting and warfare points from California. In this instance, the stems of the warfare points are designed to split the arrow shafts, and the wide shoulders (with barbs, for one point) are intended to complicate backing the points out of the wounds.

Similarly, in regard to Comanche points, Mason (1894:661) wrote, "There is more authority and reason for the assertion that the barbed arrowheads among these Indians were for war and the leaf-shaped and rhomboidal heads were for hunting, because they could be easily withdrawn from the wound and used again." Parker (1912:67) suggested that warfare- and hunting-point designs differed in their orientations relative to the nocks:

The head of the war arrow is shorter and broader than that of the hunting arrow, and is attached to the shaft at right angles with the slot which fits the bowstring, the object of this being to allow the arrow in flight more readily to pass between the human ribs, while the head of the hunting arrow, which is long and narrow, is

Figure 15. Stemmed warfare points (*center* and *left*), and side-notched hunting point (*right*); Wintu, northern California. (Redrawn after Dubois [1940:124] by the author.)

attached perpendicularly to the slot, to allow it to pass readily between the ribs of a running buffalo.

Although it is unclear whether point position at launch affected the penetration orientation (Mails 1995:429), these observations do suggest that projectiles were designed based on perceived differences in the anatomy of people and quadrupeds.

These ethnographic descriptions suggest two characteristics that can be used to distinguish points designed for warfare from those intended for hunting large game. First, big-game-hunting points may more commonly have rounded basal corners, whereas warfare points may more frequently have pointed tangs. Second, warfare points may more commonly have highly concave bases, creating barbs that resist backing out of wounds (Mason 1894:654).

To summarize, certain types of both thick-stemmed and unnotched points may have been more commonly designed for use in warfare, whereas points made for hunting large animals are more frequently corner notched or have side notches in the lower one-third of their blades. Points with side notches in middle of the blades or above are possibly hybrid types that represent a compromise between these two designs. The notch placement on these points suggests that they were deeply set into shafts, which may have tended to splinter the shafts, thus loosening the point.

Warfare- and Big-Game-Hunting-Point Design: Discussion

Human targets differ from other large animals in ways that suggest why the design of projectiles points intended for warfare may vary from the design of those intended for hunting large animals (Cotterell and Kamminga 1992:181). First, the upright posture of people alters effective shot-placement areas for projectiles. Second, humans can employ defensive armor, such as shields (Figure 16). Third, people are capable of firing projectiles in return. Fourth, the conditions of conflict between humans are likely to vary substantially from those of hunting. Fifth, people are considerably more adept than other animals at removing projectiles from their bodies, either by themselves or with help from others, and in order to create more-serious wounds, warfare projectiles were designed such that the stone tips detached on impact.

On quadruped large-game animals, the most effective shot placement is at the animal's side, where at least one lung and the heart can be penetrated (Stevens 1870:564). Because of our upright posture, however, humans present a smaller target in profile, complicating the heart-

Figure 16. Akimel O'odham war club and shield collected from the Gila River Indian Community (collected by James M. Randall, circa 1848, catalog number 24/1970, Smithsonian Institution, Washington, D.C.).

and-lung rapid-kill shot. More importantly, the heavy bone and muscle of the upper arm may cover this vital area, whereas it is possible to more readily aim behind the front leg of quadrupeds. Humans present the largest target in a frontal position. In this stance, however, the dense bone of the sternum protects the heart, and narrower gaps exist between the ribs; it is also not possible to penetrate both lungs and the heart with a single projectile. Furthermore, humans may employ shields or other armor that stops or sufficiently slows projectiles.

If defensive armor is present, then projectile points designed for warfare are expected to be narrow, deep-penetrating designs intended to pierce that protection (Cotterell and Kamminga 1992:181). If shielding is not employed, then a point with a larger cutting area would be more important than a deep-penetrating point design. Based on this reasoning, it is expected that warfare points are unlikely to exhibit the same widths as contemporaneous hunting-point designs, and depending on the type of shielding employed, warfare points may be wider or narrower than hunting designs, which are expected to be optimized for lateral penetrations on quadrupeds.

These observations are supported by data collected by U.S. Army surgeons who treated arrow wounds received by unarmored U.S. soldiers. Although most of the examples involved points made of metal (which has different performance characteristics than stone), Bill (1862, 1882) provided information regarding the locations of injuries and the survival rates for 154 soldiers who were shot with Native American arrows in the Southwest and elsewhere (Table 7). See Coues (1866) for descriptions of stone-point effects.

Although only one-third of all arrow wounds were fatal, impacts to the chest and abdomen were most dangerous. Injuries to the arms were most common, and 42 percent of all wounds were to the extremities. Only half of the chest injuries were fatal, and in 10 of those cases, the lungs and heart were not injured; all 10 of these patients survived their wounds. As noted by Bill (1862:376), "[a]n arrow sometimes goes through the chest and passes out. It would always do so if it were not that it can scarcely miss hitting a bone." The patient, however, died in both cases in which the heart was injured—instantly in 1 case and within 5 minutes in the second case (Bill 1862).

These data also suggest that arrow injuries to the abdomen were most likely to be fatal. As a result, Bill (1862) noted that "Mexicans" generally wore several layers of blankets around their stomachs for protection. Ninety percent of the instances in which the intestines were wounded resulted in death, but that generally took several days or even weeks (Bill 1862:385–386). In the instances of impacts to unprotected abdomens, wider points that were more likely to cut the intestines and vessels would be more damaging than deep-penetrating, narrow point designs.

The case described by Calvin Dewitt (1871:154) is a typical example of an arrow wound to the abdomen:

Private Courad Tragesor, Troop I, 8th Cavalry, was wounded in an engagement with Apache Indians, at Sunflower Valley, Arizona Territory, March 9,1870, by an arrow, which entered the left-side, about four inches from the spine, and above the crest of the ileum, from below upward. The kidney evidently was injured, as the patient passed bloody urine in small quantities, and frequently. His face was pale, anxious, and expressive of great pain; pulse weak. He was conveyed in an ambulance to Camp McDowell, Arizona Territory, a distance of thirty miles, over a rough, stony, and hilly road. He died the next day. At the autopsy, it was found that the arrow had transfixed the kidney, entering it on the external border, at the juncture of middle and lower thirds, emerging from the posterior surface near the internal border, a few lines below the pelvis. A large irregular piece, about one inch long, and half an inch thick, was torn from the posterior border of the kidney at the place of entrance, evidently by the traction made in extracting the arrow, leaving the head behind.

Bill (1862:366–367) described the tendency for arrow points used in warfare to detach from the shafts and the effects of that as follows:

An arrow is shot at a man at a distance of fifty yards. It penetrates his abdomen, and without wounding an intestine or a great vessel, lodges in the body of one of the vertebrae. The arrow is grasped by the shaft by some officious friend, and after a little tugging is pulled out. We said the arrow is pulled out. This was a mistake; it is the shaft only of the arrow that is pulled out. The angular and jagged head has been left buried in the bone to kill—for so it surely will—the victim.

Similarly, regarding Apache stone points, Coues (1866:352) observed:

So frail is the connection between the head and the shaft, that in all my little experience, I never saw or heard of an instance in which the former was removed on pulling out the latter. I do not see very well how it can occur, provided the head be buried beyond its barbs. For the matter of that, as the shaft produces ordinarily next to nothing of the sum total of injury, we may regard the missile as practically consisting of the head alone.

Bill also suggested that Native Americans intentionally targeted the chest and abdomen with points that were designed to detach on impact (Bill 1862:386):

Experience has abundantly shown, and none know the fact better than the Indians themselves, that any arrow wound of the chest or abdomen, in which the

Table 7. Arrow-Wound Locations and Fatality Rates

Wound Location	Severe Injuries (n)	Proportion of Wounds (%)	Died from Wounds (n)	Fatal (%)
Abdomen	34	22	21	62
Head or spinal column	13	8	7	54
Chest	30	19	15	50
Neck	13	8	1	8
Legs	18	12	1	6
Arms	46	30	2	4
Total	154	100	47	31

Note: Adapted from Bill (1882:107).

arrow-head [sic] is detached from the shaft and lodged, is mortal. From this we concluded that the danger peculiar to all arrow wounds is, *that the shaft becoming detached from the head of an implanted arrow, leaves this so deeply imbedded in a bone that it cannot be withdrawn, and that, it kills* [italics in original].

One of the main differences between the U.S. Calvary and Native Americans was that the U.S. troops did not employ defensive armor. Bill (1862:386) concluded with this recommendation: "We wish in conclusion to recommend to those in authority the plan of protecting soldiers and others exposed to arrow wounds with a light cuirass. The Indians have a method of dressing bulls' hide for shields for themselves, which renders it arrow proof."

In addition to the effects on point design, the circumstances of warfare may have resulted in a lower recovery rate for arrows, whereas hunting arrows (with broken points securely attached) may have been more commonly retrieved (Densmore 1929:61). Even if the warfare arrows were recovered, the points were more likely to have become disassociated from the arrow shaft, because they were intentionally loosely attached (Coues 1866:351). In contrast, the basal portions of side-notched points (which were removed and discarded on habitation sites) would be more readily retrieved, because they were firmly attached to shafts that were collected for reuse. This suggests that hunting points recovered from archaeological sites may more commonly be fragmentary than warfare points.

Warfare- and Big-Game-Point Design: Summary

A considerable body of ethnographic evidence, including observations of Akimel O'odham practices (see next chapter), suggests that projectile tips were designed differently for hunting and for warfare (Ellis 1997:45; Justice 2002:38–44). Human targets differ from other animals in

ways that suggest that the design of projectiles intended for warfare will vary from the design of projectiles intended for hunting. In order to create more-serious wounds, warfare projectiles were frequently made so that the tips detached on impact (Bill 1862, 1882; Coues 1866; Ellis 1997:45; Justice 2002:38–44). In contrast, hunting points designed for large game animals were securely fixed, such that they would stay on the shaft and create more damage as the projectile moved in the wound.

When attempting to tightly bind a triangular point, several problems occur if the stem is wider than the shaft (Christenson 1997:134–135). First, it is difficult to firmly fasten the point, because the binding material is cut by the sharp edges of the point (Geneste and Maury 1997:183). Second, the bindings necessarily extend over a larger area that is perpendicular to the cutting edges of the point. This perpendicular wedge is an impediment to effective penetration of the projectile (Knecht 1997:201–202). Notching is one solution for reducing the width of the stem. Notching also recesses the binding from the cutting edges of the point, which further decreases the chance that the material will be cut during penetration (Redding 1879). These observations suggest that triangular points designed for use against people may lack notches near the base. Triangular arrow points designed for hunting are expected to have notches for the bindings in the lower one-third of the blade.

Research presented above suggests additional characteristics that may distinguish warfare points from hunting points. First, hunting points may more commonly have rounded tangs to facilitate removal, whereas warfare points may more frequently have pointed tangs. Second, warfare points may have wider or narrower bases than hunting-arrow points, depending on the absence or presence of defensive armor, respectively (Cotterell and Kamminga 1992:181). Third, hunting points should more commonly be fragmentary, whereas warfare points should be more commonly whole. Observations presented in this section provided the basis for the formulation of the second hypothesis used to guide the following analyses.

Hypothesis 2: Stone projectile points were designed differently for warfare than for large-game hunting.

- Implication 2.1: Points made for hunting will have design features that facilitate secure hafting, whereas points intended for warfare will have been designed to detach from the shafts.

Obsidian Analysis Methods

The third hypothesis concerns socioeconomic interactions involved in procuring the raw materials used to make points. This hypothesis is based on considerable previous research that was summarized in Chapter 3. As a result, it is possible to more succinctly summarize the final hypothesis employed to guide this investigation. Trace-element analyses were performed in the Archaeological XRF Laboratory, Department of Earth and Planetary Sciences, University of California, Berkeley, under the supervision of Dr. M. Steven Shackley. Trace-element data were collected from each sample for a total of nine elements: titanium (Ti), manganese (Mn), iron (as FeT), thorium (Th), rubidium (Rb), strontium (Sr), yttrium (Y), zirconium (Zr), and niobium (Nb). Elemental intensities were converted to concentration estimates in parts per million by employing a least-squares calibration line established for each element from the analysis of international rock standards certified by the National Institute of Standards and Technology, the USGS, the Canadian Centre for Mineral and Energy Technology, and the Centre de Recherches Pétrographiques et Géochimiques in France (Govindaraju 1994).

Further details concerning the petrological choice of these elements in Southwest obsidians are available in reports by Shackley (1995, 2005). These quantitative determinations were then compared to known samples. The source-comparative database has been compiled as part of a long-term project to characterize obsidian sources in the Southwest (Shackley 1988, 1990, 1992, 2005).

P-MIP Obsidian Data Sampling Methods

A sample of 142 of the obsidian artifacts from the P-MIP survey collection was selected for XRF analysis. In order to obtain a spatially and temporally representative sample, the obsidian artifacts were stratified geographically and by time period. The 13 units depicted in Figure 10 were employed to stratify the sample spatially. Because too few pieces of obsidian are available from Units 3, 6, and 13, those areas were not included in the sample. Between 7 and 28 artifacts were selected for XRF analysis from

each of the areas. Both diagnostic projectile points and obsidian flakes were selected for analysis from each area. Temporal stratification was achieved by selecting roughly equal numbers of artifacts from the Hohokam pre-Classic and Classic periods and the O'odham Historic period for each of the units.

In addition to the survey data, obsidian artifacts from two recent data recovery projects conducted in the GRIC are also considered. One project included excavations at sites along the Santa Cruz River in the GRIC (Loendorf 2007). The second excavated sample was from the northern side of the Gila River and included both pre-Classic and Classic period obsidian from the Lower Santan Platform Mound village (Loendorf 2008). The third hypothesis employed to guide this research is as follows.

Hypothesis 3: Obsidian distribution patterns can be used as proxy measures for socioeconomic interactions among communities.

- Implication 3.1: Classic and Historic period populations of the Middle Gila and lower Salt Rivers procured obsidian, an important material for the production of small projectile points, through social mechanisms.

- Implication 3.2: Significant differences in obsidian frequencies at neighboring communities suggest that they maintained separate trade contacts.

Chapter Summary

The nature of Middle Gila River archaeological data, the topography of the region, and the survey methods employed during the P-MIP investigations resulted in a situation in which sites vary in size by many orders of magnitude. Therefore, it is necessary to control for site area and other sampling issues in any analyses of these data. In the research presented in Chapter 6, sampling fraction is standardized based on survey coverage, and instead of sites, large areas of roughly equal size are employed as units of analysis.

This chapter presented three hypotheses used to link material-cultural patterns with past human behavior. The first hypothesis is employed in conjunction with point shape to suggest temporal associations for projectile point assemblages. It is posited that flaked stone projectile tips generally became smaller over time in response to developments in the technology for launching these weapons. Technological changes increased the maximum attainable projectile velocity, and lighter projectiles will be launched at higher velocities than heavier projectiles. Concurrently, heavier projectiles have greater kinetic energy than lighter projectiles launched from the same mechanism, and effective projectile design requires balancing the ability to reach the target with the damage that can be inflicted by the projectile. This creates upper and lower optimal design limits for points employed with a given launching technology.

Because projectile points generally became smaller, weight can hypothetically be employed in conjunction with shape to suggest the relative ages of assemblages. Applying taxonomic classification systems without including size as a variable would result in the creation of some types that span thousands of years. The ability to more precisely control for differences in temporal association is essential when considering synchronic issues. The suggestion that stone points generally decreased in weight over time is readily testable using archaeological data, and Chapter 6 considers regional-, site-, and feature-level variation in projectile tip weight.

The second hypothesis posits that flaked stone points were designed differently for large-game hunting and for warfare. Therefore, analyses (presented in Chapter 6) of temporal and spatial variation in point design provide data regarding both subsistence practices and conflict among humans. This hypothesis is based on a large body of ethnographic research, which was summarized in this chapter. Expectations for projectile point patterning based on this research include the following: (1) hunting points should generally have rounded tangs, whereas warfare points will more frequently have pointed tangs that resist backing out of wounds; (2) in cases in which defensive armor was employed, warfare points are expected to have narrower bases than hunting-arrow points; and (3) points designed for hunting are expected to have higher fragmentation rates, whereas warfare points are anticipated to more commonly be whole. The following chapter presents ethnohistorical and ethnographic information from the study area itself. These expectations are then tested in Chapter 6.

The third and final hypothesis used in this analysis is based on extensive previous research, and it provides a means to consider socioeconomic-interaction patterns. Because XRF analyses of obsidian have been conducted for 30 years, comparative data from across the Hohokam region are available. Chapter 6 employs these data to consider patterns of cooperation among Classic and Historic period sedentary agriculturalists in the Sonoran Desert of central Arizona.

CHAPTER 5

Study Area Ethnohistorical and Ethnographic Observations

The relations of the Pimas to their neighbors had a profound influence upon their social organization and general cultural development. They held possession of the best agricultural lands in their section of the Southwest, and were compelled to fight for the privilege [Russell 1908:200].

Despite the intense conflict they faced and repeated requests for firearms, the Akimel O'odham living along the Middle Gila River possessed few guns until near the end of the nineteenth century, and flaked stone points continued to be used until the late 1800s (Ezell 1961:66, 1994:346; Hall 1907:420; Russell 1908:111). Written descriptions of Akimel O'odham cultural practices and settlement locations began in the late 1600s and continued throughout the Historic period (Darling et al. 2004:284). Thus, the situation along the Middle Gila River offers an important opportunity to compare spatial and temporal patterning among stone points with historically documented trading partners, migrations, settlement patterns, and subsistence practices.

Historic Period Projectile Technology and Hunting Practices

No one would think that a small straight stick would hurt anything or kill anybody, or that a small flat white stone would be harmful [Burns 1916:313].

In contrast to many Eastern and Plains tribes, Native Americans along the Middle Gila River only rarely employed metal arrow points, and they continued to make stone points until the late 1800s (Ferg and Tessman 1997:259–261; Mason 1894; Russell 1908; Wilson 1899:849). This is probably the result of several factors, but because the Akimel O'odham did make projectile points from man-made glass containers, it is unlikely that

this difference results exclusively from a lack of access to Euroamerican goods (Loendorf and Rice 2004).

Russell (1908:95–96), one of the only anthropologists who visited the Akimel O'odham while they were still regularly using bows, provided several observations regarding stone-point use and associated practices. However, changes in cultural traditions occurred prior to his visit, and much of the information he collected was from community elders (Roffler 2006). As Fontana (1975:xi–xv) observed in his introduction to the 1975 reprinting of Russell's work:

> *The Pima Indians* provides us with a valuable, if distorted view, of what parts of Pima life may have been in, let us say, the 1860s or 1870s. Read and understood in that context, the book is a classic of its kind. . . . The reader should know, however, that he is reading a particular kind of history and that much of the information was already history in 1901–02. It is by no means a balanced picture of Pima life in any period; it certainly is not a depiction of Pima life today [italics in original].

Although it is essential to recognize the limitations of his research, his record is the most comprehensive study available regarding the Historic period Akimel O'odham, and it is therefore extensively cited in the following discussion.

At the time of Russell's visit in 1902 and 1903, the Akimel O'odham only rarely practiced large-game hunting: "Perhaps one [deer] in two or three years would be an excessive estimate of the number killed by the men of the Gila River reservation" (Russell 1908:81). Instead, they primarily hunted locally available small game, and the arrows (*haapod*) they used for that purpose lacked stone tips (Figure 17) (Rea 2007b). Because use of the design had largely stopped, he was only able to collect one example of an arrow intended for use in warfare. This arrow was unusually long and had a stone point attached, which suggests that stone tips were used in warfare (Figure 18) (Ezell 1961:65; Rea 2007b:81). This conclusion is supported by the observations of Bancroft (1886:520), who stated: "The Pimas wing their war arrows

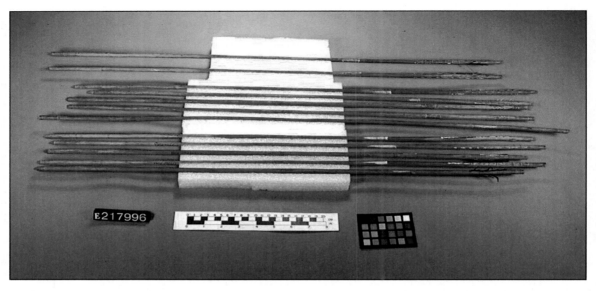

Figure 17. Akimel O'odham small game hunting *haapod* (arrows) (collected by Frank Russell, 1902, catalog number E217996-0, Smithsonian Institution, Washington, D.C.).

Figure 18. Akimel O'odham warfare *haapod* (arrows) (collected by Dr. Edward Palmer ca. 1885, catalog number E76021-0, Smithsonian Institution, Washington, D.C.).

with three feathers and point them with flint, while for hunting purposes they have only two feathers and wooden points." Similarly, Mason (1894:Plate XLII) illustrated both wooden-tipped and stone-pointed Akimel O'odham arrows (*haapod*).

Grossman (1873:416) also described similar differences between Akimel O'odham arrows (*haapod*) designed for small-game hunting and those intended for warfare, as well as the effectiveness of shields for defensives purposes:

The only weapons used by the Pimas before the introduction of fire-arms [sic] were the bow and arrow and war-club [sic]. For defensive purposes they carried a round shield, about two feet in diameter, made of rawhide, which, when thoroughly dry, becomes so hard that an arrow, even if sent by a powerful enemy at a short distance, cannot penetrate it. These weapons

are still used by them to a great extent, and, like all Indians, they are good marksmen with the bow, shooting birds on the wing and fishes while swimming in the shallow waters of the Gila River. For hunting fishes and small game they use arrows without hard points, but the arrows used in battle have sharp, two-edged points made of flint, glass, or iron.

Hodge (1910:252) observed that the Akimel O'odham had "only in recent years discarded the bow and arrow, with which they were expert. Arrowpoints [sic] of glass, stone, or iron were sometimes employed in warfare. War clubs of mesquite wood also formed an important implement of war; and for defensive purposes an almost impenetrable shield of rawhide was used." Webb (1959:25) suggested that shields were capable of effectively protecting the people who used them and described the use of this armor as follows: "If you shot an arrow at him [an Akimel O'odham warrior] he merely side-stepped, holding the shield at an angle in the path of the arrow. When it hit the shield, it only glanced off to one side."

In addition to differences in the arrow points, the Akimel O'odham used separate bow designs for small-game hunting and warfare. Self-bows were used with arrows (*haapod*) that lacked stone points for small-game hunting. As will be discussed further in the next chapter, recurved bows that are capable of higher arrow velocities were employed with stone-tipped arrows for warfare (Figure 19).

Spier (1933:134) stated that Pee Posh "war and hunting arrows did not differ in length, but in their heads and feathering. War arrows were infrequently provided with stone heads." However, Spier made these observations roughly 50 years after the manufacture of flaked points ceased, and his description of stone points was based on a single wooden model that was made for him by an informant. Furthermore, in 1849, Hayes (1976:45) observed "Maricopa warriors" armed with arrows tipped with "small arrow-heads of stone" (Figure 20). The wooden model made for Spier was "triangular but with convex edges, straight base, and notched in the edges near the base" (Spier 1933:134). These observations suggest that side-notched points were used for large-game hunting.

According to Densmore (1929:61), because of the time and effort involved in producing arrows, Tohono O'odham hunters attempted to recover lost projectiles; however, war arrows were abandoned (Rea 1998:74). Because arrowheads are very likely to break with use, portions of broken side-notched points are likely to have been attached to hunting-arrow shafts that were collected for reuse. This observation supports the suggestion that hunting points recovered from archaeological sites may more commonly be fragmentary than warfare points (see Chapter 4).

Bourke (1891:71), who lived among the Apache while they were still making stone projectile points, provided more-detailed observations regarding manufacturing techniques and shape:

Mr. Edwin A. Barber, in the American Naturalist, described nine different kinds of arrow-tips [sic]. Each of these various shapes could be seen among the Apaches to-day [sic], and often in the same quiver several shapes would be found.

This observation suggests that considerable morphological variation existed in Apache points at a given time and that point shape (i.e., style) alone may be a poor indicator of the cultural association of points made by the Apache in general.

Bill (1882:104) described the use of loosely attached, stemless points on Apache arrows used in warfare (Figure 21) as well as the tendency for stone or glass points to fragment within wounds:

These [stone or glass] arrow heads have no neck; they are about an inch long, and a third of an inch wide.

Figure 19. Depiction of two O'odham men drawn by Kino on his 1696–1697 map. The men are using recurved bows to shoot arrows at a Jesuit Missionary (redrawn by Shari Tiedens).

Figure 20. Pee Posh with bow and stone-tipped arrows, ca. 1875 (photograph by Elias A. Bonine, Smithsonian American Art Museum, Washington, D.C.; museum purchase from the Charles Isaacs Collection made possible in part by the Luisita L. and Franz H. Denghausen Endowment).

Figure 21. San Carlos Apache man with a warfare arrow (photograph by Frank Randall, SPC SW Apache NM ACC 20263, Catalog No. 129781, 100-139 02048900, National Anthropological Archives, Smithsonian Institution, Washington, D.C.).

They are fastened by gum into a notch, which is cut in a rod of wood eight inches long, and this again is fastened by gum into a reed thirty inches long; but so frail is the connection between head and shaft, that the Indian is obliged to take extraordinary care that they do not become separated in the quiver. These heads are of course brittle, and if they strike a bone, they are sure to break. Mr. V., a paymaster and clerk, was thus wounded in the arm by an Apache arrow. The glass head struck the humerus, and broke into many fragments.

Similarly, Coues (1866:353) made the following observations regarding Apache arrow wounds he treated:

The extreme friability of the head produces results which must be taken into consideration, as one of the most common and troublesome features of the wound. When the head impacts on bone—and it generally traverses soft tissue till halted in this way—the chances of its shivering into bits vastly preponderate over the probability of its becoming fixed or glancing.

Mike Burns, a Yavapai who was born in Arizona around 1864 and lived in the vicinity of the GRIC, described the Apache arrow-manufacturing process, including the use of heat treatment for making stone points (Farish 1916:289): "The arrows were made of sticks, with a little sharp stone in the end " (Burns 1916:311). "The arrow heads were made of a hard flint, which would be put close to a fire to make it chip easy, and then it would be worked down to the shape and size desired" (Burns 1916:314).

In contrast to the Akimel O'odham, some mobile populations who lived close to the Middle Gila River did practice big-game hunting on a regular basis, and meat was a more substantial portion of their diet (Burns 1916:291; Hrdlička 1908:22). As is the case for nearly all ethnographic examples, Apache arrows designed for hunting large game or warfare were tipped with stone points, but arrows intended for killing birds or other small game did not have stone points attached (Basso 2004:227; Bourke 1890:56; Coues 1866; Mason 1894:668–669). Similarly, the Yavapai also hunted large game with stone-tipped arrows that were generally side notched, and they used arrows without stone points for small-game hunting (Khera and Mariella 1983:50).

Hoffman (1878:467–468) argued that triangular, side-notched points were characteristic of one Apache group:

The manufacture of stone arrow-heads [sic] is still carried on by the Coyoterò Apachès. Various species of siliceous materials are employed. The triangular shape is characteristic of this tribe. The dart is fastened to the shaft by means of dark reddish-brown vegetable gum and sinew threads, which are brought forward over the two basal apices, above which there are usually two slight notches for their reception. Fragments

of so-called porter-bottles are frequently utilized in the manufacture of arrow-heads, making an effectual but brittle weapon.

Coues (1866:351), who was a surgeon, described Apache stone projectile points used in warfare as follows:

The head is apparently a small and trifling affair, compared with the results it is capable of producing. It is made from some species of quartz, chalcedony, obsidion [sic], etc., and is always either white or black in color. It is an inch or somewhat less in length, by about a-third [sic] of an inch in greatest width; in shape a narrow isosceles triangle. . . . There is no projecting handle for insertion into the wood. No thongs or wrapping of any sort are used; and so frail is the connection between the head and shaft, that the Indians themselves are obliged to carry their arrows with great care.

He went on to observe: "The characteristics of the Apache arrow-head [sic] are essentially these: 1, its minute size; 2, its jagged edges and angles; 3, its extreme friability; 4, its very ready separation from the shaft" (Coues 1866:353). Bourke (1890:57) described the preferred materials and manufacturing techniques for Apache points as follows:

Stone arrow-heads [sic] were preferably made of obsidian (dolguini), next of chalcedony, lastly of pieces of beer bottles, but the process of manufacture was in each case the same, and consisted in chipping small fragments from the edges of suitable pieces of material, the chipping implement being a portion of hardened deer or elk horn, held in the right hand, the silicious stone being held in the left over a flap of buckskin to protect the fingers.

Bourke (1890:57–58), who was a Calvary officer, was concerned with how long it would take "Apache Indians, whose village had been captured and destroyed by troops, to provide themselves anew with weapons." Consequently, he also recorded how long it took to make stone points:

I made it my business to determine exactly how many minutes were requisite for making a serviceable arrow-head [sic]. I singled out an Apache at random and stipulated that he should employ no tools of iron, but only allowed him to gather from the ground such pieces of chalcedony as he pleased. He made a number of barbs [stone points], the time as recorded in my note-book [sic] being five, six, seven, and eight minutes. An expert would have completed the barbs in less time [Bourke 1890:57–58].

One of the main documented differences in Apache, Pee Posh, and Akimel O'odham arrows is the materials employed to make the shafts. Pee Posh and Akimel O'odham arrows generally had solid shafts made from arrowweed (Figure 22), whereas the Apache usually employed cane shafts (Bourke 1890; Coues 1866:351; Mason 1894:668–669; Russell 1908:96; Spier 1933). Bourke (1890:58) suggested that the Apache design was superior:

The Apaches have a myth which states that they overcame all of the tribes in their path because the god, *To-va-dis-chinni* ("The Mist Rising from the Water"), placed them in a reed swamp and gave them pieces of obsidian as tips for their arrows. When read between the lines this myth relates an important truth: The

Apaches did subdue or drive the other tribes before them on account of having better arrows.

In addition to arrows, the Pee Posh also sometimes employed spears (Spier 1933), and Russell (1908) described similar weapons for the Akimel O'odham, as did Bourke (1890:56), Cozzens (1874:119), and Hoffman (1878:468) for the Apache. The use of spears in warfare is also described in the calendar-stick records Russell (1908:40–41) reported. Charlie Redbird, one of Spier's (1933) informants, told him that stone points were sometimes used on these spears.

Figure 22. Akimel O'odham woman collecting arrow weed (photograph by Edward Curtis).

Bourke (1890:56) reported that Apache spears were "tipped with a flint barb, two or three inches in length by an inch in breadth, sometimes with serrated, sometimes with plain edges, fasted to the staff with sinew and gum." He added that a good lance head "could be made in a very short time, but in exactly how many minutes I am unable to say" (Bourke 1890:58). These observations suggest that in addition to small arrow points, substantially larger spear points should also occur in Historic period projectile point collections from the Middle Gila River region. The following section presents additional details regarding big-game-hunting practices in the study area.

Akimel O'odham Big-Game-Hunting Practices

Ethnographic and ethnohistorical records suggest that the Akimel O'odham and Pee Posh rarely hunted large animals during the Historic period (Ezell 1961; Rea 2007b:72; Russell 1908; Whittemore 1898). For example, Russell (1908:82) related an anecdote that is consistent with his suggestion that the Akimel O'odham only rarely hunted big game:

When climbing in the Sierra Estrella, in March, 1902, the writer saw a flock of five [mountain sheep] which did not manifest any such fear at the sight of man as do the mountain sheep of British Columbia and the more northern Rockies. Indeed, the Pima chief at the foot of the mountains explained the reason for their indifference very adequately when he declared the sheep were game fit only for the Papagos [Tohono O'odham], who had no fields to look after.

Over 60 years later, regarding this statement Rea (1998:60) wrote:

It was not a flippant remark that the Pima leader at the foot of the Sierra Estrella made in 1902. . . . Even when I arrived and took up residence at the base of the Estrella in 1963, only several men were known to be big-game hunters in the four local villages, and individual hunters were remembered by name.

The possibility that the Historic period Akimel O'odham rarely hunted large game is supported by the observations of Hayes (1976:45), who visited the Middle Gila River in 1849:

The interpreter was asked if there (are) many deer or bear in the neighborhood [in the vicinity of the Akimel O'odham villages along the Middle Gila River]; he replied there were, but the Pimos [Akimel O'odham] preferred work to hunting.

Similarly, Cremony (1868) related a Pee Posh (i.e., Maricopa) story regarding their migration to the Middle Gila River that says that the Akimel O'odham made the cessation of large-game hunting part of the agreement that allowed the Pee Posh to move next to the O'odham villages. It also provides an explanation for why these people did not regularly practice large-game hunting:

[I]t was agreed that the Maricopas should inhabit certain lands of the Pimos [Akimel O'odham]; but it was made a sine qua non that the new-comers [sic] must forever renounce their warlike and hunting propensities, and dedicate themselves to tillage—for, said the Pimos, we have no hunting grounds; we do not wish to incur the vengeance of the Tontos, the Chimehuevis, the Apaches, and others, by making useless raids against them; they have nothing to lose, and we have, and you must confine yourselves solely to revenging any warlike incursions made either upon us or upon yourselves [Cremony 1868:90–91].

Whittemore (1898:56) also suggested that large-game hunting could cause conflicts to arise with the Apache: "Formerly, there were some deer and mountain sheep in the vicinity, but the latter are nearly extinct, and in hunting them there was danger of trespassing on the hunting-ground [sic] of the war like [sic] Apache." He also related an anecdote that suggests that the Akimel O'odham hunted big game in some circumstances but that it was a dangerous activity that required traveling from the Middle Gila River: "Once the Pimas, being hungry, went to the San Pedro to hunt deer. They took their wives with them and a few ponies. They left the women in the morning and on their return in the evening, all had been taken captive by the Apaches" (Whittemore 1898:56).

Ezell (1961:42) found little evidence in Hispanic sources that the Akimel O'odham practiced large-game hunting. The only reference he identified consisted of a large pile of mountain-sheep horns that was reported at one village, and he went on to relate:

The American accounts contain many more references to game, but they are chiefly to small game such as quail. Emory's party was the only one to report large game. . . . This, however, occurred at the western edge of Maricopa territory near the Mohawk Mountains, and no other American diarist reported either seeing or taking any large game while traveling through Pima territory.

These observations indicate that the Historic period Akimel O'odham rarely if ever hunted big-game animals. Consequently, stone projectile points with big-game-hunting design features are expected to rarely occur in Historic period assemblages, and instead, stone points in these contexts are expected to largely consist of warfare designs. The following section summarizes other tasks that stone points were occasionally used for, in addition to hunting or warfare.

Noneconomic and Non-Conflict-Related Aspects of Projectile Points

There is evidence in the ethnographic record that the O'odham and other southwestern peoples placed ritual significance on projectile points. These practices may have impacted patterning in the archaeological record in several ways, and this section explores possible effects of beliefs concerning projectile points. For example, McGee (1898:245) observed that the Tohono O'odham

> warrior goes confidently to battle against the Apache when protected by a fetish including an Apache arrowpoint [sic] taken in conflict, and feels sure of victory if his warclub [sic] is made in imitation of that of the enemy and potentialized by a plume or inscription appealing to the Apache deity. This indicates the real essence of piratical acculturation; it represents the aim of shamans and warriors to obtain favor from the mystical powers of the enemy, and thus to win easy victory;

and it results, incidentally, in painstaking imitation of articles seen and captured in battle.

The reuse of Apache arrow points by the Tohono O'odham may have resulted in their inclusion within O'odham household assemblages. Further, the tendency to copy the designs of enemies may have resulted in morphological similarities among artifacts produced by different groups of people who were in conflict.

Instances in which arrows were shot into or left at shrines or other features were also recorded. For example, Russell (1908:255) observed "decaying fragments of arrow shafts" at a shrine called Puma Lying, which was located near Gila Butte, in the center of the study area (Figure 23). This suggests that concentrations of arrows were present at some locations away from habitation areas or at other locations associated with their manufacture, maintenance, or use.

Bourke observed several instances in which supernatural properties were attributed to arrowheads (Wilson 1899:849). For example, he witnessed an Apache woman who wore on her

> neck [a] stone amulet, shaped like a spear [projectile point], which is figured in the illustrations of this paper. The material was the silex from the top of a mountain, taken from a ledge at the foot of a tree

Figure 23. Puma Lying shrine (photograph by Frank Russell, Negative 2704 C, National Anthropological Archives, Smithsonian Institution, Washington, D.C.).

which had been struck by lightning. The fact that siliceous rock will emit sparks when struck by another hard body appeals to the reasoning powers of the savage as a proof that the fire must have been originally deposited therein by the bolt of lightning. A tiny piece of this arrow or lance [projectile point] was broken off and ground into the finest powder, and then administered in water to women during time of gestation [Bourke 1892:468–492].

The artifact illustrated by Bourke (1892:468) was a large teardrop-shaped projectile point, and he noted that he also saw Pueblo people using similar items. His observations suggest that the sparks resulting when cryptocrystalline silicates are struck played a role in the power that was attributed to projectile points. Their use by women in fertility ceremonies is also interesting. Although projectile points are generally associated with male activities, Bourke's observations indicate that in at least some situations, projectile points were also used by women.

Carl Lumholtz (1912:180) also observed the use of arrow points in Tohono O'odham curing ceremonies:

From the Indians and Mexicans of Sonoita I gathered several ancient stone artifacts such as axes, lance and arrow points, which undoubtedly belonged to predecessors of the Papago, having the same general character as the rest of the prehistoric remains found in the Papagueria and already alluded to. The Indians of the present day know nothing about them, but the magic qualities attributed to them are used for healing purposes. To this end the lance or arrow points are left in water, which afterward is taken internally and applied externally, while the medicine-man [sic] waves the stone object over the patient, holding it by a string attached to it, and at the same time he blows his breath over the sick man repeatedly.

Lumholtz (1912:110–111) also noted similar Tohono O'odham beliefs regarding lightning and projectile points:

The wellnigh [sic] universal superstition relating to flint in arrow-heads [sic] is also found among the Papagoes [sic], though one would think that sufficient time had not elapsed since the days when the natives themselves made such objects. Their very name is lightning stone (*vthom*) [italics in original], and one man who presented me with one assured me that he found it by searching the ground after lightning had struck near his house. Sometimes, when lightning strikes a tree, the Indians will dig in the ground underneath for arrow-points [sic].

Ethnographic observations also have suggested that the gifting of arrows happened in certain circumstances (Hallenbeck 1940:91, 228). Griffen (1969:123–124)

reported that exchanges of bows and arrows occurred and were important for cementing alliances. Further, he also suggested that obsidian-tipped arrows were used in ritual dances by both males and females as parts of renewal ceremonies. These observations underscore the ritual and symbolic importance placed on projectile points by the people who made them. These beliefs may have affected both the raw materials selected for the manufacture of projectile points and aspects of point shape.

DISCUSSION

Although practices discussed in this section may have resulted in mixing among artifacts made by different groups, it is unlikely that statistically significant numbers of projectile points were transferred via these mechanisms, for several reasons. First, the ethnographic descriptions indicate that only certain people employed individual artifacts as talismans or in medicinal practices, that many more archers were present in groups, and that an individual archer owned 50 or more arrows (Rea 2007b:83), which were replaced on a regular basis. Consequently, enemy or magical arrow points are expected to be substantially outnumbered by projectile points employed for mundane purposes. Second, in order for an arrow to work effectively, it must be the correct length and stiffness for a given bow (Hamm 1991:89–134; Pope 2000:81–100). Furthermore, the arrow shaft also needs to be the correct length for the draw of the archer, and customized arrows were produced based on the body sizes of individual archers (Burns 1916; Rea 2007b:80; Russell 1908:96). Therefore, arrows were not freely interchangeable among bows or archers. Third, as discussed in Chapter 4, arrows of different masses will have different points of impact, and it is necessary to carefully control for consistency in the sizes of projectiles, a suggestion that is also supported by ethnographic observation (Coues 1866:351; Mason 1894:660). Fourth, specialized arrows employed for nonmundane purposes often do not have stone points attached. For example, arrows that were used by the Apache for gambling purposes are decorated with unique and elaborate, painted designs, but they lack stone points (Mason 1894:Plate XLIV). Fifth, dense concentrations of projectile points potentially associated with offerings were not identified during the survey (Loendorf and Rice 2004).

Furthermore, archaeological data do not support the suggestion that arrows with finished stone points attached were commonly transferred among or reused by different groups of people. If this occurred, then variation would be expected between stone points and the manufacturing debris found in archaeological assemblages. However, assemblages in the study area generally have evidence for on-site manufacture of points, and the material types for finished points and manufacturing debris are consistent in most cases (Loendorf et al. 2004).

In some instances, small numbers of projectile points made from material types that are not present in site assemblages have been identified, but researchers have generally taken these data as evidence for trade among populations (e.g., Peterson et al. 1997). However, ethnographic data presented in this section suggest that these points may have been introduced into sites via other mechanisms, potentially including during conflict among populations (Seymour 2011). Furthermore, although other goods may have been more readily exchanged among groups, the use of projectile points as warfare weapons may have affected patterns of exchange for the raw materials necessary to manufacture them. The following section further explores aspects of Historic period trade within the study area.

Historic Period Socio-economic Interactions

This discussion considers Historic period exchange relationships, which are used to generate expectations for Historic period obsidian acquisition patterns. The Akimel O'odham exchanged goods largely with the Pee Posh and Tohono O'odham and were in conflict with other surrounding groups (Ezell 1961:28–31; Russell 1908:93). They also bartered or sold goods to Hispanic populations to the south, and by the 1850s, they traded large amounts of goods with settlers and others who traveled through the area on their way to the West Coast. Prior to 1833, Pee Posh from Gila Bend came at harvest time to trade with the Akimel O'odham (Russell 1908:93). After the Pee Posh moved to the area adjacent to the Akimel O'odham communities in the early 1800s, the Tohono O'odham were their primary external trading partners. Although the Tohono O'odham lived in more-arid desert environments to the south, they brought both food and other items for exchange (Webb 1959:65).

Russell (1908:93) observed that in addition to salt, the Tohono O'odham also brought a wide variety of other items:

the trade which they carried on with the Pimas was by no means one-sided, as may be seen from the following list of products that were formerly brought to the Gila at the time of the June harvest. Of vegetable products there were saguaro seeds, the dried fruit and sirup [sic]; tci´aldi, a small hard cactus fruit; agave fruit in flat roasted cakes; agave sirup; rsat, an unidentified plant that grows at Santa Rosa; prickly pear sirup; wild gourd seeds; a small pepper, called tcĭl´tipĭn; acorns of Quercus oblongifolia; baskets of agave leaf; sleeping mats; kiâhâs and fiber to make them; maguey fiber for picket lines. . . . Of mineral products they brought red and yellow ochers for face and body paint, and the buff

beloved by Pima weavers. . . . In exchange for the objects of barter brought to them the Pimas gave wheat, which was also given the Papagos for aid in harvesting it; corn; beans; mesquite beans; mesquite meal, roasted in mud-lined pits; cotton blankets and cotton fiber, with the seed; dried squash, pumpkin, and melon; rings of willow splints and of devil's claw for baskets; besides articles of lesser consequence. In recent years there has been some trade carried on in colored earths and salt with the once hostile Yumas and Mohaves.

Few of the items Russell listed are likely to be preserved in archaeological sites, and only the pigments would remain, unless they were charred. It is interesting that the traded items were largely foodstuffs (Webb 1959:65). However, Russell (1908:92) also listed exchange rates as follows:

For purposes of trade or in gambling the following values were recognized: A gourd was equivalent to a basket; a metate, a small shell necklace, or the combination of a basket and a blanket and a strand of blue glass beads was equivalent to a horse; a string of blue glass beads 4 yards long was equivalent to a bag of paint; and a basket full of beans or corn to a cooking pot.

This list suggests that baskets full of food were exchanged for cooking pots and that decorated ceramics were also obtained as containers through exchange interactions. "Furthermore, many of the smaller decorated [ceramic] pieces are traded from both the Kwahadk's and the Papagos, the latter bringing them filled with cactus sirup [sic] to exchange for grain" (Russell 1908:124).

These observations suggest that by the late Historic period, exchange relationships among the Akimel O'odham and other surrounding groups were predominantly with people who lived to the south and west of the study area. The next section develops expectations for the spatial distribution of Historic period projectile points within the GRIC.

Historic Period Settlement-Pattern Descriptions

The Akimel O'odham did not experience intensive colonial contact during most of the Historic period (Eiselt 2002:10; Ezell 1994:319). Initial historical documentation of the Middle Gila River area was not until 1694, and written records after that time were sporadic and limited in scope until the arrival of Americans in the mid-1800s. Sufficient references exist, however, to make a number of inferences regarding Akimel O'odham settlement patterns and population movements between roughly 1700 and the time that stone-point manufacture largely ceased, sometime in the late nineteenth century (cf. Russell 1908:111).

The Spanish missionary Father Kino was the first European to visit the Akimel O'odham communities along the Middle Gila River (Wilson forthcoming). Figure 24 shows a detail from one of the maps he drew based on his travels. He made four trips through the area, spending a maximum of 10 days over the course of these encounters (Wilson forthcoming). Of this time, Ezell (1983:150) wrote:

[I]t can be argued that disease did not wait upon Spanish explorers but preceded them by being spread by fugitives from infected communities and that one or more epidemics had struck Pimeria by 1524. Proceeding on that assumption, it is argued that the Spaniards met in 1694 a society reeling under the onslaughts of repeated epidemics over a period of approximately 170 years.

At least six areas of settlement were documented along the Middle Gila River during that period (Ezell 1961,

1983; Russell 1908; Wilson forthcoming). According to Manje, who accompanied Kino, the Akimel O'odham lived in scattered houses in 5–10 locations (Bolton 1948). Although exact locations for all of these communities remain uncertain, Wilson (forthcoming) suggested that they "were restricted to a nineteen-league (c. 47–48 miles) stretch of the valley, beginning at 3 leagues [ca. 12.1 km] above the junction of the Salt and Gila [Rivers] and ending one league [ca. 4 km] from Casa Grande." It appears that these communities were dispersed along the river, which partially accounts for difficulties in determining settlement locations and numbers. Distances were given relative to one another, and it is unclear exactly when the Spaniards would decide they were arriving at and leaving a given community, because their descriptions suggest that houses were scattered in loose clusters that varied in size and density (Ezell 1961:110).

Neither Kino nor Manje provided population estimates for all of the Middle Gila River communities, and at the time of their visits, people were still living in the Gila Bend area, farther to the west, along the river (Wilson forthcoming). Despite the epidemics that spread through the area, there are indications that the population along the Middle Gila River grew rapidly over the course of Kino's

Figure 24. Detail of a map drawn by Kino of southern and central Arizona (1701–1702), showing the location of Casa Grande and the confluence of the Salt River with the Gila River near the top center. Native American communities are indicated with circles.

visits: "In his 1694 entry, Father Kino mentioned only two settlements. In 1697 and in the context of Casa Grande he said 'There are nearby six or seven *rancherías* of Pimas Sobaipuris.'" (Wilson forthcoming).

During the seventeenth century, the Spanish applied the name "Sobaipuri" indiscriminately to people residing along the San Pedro, Santa Cruz, and Gila Rivers in southern Arizona, which has created considerable confusion regarding the use of this designation (Hackenberg 1974:63; Seymour 2011; Vint 2005). It appears that the San Pedro and Santa Cruz River populations were culturally similar to the ancestors of the Akimel O'odham living along the Middle Gila River, but the people along the San Pedro River experienced more intensive contact with the Spanish and suffered greater conflict with the Apache during the first part of the eighteenth century.

Hackenberg (1974:70) found few reasons to differentiate among these peoples: "All of these Pimas, or Pimas Sobaipuris, spoke a mutually intelligible language, were riverine agriculturalists, and were settled in scattered villages." He went on to conclude that the main differentiation between the people along the Gila River and those on the San Pedro River was based on the

> divergent courses of events which befell the two groups in the Eighteenth Century. During this time, the Gila Pimas consolidated their settlements to a range of less than twenty miles, and formed a united defense perimeter against Apaches which permitted them to survive. The San Pedro Sobaipuri, on the other hand, quarreled among themselves, failed to unite even in the face of large scale Apache attacks, [and] remained in sprawling settlements scattered for 90 miles along the San Pedro River [Hackenberg 1974:70].

When discussing relationships among the Akimel O'odham and other Native American groups, Ezell (1961:21) stated:

> [T]he Sobaipuris of the San Pedro and Santa Cruz valleys, were most like the Gila Pimas, since the Spaniards, visiting the latter for the first time after having known the Sobaipuris, at first identified the Gila Pimas as Sobaipuris also. By 1762 Nentvig (Arizona Silhouettes 1951:79) reported that the Sobaipuris had abandoned the San Pedro Valley, some joining the Gila Pimas and some moving to the Santa Cruz Valley, although some of these later left to join the Gila Pimas.

Population estimates for the Akimel O'odham given by the Spanish missionaries also suggest that a portion of the San Pedro populations and surrounding areas moved to the Gila River (Ezell 1961:116). In 1768, Father Garcés reported a population of approximately 4,000 people along the Middle Gila River, which Wilson (forthcoming) suggested was "several fold from the numbers in Kino's time." He went on to write, "[I]t appears that the population of the Middle Gila was increasing by the 1740s if not before and that this increase continued until at least the 1770s. The new people were initially refugee Sobaipuris who came directly or indirectly (or both) from the San Pedro valley" (Wilson forthcoming).

Between 1744 and 1775, the occupied area along the Middle Gila River contracted by at least half. By the time Anza and Garcés visited the Middle Gila River area in 1775, the first village was not encountered until the vicinity of Gila Butte, but locations to the east, in the Santa Rosa area, had been occupied during a visit just a year earlier. The last settlement was encountered near Pima Butte (Wilson forthcoming).

Akimel O'odham settlements had become the target of more frequent raiding during that time (Ezell 1983; Russell 1908; Wilson forthcoming). To defend against these constant threats, the Akimel O'odham adopted the denser settlement pattern, introduced mandatory military service for all males, and conducted punitive campaigns. Village locations provided by Bringas in 1795 suggest that the locations of the settlements remained stable from 1775 until that time (Wilson forthcoming).

The next written record of habitation areas along the Middle Gila River came during the Romero expedition in 1823. He reported four villages that appear to have been along the same stretch of the river between Gila and Pima Buttes where Garcés and Anza had reported O'odham settlements to be approximately 48 years earlier (Wilson forthcoming). Romero also made the earliest reference to the Pee Posh village of "Standing Bone," which apparently was located along the Santa Cruz River, immediately west of the O'odham villages (Wilson forthcoming). It is unclear when the area was first occupied by the Pee Posh, although Spier (1933:26) suggested that Pee Posh occupation first occurred at the beginning of the nineteenth century.

Hackenburg (1974:38) stated that by 1846, the Akimel O'odham and Pee Posh were living in a short stretch of land south of the Gila River, in the vicinity of Casa Blanca, extending no farther west than the Salt-Gila confluence. He went on to observe, "Pimas were afraid to venture any farther than five or six miles east of Casa Blanca" because the Apache posed a constant threat (Hackenburg 1974:39). Although the number of reported villages increased, suggesting possible population expansion, the Akimel O'odham appear to have occupied the same stretch of the river from Gila to Pima Buttes in 1846–1849 as they had in 1775, and the limited expansion in settlement outside the core area consisted of Pee Posh communities (Wilson forthcoming).

As late as 1850, all "Pima Indian villages were still on the south side of the Gila River" (Hackenberg 1974:100). Bartlett (1854:232) described the area in 1852 as follows:

The valley or bottom-land [sic] occupied by the Pimos [Akimel O'odham] and Coco-Maricopas [Pee Posh] extends about fifteen miles along the south side of the Gila [River], and is from two to four miles in width, nearly the whole being occupied by their villages and cultivated fields. The Pimos occupy the eastern portion. There is no dividing line between them, nor anything to distinguish the villages of one from the other. The whole of this plain is intersected by irrigating canals from the Gila, by which they are enabled to control the waters, and raise the most luxuriant crops.

After that time, however, Apache raiding began to abate, and as a consequence of external pressures exerted by Euroamerican settlers, the Akimel O'odham returned to a more dispersed settlement pattern (Dejong 2009; Shaw 1994:58–65; Webb 1959:38). John Reid, a traveler from Texas, reported settlements on both sides of the Gila River in 1857 (Wilson forthcoming). The Pee Posh established a settlement at Sacaton perhaps in 1848–1849 (Spier 1933). By that time, the O'odham core area appears to have been bordered on the east, west, and north by Pee Posh settlements.

The most devastating effect of the migration of Euroamerican settlers into the region was the construction of upstream canals in the 1870s that diverted much of the water to non–Native American farmers along the Gila River (Dejong 2009; Ezell 1983). As a result, during subsequent periods of drought, the lack of water led to the further dispersal of the Akimel O'odham, including the relocation of some settlements to areas of former occupation in the Salt River Valley (Ezell 1983; Webb 1959:45). Russell (1908:33) concluded:

[N]o effective efforts were made to prevent the water from being diverted from the reservation, and the result was nearly as predicted—a result that should bring a blush of shame to every true American. A thrifty, industrious, and peaceful people that had been in effect a friendly nation rendering succor and assistance to emigrants and troops for many years when they sorely needed it was deprived of the rights inhering from centuries of residence. The marvel is that the starvation, despair, and dissipation that resulted did not overwhelm the tribe.

Middle Gila River Historic Period Conflict

Although the nature and intensity of warfare varied substantially over time and space, conflict was endemic among southwestern Historic period populations (Basso

2004; Ezell 1961; Jacoby 2008; Kroeber and Fontana 1986; Rice 2000; Russell 1908; Shaw 1994:10–14; Spier 1933; Webb 1959:22–25). During the nineteenth century, the Akimel O'odham experienced two primary forms of violence that are generally classified as raiding and warfare. The Pee Posh, for example, distinguished between "formally arranged pitched battles" (Spier 1933:168) and small raiding attacks, the intents of which were brief assault and rapid disengagement (Kroeber and Fontana 1986; Spier 1933).

The Western Apache also differentiated between raids, of which the primary objective was to obtain property, and vengeance attacks, the intent of which was to kill enemies (Basso 2004). Apache raiding parties tended to be small groups of 5–15 men who moved stealthily and tried to avoid combat (Kroeber and Fontana 1986:36). Warfare expeditions, on the other hand, could include 200 or more men who attempted to kill adversaries and even destroy entire settlements (Kroeber and Fontana 1986). These attacks were generally organized in retaliation for their own losses.

Both Yavapai and Apache groups raided the Akimel O'odham villages along the Middle Gila River (Gifford 1936; Russell 1908). Russell (1908:201) noted, "Every three or four days small parties of five or ten would come steal live stock or to kill any individual that might have gone some little distance from the villages." As discussed in the previous section, although the individual attacks were generally minor, conflict with these groups impacted Akimel O'odham settlement patterns along the Middle Gila River and led to the abandonment of large areas of former habitation (Russell 1908:201).

In response to these raids and larger attacks, the Akimel O'odham organized punitive campaigns against the Apache on a periodic basis (Webb 1959:30). Many facets of these campaigns were highly ritualized. For example, carefully prescribed and detailed speeches based on their creation story were made each evening while they traveled (Bahr 1975). These raids usually ended with the death of one or two Akimel O'odham, the destruction of an Apache camp, and "perhaps half a dozen of the enemy killed and a child taken prisoner" (Russell 1908:202).

In contrast to the Apache, the Akimel O'odham did not conduct raids in order to acquire goods, and their intent was usually, instead, to inflict deaths and injuries. Bourke (1890:59), who lived with the Apache, described Akimel O'odham and Pee Posh tactics as follows:

Having located a *ranchería*, or village, of their enemies, they [the Akimel O'odham and Pee Posh] would surround it at night and when first light appeared in the east would raise a yell, shrill and unmistakable in its blood-curdling significance. The terror-stricken foe, rushing out pell-mell from their frail jacales were obliged to go down on their hands and knees to get out of the low openings. Crouched in this defenseless position, they would hardly have protruded their heads, when crack! would come the macan or war-club of the blood-thirsty assailants. The Pimas and Maricopas used to be greatly addicted to plundering, in which they rivaled the Prussians.

After describing similar depredations inflicted by the O'odham against the Apache, Burns (1916:311) wrote, "Treatment like this will, of course, make any human being feel like getting even in some way. The Apaches, however, did not have many weapons to protect themselves; they only had bows and arrows."

The Akimel O'odham, who had a different perspective, recorded details of these conflicts in the calendar-stick records they kept (Russell 1908:34–66) (Figure 25). For example, the record written by McClatchie for the year 1837 described a raid in which the assailants used armor to defend themselves:

In the summer a Pima woman went out to gather some cactus fruit and Apaches chased her back. In

trying to jump a ditch she fell in and they killed her. Our men who were in the field pulling white-head weeds out of the corn, saw the woman running toward them and wondered why she ran. Then they saw the Apaches and ran to the homes and got more men and went after the Apaches. On the south side of where Mesa now is, they overtook the Apaches and killed five. The rest escaped. None of the Pimas were killed. As soon as the fight was over they sent back a man to tell the women how many Apaches they had killed. This was a very hard fight. The Pima Chief See-o-Ke kept telling his men not to run away, to stand and fight. But the Apaches did run, and got mixed up with the Pimas, and the dust was so thick it was hard to tell which was [sic] Apaches and which was [sic] Pimas. The Apaches fought with bows and arrows, and the Pimas with sharp sticks, very few of them having a bow or arrow. Some Pimas living near where the fight was, saw the dust and came to see what was the matter. The fight was at its thickest,

Figure 25. Pima calendar stick (from Russell 1908).

so they joined in and helped the other Pimas. The Apaches wore cowhides for shirts and blankets on top, so the sharp sticks would not go into their bodies, but the Pimas killed five by hitting them on their faces [Hall 1907:416].

Russell (1908:203) summarized Historic period conflict among the Native Americans from the Middle Gila River region as follows:

These raids [by the Akimel O'odham] were not infrequent, but they could hope to reap no better reward for their efforts than revenge for past injuries, whereas the Apaches were spurred on to constantly renewed attacks for the sake of plunder that they might secure. Thus the feral pauper preyed upon the sedentary toiler, but paid dearly in blood for his occasional prize of grain or live stock. The effect upon the two tribes of so strenuous a life was beginning to manifest itself in an interesting manner at the time of the intervention of the Americans. The Spaniards and Mexicans had shown utter incapacity to cope with the Apaches, and their presence in Sonora was rather an aid to the enemy than otherwise. The Pimas were compelled to fight their own battles. In doing so they learned the advantage of concentrating their fields. They perfected a system of attack, appointed runners for bringing in assistance, and organized a fairly satisfactory method of defense. They never used smoke signals except to announce the victory of an incoming war party. They kept themselves constantly in fit condition by their campaigns, and even engaged in sham battles for practice. These have been held within the last decade at the lower villages on the reservation. Their daily duties were ordered with reference to the possibility of attack. Their arts were modified by the perpetual menace. Their myths were developed and their religion tinged by the same stress.

Settlement Patterns and Archaeological Visibility

The ongoing conflict among Historic period populations in the Middle Gila River region had substantial effects on the settlement patterns of different groups, which, in turn, have variously affected the archaeological visibility of these people. In short, warfare between sedentary agriculturalists (e.g., Akimel O'odham and Pee Posh) and people who practiced raiding (e.g., Apache and Yavapai) resulted in the concentration of the former populations for defense, and the latter groups instead practiced a dispersed and mobile settlement pattern as a defensive mechanism

(Jacoby 2008:143–188; Nabokov and Easton 1989:338). This observation is supported by the fact that although extensive historical records exist regarding the results of conflict between them, no archaeological sites attributed to the Apache have been recorded in the study area, whereas Akimel O'odham sites are common.

For many reasons, sedentary populations are more readily visible in the archaeological record than are highly dispersed, mobile populations (Herr et al. 2009; Pinter and Stokes 2009; Seymour 2009; Upham 1988). First, concentrated populations leave behind much denser accumulations of cultural material (e.g., large middens) that are more readily identifiable on the modern ground surface than are diffuse, low-density remains left behind by scattered populations. Second, in order to travel efficiently, populations that frequently move are restricted in the materials that they can carry. In contrast, sedentary populations are not similarly constrained, and it is therefore possible to accumulate more possessions (Andrefsky1994). Third, year-round habitations are more likely to be built in geomorphological settings that facilitate their preservation (Loendorf and Rice 2004:8–10). Fourth, Seymour (2009) argued that the archaeological remains from Historic period mobile people tend to co-occur with the remains of Archaic period populations. Archaeologists have generally assumed that all of these materials are from the Archaic period and have therefore failed to recognize data from mobile Historic period peoples (Seymour 2009).

Most importantly, because the Akimel O'odham and the U.S. Government troops regularly organized military campaigns against hunter-gatherers who raided sedentary populations, these seasonally transhumant populations went to considerable lengths to conceal their presence on the landscape (Basso 2004; Herr et al. 2009:39). They undertook such practices as camping in different locations every night and even walking in each others' tracks while traveling (Basso 2004). Another way they hid their activities and obtained materials for tools in the process was to intentionally reoccupy prehistoric sites, which further complicates identification of the remains that they did leave behind (Ferg and Tessman 1997; Herr et al. 2009:45; Pinter and Stokes 2009; Whittlesey et al. 1997:212).

The Apache were so successful at hiding that it was difficult to find any evidence whatsoever of their existence, even at the time they were occupying much of southern Arizona (Shaw 1994:39–42). A contemporary observer, John C. Cremony (1868:138), put it this way:

Remember that a well appointed and careful party may travel through Arizona from one year's end to the other, without ever seeing an Apache, or any trace of his existence, and from this cause travelers frequently become careless and fall an easy prey to their sleepless watchfulness. Indeed, it is not difficult to point out many who have no faith in their apparent ubiquity, but believe they must be sought in their strongholds. There are others again who will not be convinced that the eyes of these Indians are always upon them, because they see nothing to indicate that fact; but the truth is, every move you make, every step you advance, every camp you visit, is seen and noted by them, with the strictest scrutiny.

He went on to argue:

Casual observers have, unintentionally, done serious evil by underrating their [Apache] real strength, to an extent almost inconceivable among those who are better informed. I have been in company with a body of fifteen hundred at the very time that intelligence was received that half a dozen other parties, numbering from twenty to three hundred each, were actively engaged in committing depredations at other points embraced in a radius of five hundred miles, and yet I have seen the number of Apaches estimated as low as fifteen hundred and two thousand. Nearly eight years of personal experiences have satisfied me that the Apache race, collectively, will number fully twenty-five thousand souls [Cremony 1868:142].

Burns (1916:325) provided an anecdote regarding difficulties that the U.S. troops had when attempting to find Apache camps (Figure 26): "Once in the winter of 1872, the soldiers passed right by a camp of Indians on a thick flat of cedar; it was snowing and the wind was blowing right in the soldiers' faces. They never looked down on the ground to see if there were any tracks of the Indians, and went right on by."

Because the Apache went to considerable lengths to conceal their presence on the landscape, they left behind comparatively little evidence of their existence in the archaeological record. Furthermore and for the same reason, their existence is also underrepresented in the historical records written by Euroamericans who traveled through the region.

In addition to the effects of settlement patterns on archaeological visibility, differences in material culture (especially architecture and ceramics) between sedentary people and groups with high residential mobility also differentially affect archaeological visibility (Upham 1988). For example, Apache groups were generally small, and they built ephemeral brush structures (Figure 27) that are less likely to have left evidence in the archaeological record than are adobe and especially masonry structures (Nabokov and Easton 1989:338).

Indeed, one current database that is designed to track populations between A.D. 1200 and 1700 only includes archaeological sites with more than 12 rooms (Clark et al. 2008:2). Therefore, people such as the Apache who usually traveled in small groups and built structures that did not commonly leave evidence in the archaeological record are excluded from this database by definition, and they are consequently archaeologically invisible.

Figure 26. Apache village (photograph by Edward Curtis).

Figure 27. Apache brush structure (photograph by Edward Curtis).

Furthermore, the Apache less commonly used ceramic vessels, which are fragile and difficult to transport (Herr et al. 2009:41). The few ceramics that were made by the Apache were plain wares, which are more difficult to identify and may not be recognized as Apache products (Herr et al. 2009:41). Decorated ceramics play a central role in chronological control within southern Arizona, and sites that lack diagnostic ceramics and surface evidence of architecture are almost invariably designated as "artifact scatters" of unknown age (Wells, Rice, et al. 2004). Therefore, even if Apache sites are identified during archaeological survey, they are unlikely to be recorded as such. As a result, mobile populations who did not regularly use decorated ceramics and who lived in ephemeral structures are quite literally archaeologically invisible.

Archaeological Visibility Discussion

Although people such as the Apache are difficult to identify in the archaeological and even the historical record, their raiding had thoroughly documented and dramatic effects on sedentary populations. As a consequence, in order to examine conflict and cooperation among the people who lived along the Middle Gila River, it is necessary to consider the role that highly mobile populations (e.g., the Yavapai and Apache) played.

In spite of what appeared to be an inconsequentially small population to many observers, the Apache forced the Sobaipuri to abandon the San Pedro River, and the Akimel O'odham found it necessary to concentrate their habitations in a small area for defense. The Apache and other archaeologically invisible peoples successfully stopped and then reversed Euroamerican expansion into southern Arizona for hundreds of years and were not subdued until the late 1800s, despite concerted and prolonged efforts by state-level societies (e.g., placing large bounties on Apache scalps) as well as by other Native Americans (Cozzens 1874:38–39; Kozak and Lopez 1999:42–43). Although these dramatic effects of Apache raiding are clearly documented in the historical record; until recently, the methodology southwestern archaeologists have employed has meant that these people and other mobile groups were archaeologically invisible (Herr et al. 2009; Seymour 2009, 2011).

Chapter Summary

This chapter has presented ethnographic and ethnohistorical descriptions of projectile technology, socioeconomic interactions, settlement patterns, conflict, and subsistence practices of Historic period people who lived within or in the immediate vicinity of the Middle Gila River study area. Although relatively few Euroamericans visited the region until the 1850s and initial contact was not until A.D. 1694, it is possible to infer numerous expectations for patterning in the archaeological record that are based on written documentation. Table 8 summarizes expectations for Historic period arrow-point technology that are based on the observations of people who visited the Middle Gila River at this time.

Ethnographic observations for study area populations also have suggested several other factors that may have affected patterning in the archaeological record. These data indicate that noneconomic or warfare uses of projectile points occurred in some circumstances. Although these factors are unlikely to have resulted in systematic alterations to point morphology, such practices as using enemy projectile points as talismans may have resulted in some intermixing among point assemblages. Because points are small portions of a complex system (including the arrow, bow, and archer) that must be carefully balanced to function effectively, it is unlikely that completed projectile points were commonly exchanged among different groups of people. Instead, the raw materials necessary for point manufacture may have generally been traded. The use of points in warfare is also expected to have affected patterns of projectile raw-material exchange.

Historic period exchange consisted largely of foodstuffs, although decorated ceramics and cooking vessels were also traded. Prior to the 1830s, Pee Posh from the Gila Bend area conducted trade with Akimel O'odham. After that time, these Pee Posh populations relocated to the Middle Gila River area, and this external trade no longer occurred. Conflict between the Akimel O'odham and surrounding populations limited economic interactions, and the Tohono O'odham, who were located to the south of the study area, were their primary trading partners.

Settlement-pattern expectations based on historical documentation include the following observations: (1) Historic period settlement was largely on the southern side of the Gila River until 1850, suggesting that projectile points from that time should be concentrated on that side of the river. (2) The dispersal of Akimel O'odham settlements that occurred after the arrival of Euroamericans in the mid-1800s suggests that Historic period points found on the northern side of the river should generally be more recent and therefore, by inference, lighter than older Historic period points from the southern side. (3) The contraction of Akimel O'odham settlement to a small stretch of the Gila River between Gila and Pima Buttes that occurred by 1775 and continued until the 1850s suggests that Historic period projectile points should be most highly concentrated in the Casa Blanca area. (4) Pee Posh migrants to the Middle Gila River settled on the margins of the Historic period settlement core area, suggesting that point types associated with people moving into the area may be more common on the immediate peripheries of Casa Blanca. (5) Some San Pedro Sobaipuri moved to the Middle Gila River area during the mid-1700s, which suggests that they might have introduced point types at that time.

Until recently, the methodological approach of southwestern researchers has meant that highly mobile hunter-gatherer populations have been archaeologically invisible. Conflict among hunter-gatherers and sedentary agriculturalists had profound effects on both groups, which were extensively documented in the historical record. Because mobile populations actively concealed their locations on the landscape, these people are hard to recognize in the archaeological record. Although they are difficult to identify, diachronic trends in obsidian utilization presented in the next chapter suggest evidence that hunter-gatherers may have moved into the Sonoran Desert before the Historic period and that they may therefore have played a role in the changes in settlement patterns and cultural practices that occurred between the Classic and Historic periods.

Table 8. Warfare and Hunting Expectations Based on Ethnohistorical Observations

Group	Large-Game Hunting	Hunting-Point Types	Warfare	Warfare-Point Types
Apache/Yavapai	Commonly.	Wooden arrow tips for small game and side-notched stone points for large game.	Raiding and skirmishes; large battles only rarely.	Small stone arrow points with a wide variety of shapes and stone-tipped spears.
Akimel O'odham	Very rarely.	Wooden arrow tips for small game only.	Skirmishes and large battles regularly.	Small stone arrow points (Sobaipuri points were serrated) and stone-tipped spears.
Pee Posh	Before immigrating to the Middle Gila River.	Wooden arrow tips for small game and side-notched stone points for large game.	Skirmishes and large battles regularly.	Small stone points (?) and stone-tipped spears.

CHAPTER 6

Middle Gila River Projectile Point Data

After considering the overall distribution of projectile points within the study area, this chapter begins with an analysis of projectile points that have been suggested to be Historic period types, based on previous research in the region (Brew and Huckell 1987; Bronitsky 1985; Canouts et al. 1972; Di Peso 1953; Doyel 1977; Gilpin and Phillips 1998; Haury 1950; Justice 2002; Loendorf and Rice 2004; Masse 1981; Ravesloot and Whittlesey 1987; Rosenthal et al. 1978; Seymour 1993, 2009, 2011; Vint 2005). Patterns in these data are compared to ethnohistorical and ethnographic descriptions of Akimel O'odham settlement locations (Bolton 1948; Ezell 1961, 1983; Hackenberg 1974; Russell 1908; Spier 1933; Upham 1983; Wells 2006; Wilson forthcoming; Winter 1973). Following these investigations, the distribution of Historic period ceramic types is compared to patterning in the point collection. Classic period ceramic data and platform-mound locations are then used to generate exceptions in the distribution of stone projectile points made at that time.

The following sections present attribute-based analyses of the P-MIP projectile point collection that further explore both temporal and spatial variability in these remains. This research attempts to better define and understand the underlying characteristics employed to define categories in the typological system (Loendorf and Rice 2004). The hypothesis that points generally became smaller over time as a result of improvements in delivery systems is tested through analyses of point-size data at a range of spatial scales, beginning with study-area-wide analyses, continuing through intrasite patterning, and finally considering variation among individual features. Both survey and excavation data are considered; however, the available sample of excavated Historic period features was small.

The next portion of the analysis tests several expectations for warfare- and hunting-point designs. The distribution of these two different point types is then considered. Next, temporal and spatial patterns in serration data are examined. These analyses suggest that some point attributes generally employed to define "styles" in classification schemes are actually more closely associated with differences in the intended functions of the projectile points. At the same time,

evidence is identified that suggests that other attributes, especially those associated with the blade margins, may be more closely associated with style, in the sense that they appear to have been intentional expressions of cultural associations. The final portion of this chapter employs obsidian source data to examine synchronic and diachronic variation in socioeconomic cooperation among social groups within the study area and in surrounding locations.

GRIC Projectile Point Densities

Projectile points were rarely collected as IOs, and more than 95 percent of the collection was recovered from contexts that had site-level artifact densities. Projectile points collected from the surfaces of these sites probably entered the archaeological record as a result of many different processes. First, points may have been accidentally disassociated from shafts in habitation areas. Ethnohistorical documentation summarized in Chapter 5 suggests that warfare points readily detached from arrows and that the small size of the points would have complicated recovery of separated projectile tips. Second, some points were intentionally discarded after breakage. Third, projectile points were sometimes included as intentional or unintentional (e.g., because they were lodged in the body of the deceased) burial accompaniments. Fourth, some projectile points may have been lost during use when the arrow was fired at a target. Fifth, points may have been in such contexts as structures that burned or otherwise collapsed and were therefore not recovered. For example, flooding and resultant deposition may have buried functional artifacts. Sixth, points may have been buried in caches for later use. Seventh, projectile points may have been used as offerings in ritual contexts. These explanations are not mutually exclusive, and these and other factors resulted in the deposition of artifacts in the archaeological record.

Table 9 presents projectile point counts by portion of the study area, and Figure 28 shows the overall point density within the study area. Table 9 does not include 28 small, indeterminate biface fragments in the study collection that were too incomplete to determine point size. Point densities are low throughout the community, and areas with the highest concentrations still have less than 50 points per 1,000 ha of survey. This probably results in part from the limited large-game-hunting opportunities in the lowland-desert environment of the study area (James 2003:76). Furthermore, faunal analyses suggest that there was less reliance on large game after the Middle Archaic period, whereas the importance of small-game hunting, which did not require the use of stone points, increased in the Hohokam region (Dean 2003, 2005; Greenspan 2001:14; James 2003). Although point densities are low throughout the GRIC, nearly 1,000 projectile points or point preforms were collected from the community, in total, because over 50,000 ha were surveyed as part of P-MIP investigations.

Projectile points in the surface collection were more concentrated on the southern side of the river than the northern, and the southern-side density of all projectile points is over two times higher than the density on the northern side of the river. The Snaketown area (Unit 7) has the highest small-point density on the northern side of the river, and the Borderlands area (Unit 9) has the highest large-point density. Similarly, Casa Blanca (Unit 8) has the highest small-point density on the southern side of the river, and large points are most dense in the Santa Cruz area (Unit 11), which has the highest density of large points found in the study area.

Several factors may account for the tendency of overall point densities to be higher on the southern side of the river. The Akimel O'odham collected points from earlier occupations (Russell 1908:95), and that practice may have depleted surface artifacts in areas outside their habitations. As will be discussed further below, the Historic period population was concentrated on the southern side of the river, and their collecting activities may consequently have lowered point counts elsewhere while increasing densities in their habitation areas.

As will be considered further below, it also appears that some parts of the community afforded better access to big-game-hunting opportunities or were peripheral areas that were more exposed to attack, and the people in these areas may therefore have made more stone points per capita than did those in other locations. The Santa Cruz area, in particular, has the highest density of Archaic period points, the second-highest density of small points, and the highest overall point density. In addition to riparian-area access along the Santa Cruz and Gila Rivers, this area is adjacent to upland locations in the Sierra Estrella that currently support large game animals, including bighorn sheep (Rea 1998; Webb

Table 9. Projectile Point Size, by Study Unit within the Gila River Indian Community

Site Group	Map Unit	Survey Area (ha)	Large Point or Preform		Small Point or Preform		Total	
			n	Points/ 1,000 ha	n	Points/ 1,000 ha	n	Points/ 1,000 ha
Northern Side								
Maricopa	12	5,223	4	0.8	27	5.2	31	5.9
Borderlands	9	13,752	88	6.4	27	2.0	115	8.4
Blackwater	1	1,778	—	—	3	1.7	3	1.7
Santan	4	3,052	5	1.6	28	9.2	33	10.8
Lone Butte	10	3,432	8	2.3	26	7.6	34	9.9
Snaketown	7	8,267	45	5.4	214	25.9	259	31.3
Total, northern side		35,504	150	4.2	325	9.2	475	13.4
Southern side								
Sacaton	5	1,535	10	6.5	13	8.5	23	15.0
Santa Rosa	2	5,449	43	7.9	50	9.2	93	17.1
Santa Cruz	11	3,047	31	10.2	108	35.4	139	45.6
Casa Blanca	8	5,325	24	4.5	198	37.2	222	41.7
Total, southern side		15,356	108	7.0	369	24.0	477	31.1
Southern-to-northern ratio		0.4	0.7	1.7	1.1	2.6	1.0	2.3

Note: Excludes indeterminate-size points.

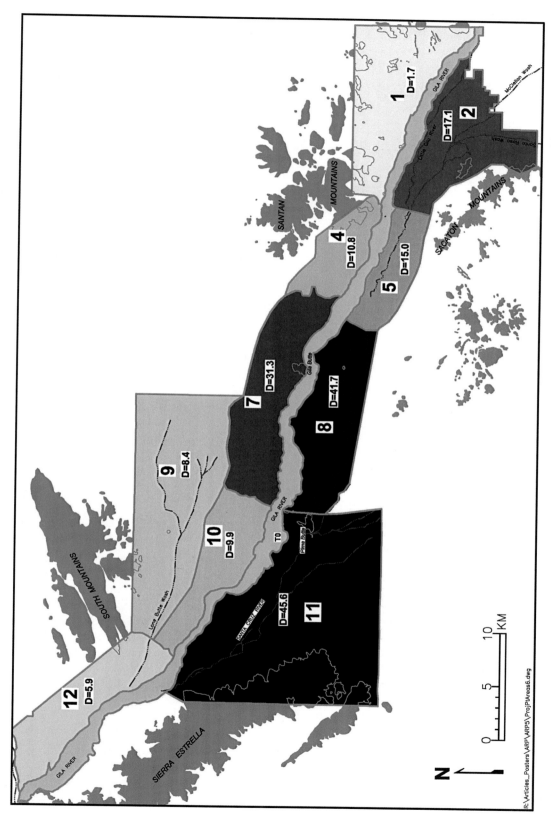

Figure 28. Map of overall point densities, Pima-Maricopa Irrigation Project collection. Units are shaded based on point density, and black represents the greatest. D = projectile point density in points per 1,000 ha of survey in the unit.

1959:76). This possibility is supported by recent excavation data from the Santa Cruz unit. Clark (2007:18.15) found that "[l]arge game animals (order Artiodactyla) are the third most abundant mammalian order." This is also the portion of the community in which Rea (1998) found a small number of big-game hunters within the GRIC, and big-game hunting is a practice that continues to this day (Barnaby Lewis, personal communication 2010).

Typological Classification Analyses

This section analyzes the spatial distribution of projectile points suggested to be from the Historic period, based on a classification system that was developed to seriate points from the study area (see Chapter 4 for descriptions and illustrations of the types). Table 10 lists densities across the GRIC for the types thought to be Historic period points, based on previous research. For this analysis, a subset of the U-shaped Based Triangular points that most closely match the previous definitions of the Huachuca points is reclassified. These small, triangular points have straight blade margins, serration, and highly concave bases. The combined density of all other classified projectile points is also included. Survey coverage is available for relatively large portions of each area, but few points were collected from the Blackwater area (Unit 1).

Historic period settlement was largely on the southern side of the Gila River until at least 1850 (Bolton 1948; Eiselt 2002; Ezell 1983:151; Hackenberg 1974:236; Russell 1908; Wells 2006:22–25; Wilson forthcoming), suggesting that projectile points from that time should be concentrated on that side of the river. The density of the three Historic period types on the southern side of the Gila River is nine times higher than the density on the northern side, whereas the combined density of other classified points is more similar for the two sides of the river. Historic period types account for over 40 percent of all points collected on the southern side. In contrast, these points compose just 13 percent of the collection from the northern side of the river. These observations are consistent with the historically documented tendency for settlements to be located on the southern side of the Gila River until roughly 1850.

Akimel O'odham settlements contracted to a short stretch of the Gila River between Gila and Pima Buttes before 1775, and that continued until the 1850s (Ezell 1961:115; Russell 1908:29–30; Upham 1983:56–57; Wells 2006:25; Wilson forthcoming), suggesting that Historic period projectile points should be most highly concentrated in the location known today as Casa Blanca. As expected, the highest Historic period point density occurs in that area, where Spanish sources suggest that people were concentrated from at least the middle 1700s until the 1850s

(Figure 29). Furthermore, the area of highest Historic period point density on the northern side is the Snaketown area, opposite Casa Blanca.

Pee Posh [Maricopa] migrants to the Middle Gila River in the early 1800s settled on the margins of the Casa Blanca area (Hackenberg 1974:113; Spier 1933:26; Wilson forthcoming), suggesting that point types associated with people who moved into the area may be more common on the immediate peripheries of the core area for Historic period occupation. In contrast to the other two Historic period point types, Huachuca points occur at higher densities in locations surrounding Casa Blanca (see Table 10); areas to the north, west, and east have both higher densities and higher proportions of Huachuca points (Figure 30).

The concentration of these points on the margins of the Casa Blanca area suggests that Huachuca points were introduced by people who immigrated to the Middle Gila River to join existing populations. In part because similar points have been found at sites on the San Pedro River and farther southeast, along the Santa Cruz River (Di Peso 1951; Justice 2002; Ravesloot and Whittlesey 1987; Vint 2005), it appears that these artifacts may have been associated with Sobaipuri immigrants from those areas. Spanish sources have documented the movement of people from those areas to the Middle Gila River as a result of disease and warfare (Ezell 1961:116; Hackenberg 1974:116–126; Russell 1908:23; Wilson forthcoming).

Ceramic Data

Another way to consider settlement patterns is to compare other lines of evidence to the point distributions presented in the previous section. Table 11 shows survey data for Historic period sherd counts and densities by portion of the GRIC (see Simon 2003 for a discussion of the types). All of the Historic period ceramic densities are substantially higher on the southern side of the river, and every type is most concentrated within the Casa Blanca area (Figure 31).

Black-on-red and red-on-buff sherds are the most equally distributed by side of the river, but these ceramics are still over 10 times more common on the southern side than on the northern side. Because these (Historic period) types were not made during the Classic period, it appears that these varieties may have been more common during the late Historic period, when populations began to disperse across the GRIC. Red-on-brown and plain ceramics are more concentrated on the southern side of the river, suggesting the possibility that these types were more common when the population was highly concentrated in the Casa Blanca area, during the eighteenth and early nineteenth centuries. These possibilities are generally consistent with site-based multivariate analyses of Historic period artifacts (Wells 2006; Wells, Loendorf, et al. 2004).

Table 10. Historic Period Point Densities, by Study Unit within the Gila River Indian Community

Site Group	Map Unit	Survey Area (ha)	Straight Base		U-Shaped Base		Huachuca		Subtotal, Historic Period		Other Points		Total	
			n	Points/ 1,000 ha	n	Points/ 1,000 ha	n	Points/ 1,000 ha	n	Points/ 1,000 ha	n	Points/ 1,000 ha	n	Points/ 1,000 ha
Northern side														
Maricopa	12	5,223	—	—	—	—	—	—	—	—	26	5.0	26	5.0
Borderlands	9	13,752	—	—	2	0.1	—	—	2	0.1	23	1.7	25	1.8
Blackwater	1	1,778	1	0.6	—	—	—	—	1	0.6	1	0.6	2	1.1
Santan	4	3,052	3	1.0	—	—	—	—	3	1.0	23	7.5	26	8.5
Lone Butte	10	3,432	1	0.3	1	0.3	1	0.3	3	0.9	25	7.3	28	8.2
Snaketown	7	8,267	9	1.1	13	1.6	10	1.2	32	3.9	176	21.3	208	25.2
Total, northern side		35,504	14	0.4	16	0.5	11	0.3	41	1.2	274	7.7	315	8.9
Southern side														
Sacaton	5	1,535	1	0.7	2	1.3	1	0.7	4	2.6	9	5.9	13	8.5
Santa Rosa	2	5,449	—	—	12	2.2	7	1.3	19	3.5	32	5.9	51	9.4
Santa Cruz	11	3,047	6	2.0	13	4.3	18	5.9	37	12.1	76	24.9	113	37.1
Casa Blanca	8	5,325	41	7.7	54	10.1	5	0.9	100	18.8	105	19.7	205	38.5
Total, southern side		15,356	48	3.1	81	5.3	31	2.0	160	10.4	222	14.5	382	24.9
Southern-to- northern ratio		0.4	3.4	7.9	5.1	11.7	2.8	6.5	3.9	9.0	0.8	1.9	1.2	2.8

Note: Excludes isolated occurrences. "Other Points" includes all additional points that were assigned styles.

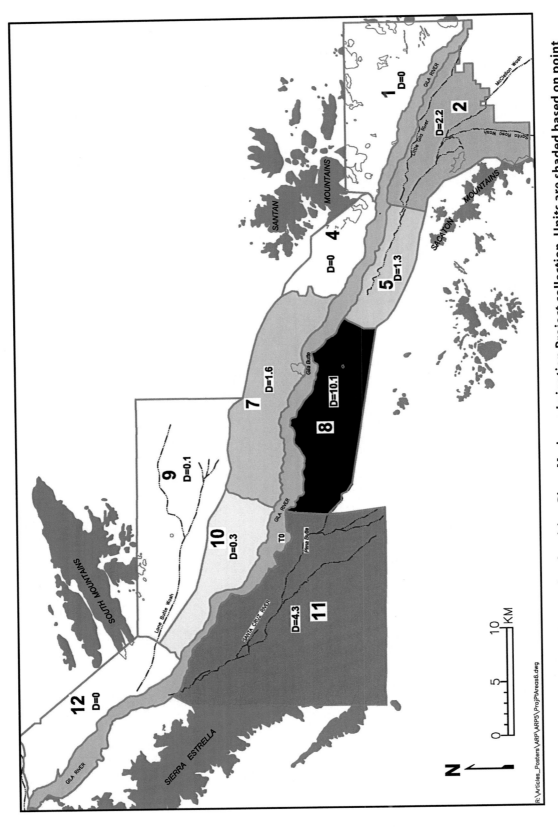

Figure 29. Map of U-shaped-base point densities, Pima-Maricopa Irrigation Project collection. Units are shaded based on point density, and black represents the greatest. D = projectile point density in points per 1,000 ha of survey in the unit.

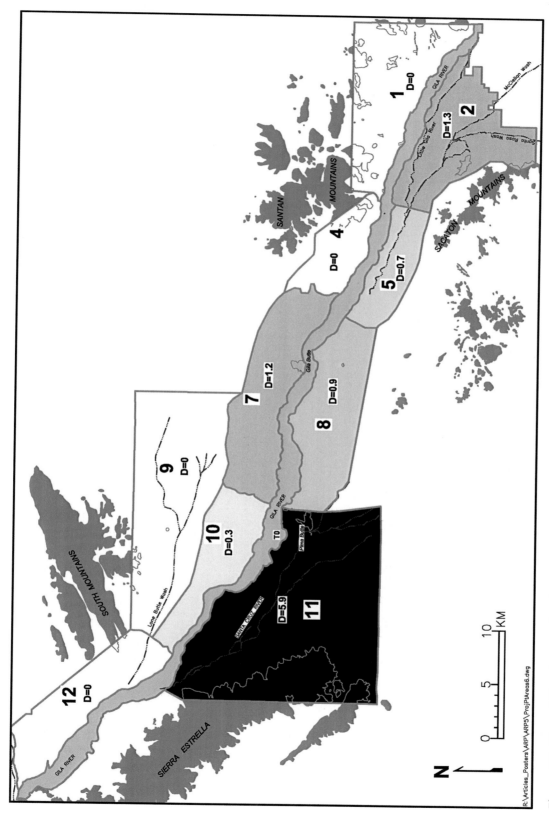

Figure 30. Map of Huachuca point densities, Pima-Maricopa Irrigation Project collection. Units are shaded based on point density, and black represents the greatest. D = projectile point density in points per 1,000 ha of survey in the unit.

R:\Articles_Posters\ARP\ARP5\Proj\PtArea6.dwg

Table 11. Historic Period Ceramic Counts, by Study Unit within the Gila River Indian Community

Site Group	Map Unit	Survey Area (ha)	Black-on-Red		Red-on-Buff		Red		Plain		Red-on-Brown		Total	
			n	Sherds/ 1,000 ha	n	Sherds/ 1,000 ha	n	Sherds/ 1,000 ha	n	Sherds/ 1,000 ha	n	Sherds/ 1,000 ha	n	Sherds/ 1,000 ha
Northern side														
Borderlands	9	13,752	73	5	1,113	81	21	2	203	15	65	5	1,475	107
Maricopa	12	5,223	40	8	710	136	243	47	176	34	172	33	1,341	257
Blackwater	1	1,778	3	2	5	3	3	2	42	24	—	—	53	30
Lone Butte	40	3,432	3	1	305	89	206	60	77	22	3	1	594	173
Santan	4	3,052	78	26	308	101	356	117	164	54	29	10	935	306
Snaketown	7	8,267	73	9	1,817	220	204	25	411	50	733	89	3,238	392
Total, northern side		35,504	270	8	4,258	120	1,033	29	1,073	30	1,002	28	7,636	215
Southern side														
Santa Cruz	11	3,047	30	10	1,405	461	1,652	542	1,586	521	267	88	4,940	1,621
Santa Rosa	2	5,449	254	47	715	131	389	71	499	92	226	41	2,083	382
Sacaton	5	1,535	129	84	889	579	52	34	180	117	143	93	1,393	907
Casa Blanca	8	5,325	856	161	20,904	3,926	4,266	801	7,638	1,434	9,681	1,818	43,345	8,141
Total, southern side		15,356	1,269	82.6	23,913	1,557	6,359	414	9,903	645	10,317	672	51,761	3,371
Total		50,860	1,539	30.3	28,171	554	7,392	145.3	10,976	215.8	11,319	700	59,397	3,586
Southern-to-northern ratio		0.4	4.7	10.9	5.6	13.0	6.2	14.2	9.2	21.3	10.3	23.8	6.8	15.7

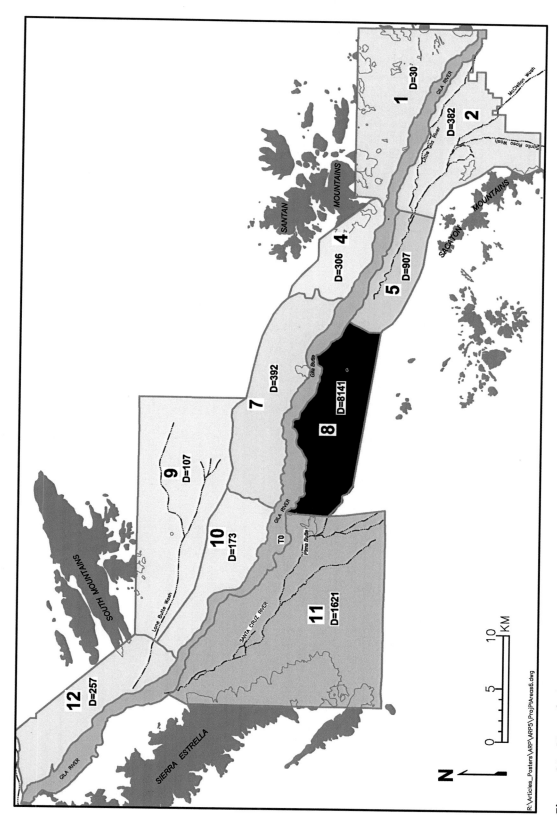

Figure 31. Map of Historic period ceramic densities, Pima-Maricopa Irrigation Project collection. Units are shaded based on ceramic density, and black represents the greatest. D = ceramic density in sherds per 1,000 ha of survey in the unit.

As can be seen in Figure 31, Historic period ceramics are concentrated in the Casa Blanca area, and densities tend to drop with distance from that location. The highest density on the northern side is in the Snaketown area, which is opposite Casa Blanca. This patterning is similar to that observed for Historic period projectile point types discussed in the preceding section (compare Figures 29 and 31). Figure 32 depicts this tendency graphically. Because of the difference in sample size, ceramic counts were log-transformed for the graph. The Pearson's correlation coefficient for the untransformed sherd and point counts is 0.94 (significance < .01), which suggests that Historic period point types and ceramics tend to be concentrated in the same locations.

Classic Period Diagnostic Ceramic Data

Classic period ceramics have distributional patterns that are different from those of Historic period artifacts and that are consistent with other lines of evidence regarding settlement locations during that period (Table 12). In contrast to Historic period ceramic densities, Classic period sherds are more concentrated on the northern side of the river (Figure 33). The densest areas on that side occur in the Snaketown and Santan units, and the highest density for all three types on the southern side occurs in the Casa Blanca area, which lies opposite those units. Five of the six platform mounds in the area occur within or immediately adjacent to these locations.

Public-architecture size has been employed as a proxy measure of Classic period settlement-complex size (Rice and Ravesloot 2003:18), and these data are consistent with the ceramic data. Four platform mounds were built on the northern side of the river, and only two mounds occur on the southern side of the river in the study area (Ravesloot and Rice 2004; Rice and Ravesloot 2003:24). The platform-mound sizes are indicated in Table 12, and their locations are shown in Figure 36. The total volume of the mounds on the northern side of the river is roughly 2.5 times greater than the southern-side volume, which also suggests that the population on the northern side of the river was higher than on the southern side during the Classic period, and this ratio is similar to the one observed for the ceramic data.

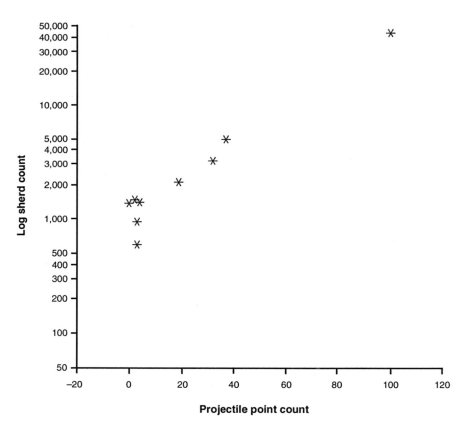

Figure 32. Scatter plot of log-10-transformed Historic period ceramic counts and Historic period point-type counts, by study unit, Pima-Maricopa Irrigation Project collection.

Table 12. Classic Period Ceramic Counts and Densities, by Study Unit, Pima-Maricopa Irrigation Project Collection

Site Group	Map Unit	Survey Area (ha)	Casa Grande		Gila Polychrome		Tonto Polychrome		Total		Platform-Mound Area (Square Meters)
			n	Sherds/1,000 ha	n	Sherds/1,000 ha	n	Sherds/1,000 ha	n	Sherds/1,000 ha	
Northern side											
Borderlands	9	13,752	17	1.2	19	1.4	1	0.1	37	2.7	—
Maricopa	12	5,223	6	1.1	53	10.1	4	0.8	63	12.1	625
Blackwater	1	1,778	7	3.9	105	59.0	4	2.2	116	65.2	—
Lone Butte	10	3,432	113	32.9	392	114.2	37	10.8	542	157.9	1,225
Santan	4	3,052	1,005	329.3	909	297.9	71	23.3	1,985	650.5	1,720
Snaketown	7	8,267	1,911	231.2	3,315	401.0	322	39.0	5,548	671.1	—
Total, northern side		35,504	3,059	86.2	4,793	135.0	439	12.4	8,291	233.5	3,570
Southern side											
Santa Cruz	11	3,047	5	1.6	98	32.2	8	2.6	111	36.4	—
Santa Rosa	2	5,449	55	10.1	339	62.2	34	6.2	428	78.5	—
Sacaton	5	1,535	136	88.6	213	138.7	15	9.8	364	237.1	—
Casa Blanca	8	5,325	482	90.5	828	155.5	55	10.3	1,365	256.4	1,400
Total, southern side		15,356	678	44.2	1,478	96.2	112	7.3	2,268	147.7	1,400
Total		50,860	3,737	73.5	6,271	123.3	551	10.8	10,559	207.6	4,970
Southern-to-northern ratio		0.4	0.2	0.5	0.3	0.7	0.3	0.6	0.3	0.6	0.4

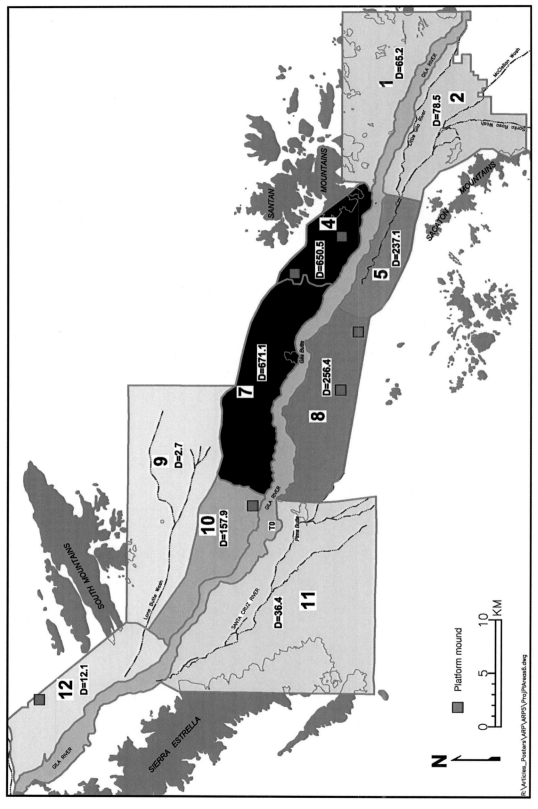

Figure 33. Map of Classic period ceramic densities and platform-mound locations, Pima-Maricopa Irrigation Project collection. Units are shaded based on ceramic density, and black represents the greatest. D = ceramic density in sherds per 1,000 ha of survey in the unit.

Classic Period Projectile Point Distribution

Table 13 shows Classic period projectile point densities by portion of the study area. Although the overall southern-to-northern ratio for points that are suggested to be from the Classic period is almost three times lower than the Historic period ratio, it appears probable that some of the Classic period types may have been misclassified. Ceramic and architectural data suggest that Classic period habitation was denser on the northern side of the river. Unnotched Classic period point types, in particular, are substantially more concentrated on the southern side of the river.

Ravesloot and Whittlesey (1987:96) argued that "small, triangular, concave-based points with serrated edges were being produced in the Classic Period." These points are highly similar to the types suggested to be associated with the Historic period. Indeed, it is this lack of differentiation in shape that has complicated the identification of early Historic period points. At the same time, this strong continuity in projectile point forms from the Classic period to the Historic period is one example of the close links between the Hohokam and the Akimel O'odham.

Middle-side-notched points constitute the only type with a higher density on the northern side of the river, suggesting that points with notches in the middles of the blade margins may be distinctive to the Classic period. Sliva (1997:54) argued that these points were made between A.D. 1050 and roughly 1350 in southern Arizona. Justice (2002) illustrated four categories that include middle-side-notched examples, but he did not use notch placement along the blade margin to distinguish types. Interestingly, all four of these varieties are from the Pueblo area of the southwest, which is also the location in which ceramic and architectural influences have been suggested to have originated during that time. Sliva (2006:59) suggested that this distinctive variety is one of the most widely distributed point types in Arizona, similar to the widespread distribution of Classic period Salado polychromes at that time (Crown 1994).

Diachronic Variation in Projectile Point Size

This section tests the point-size hypothesis through analyses of both survey and excavation data. Research presented in this section does not prove that projectile points generally decreased in size over time but, instead, merely suggests that the hypothesis requires further testing. The following analyses also suggest that the resolution of the size-weight data is limited; however, diachronic variation among points from the Hohokam core area is currently poorly understood, and it appears possible that employing size may improve our understanding of the temporal systematics of points from the region. Figure 34 shows box plots of weight for all complete points that were assigned to Classic or Historic period categories in the typology (see Chapter 4 for a description of the types). The Historic period artifacts are significantly lighter than the Classic period types (t-test: p = .02; equal variances not assumed).

Although the Historic period types are all unnotched, the difference in size does not appear to have been the result of notching patterns, because unnotched small projectile points are not significantly different in weight from notched small projectile points (Figure 35) (t-test: p = .74; equal variances not assumed). Furthermore, if only unnotched points are considered, the Historic period types are significantly different from the Classic period unnotched points (Figure 36) (t-test: p <.001; equal variances not assumed).

Other researchers have also identified a tendency for projectile points from the Sonoran Desert to have declined in weight over time (Bustoz et al. 2009; Craig 1992; Marshall 2001b). For example, Craig (1992:231) found that the Classic period projectile points were lighter than the earlier types and that they also generally had a lower size index (Length × Width/Thickness), which he suggested was the result of "increased standardization or specialization during that time period." This analysis has considered the possibility that the general decrease in weight is the result of diachronic technological changes.

The suggestion that points from the Historic period are generally smaller than Classic period artifacts is consistent with evidence that a new bow technology that increased potential arrow velocities was introduced during the Classic period. LeBlanc (1999:99–100) argued that arrows shot from recurved bows are 25–50 percent faster than arrows shot from self-bows. Empirical data provided by Baker (2001:108) showed a nearly 20 percent increase in arrow velocity for a recurved bow design, and Cotterell and Kamminga (1992:185) suggested that these bows can "store 50 percent more energy than a simple longbow [i.e., self-bow] of the same weight."

LeBlanc (1999) reviewed bows recovered from dry caves and depicted on pottery and in kiva mural images, and he concluded that the recurved bow was introduced to the Southwest somewhere between A.D. 1200 and 1450. However, according to Schaafsma (2000:48), "[t]he recurved bow, which may have been sinew backed, does not appear in the art before the fourteenth century." Although LeBlanc suggested that sinew backing and recurving almost always co-occurred in the Southwest, Schaafsma (2000:48) maintained that Puebloan recurved bows were not sinew backed (nor were they made by the Akimel O'odham) (Rea 1998:74–76; Russell 1908:95).

Table 13. Classic Period Projectile Point Counts and Densities, by Study Unit within the Gila River Indian Community, Pima-Maricopa Irrigation Project Collection

Site Group	Map Unit	Survey Area (ha)	Classic Period Types							
			Middle-Side Notched		Lower-Side Notched		Unnotched		Total	
			n	Points/ 1,000 ha	n	Points/ 1,000 ha	n	Points/ 1,000 ha	n	Points/ 1,000 ha
Northern side										
Maricopa	12	5,223	1	0.2	1	0.2	3	0.6	5	1.0
Borderlands	9	13,752	1	0.1	1	0.1	1	0.1	3	0.2
Blackwater	1	1,778	—	—	—	—	2	1.1	2	1.1
Santan	4	3,052	2	0.7	2	0.7	5	1.6	9	2.9
Lone Butte	10	3,432	1	0.3	1	0.3	7	2.0	9	2.6
Snaketown	7	8,267	14	1.7	19	2.3	29	3.5	62	7.5
Total, northern side		35,504	18	0.5	23	0.6	47	1.3	90	2.5
Southern side										
Sacaton	5	1,535	1	0.7	1	0.7	1	0.7	3	2.0
Santa Rosa	2	5,449	—	—	—	—	4	0.7	4	0.7
Santa Cruz	11	3,047	—	—	13	4.3	13	4.3	26	8.5
Casa Blanca	8	5,325	1	0.2	9	1.7	60	11.3	70	13.1
Total, southern side		15,356	2	0.1	23	1.5	78	5.1	103	6.7
Southern-to-northern ratio		0.43	0.11	0.26	1.00	2.31	1.66	3.84	1.14	2.65

Note: Excludes points collected as isolated occurrences. Classic period styles were defined following Sliva (1997).

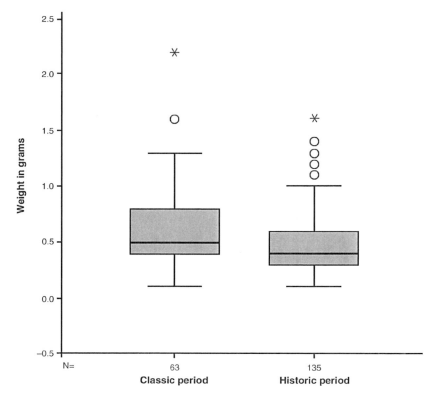

Figure 34. Box plots of projectile point weight for all finished and complete projectile points in the collection that were assigned to Classic or Historic period types.

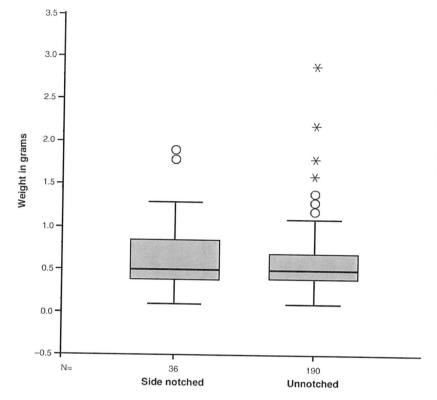

Figure 35. Box plots of projectile point weight for small finished and complete projectile points, by presence or absence of notching (excludes atlatl-dart-sized points).

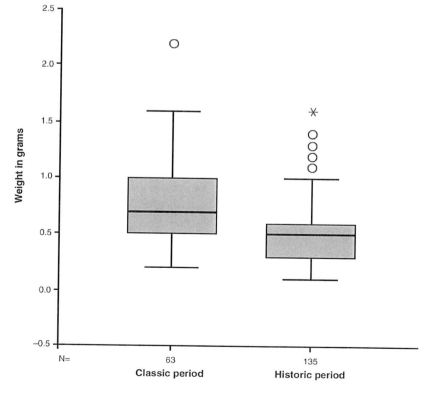

Figure 36. Box plots of projectile point weight for unnotched projectile points assigned to Classic or Historic period types.

Baldwin (1997:4), who reviewed data for bows recovered from dry caves and depicted on pottery, in kiva murals, and in petroglyphs, concluded, "Archaeological evidence documents the presence of only the self-bow in the Southwest before A.D. 1300." Counter to Schaafsma (2000:48), Baldwin (1997:3) suggested that "ethnographic data show the sinew-backed bow to be limited in production and use to the Pueblo Indians, the Navaho, and the various Apache groups . . . and lacking among the Yuman-speakers and the Pimas and other Uto-Aztecan-speakers of Southern Arizona and northern Mexico." Based on his analysis of the data, Baldwin (1997:6) suggested "that the appearance of 'double-curved' [i.e., recurved] bow forms in the depictions dating after A.D. 1300 is a symptom of the arrival of the sinew-backed bow technology." Baldwin associated the introduction of this technology with the arrival of Apacheans, which he placed at around A.D. 1400, based on analyses of several lines of evidence. LeBlanc (1999:102) argued that "the arrival of the Athapaskans appears to have been too late for them to have been vectors" for the introduction of the technology. However, LeBlanc did not cite any evidence regarding when Athapaskans first appeared in the region, and the date range he suggested for the introduction of the recurved bow technology overlaps with Baldwin's interpretation of the data. There is also ethnographic support for the possibility that the Apache introduced the recurved bow to the southern Southwest (Baldwin 1997:8). For example, one of Goodwin's Apache informants told him, "The double arc bow we had before the single arc bow" (Basso 2004:224).

The A.D. 1400 date suggested by Baldwin (1997) corresponds with Schaafsma's (2000:48) argument and places the introduction of this technology in the Southwest at or near the end of the Classic period Hohokam sequence. Baldwin (1997:7) observed, "It should also be noted that D-shaped bows [i.e., self-bows] continue to appear in kiva murals and rock art, frequently side by side with the 'double-curved bows' [i.e., recurved bows]." This suggests that recurved designs did not rapidly replace earlier bow technology, which is supported by the observation that both types continued to be employed by the Akimel O'odham in the late nineteenth century (Russell 1908).

If the technology was introduced sometime during the Classic period, this suggests that subsequent decline in point weights may have occurred during the Historic period. Because the design did not immediately replace earlier technologies, a period of transition is expected when larger points designed for self-bows were replaced by smaller points intended for recurved bows. Therefore, transitional assemblages with a mixture of sizes are expected, and as recurved designs became more common because of their superior performance, the average weights for point assemblages are expected to have declined gradually over time.

Support for the possibility that the Akimel O'odham were emulating introduced designs is provided by differences in construction techniques among recurved bows in the Southwest, including the lack of sinew backing on the Akimel O'odham bows. If the Akimel O'odham copied the Apache design, then they may have gone through a period of experimentation during which they improved the performance of their design. The effects of the lack of sinew backing on recurved-bow performance are unclear. Spier (1933:132) suggested that the Pee Posh used both sinew-backed bows and self-bows, and his informants said that sinew-backed bows did not draw harder or give more penetration. Similarly, experiments done by Pope (2000:68–69) suggested that sinew backing had little effect on arrow cast and, instead, primarily prevented the bow from breaking (see also Baugh 2001:117; Heath 2001:106; Laubin and Laubin 1980:53–72).

Hamm (1991:49–51), however, argued that sinew backing makes the bow faster and that the high tensile strength of the material prevents breakage of recurved bows that might occur as a result of the increased stress caused by curving the tips (see also Bergman and McEwen 1997): "The sinew will cure almost any problem on the back of the bow, such as knots, cutting through the grain, or cracks" (Hamm 1991:49). Without the sinew backing, it would have been necessary for the Akimel O'odham to carefully shape and cut bows such that the grain structure of the wood provided greater strength (Baugh 2001:117; Burch 2004:89–122; Spotted Eagle 1988; Hamm 1991:22–49; Heath 2001; Pope 2000:55–80), and this also may have slowed adoption of the technology. Furthermore, Akimel O'odham recurved bows were made with mulberry wood that was not locally available (Rea 1998:75, 2007b:80; Russell 1908), which also may have complicated, and therefore slowed, adoption of the design.

Rea (1998:75) quoted an O'odham story recorded by Densmore (1929) regarding the construction techniques for recurved bows that describes an interesting juxtaposition of roles:

[Coyote] went east, cut two [mulberry] saplings for the children and one for himself and brought them home. He threw down the two for the children and their mother pulled off the bark, curved them by the heat of the fire, and put strings on them, doing this at once. Coyote cleaned the wood of his tree nicely and bent his bow by leaning the tree against another tree so that when dry it would be in the proper form. The mother had used the whole tree except the rough outer bark but Coyote scraped off part of the wood on each side of his bow. He told the woman she was doing something that no one ever did and that his way was right.

Rea (1998:76) observed, "While Coyote is usually the paradigm of the bungler, in this case he is making the bow correctly, in contrast to the mother."

GRIC Surface Data by Weight

Because Historic period settlement was largely on the southern side of the Gila River, it is expected that points from that time should be concentrated on that side of the river. Figure 37 compares weight by side of the Gila River for all finished and unbroken projectile points in the GRIC collection, regardless of morphology. Projectile points from the southern side are significantly lighter, on average, than projectile points from the northern side, which is consistent with the expectation that small points should be concentrated on the southern side of the Gila River (t-test: $p < .001$; equal variances not assumed). This analysis involves the fewest assumptions and includes all points from throughout the archaeological sequence. Different patterning, however, is apparent if only points that were assigned Historic period types are considered, and all of the following analyses in this section exclude large atlatl tips.

The Akimel O'odham returned to a more dispersed settlement pattern after the arrival of Euroamericans in the mid-1800s (see Chapter 5), suggesting that Historic period points found on the northern side of the river should generally be more recent and therefore lighter than points from the southern side. Within the artifacts classified as Historic period points based on the typological classification system, the data are consistent with the expectation that Historic period points from the northern side should generally be smaller because they are more recent than those from the southern side (Figure 38) (t-test: $p < .001$; equal variances not assumed).

Sacate Site Data

Another way to examine variability in Historic period projectile points is to examine patterning in surface-collection data from a single site. The Sacate site (GR-909) is a roughly 3-km-long and 0.8-km-wide Historic period Akimel O'odham village located near the center of the modern GRIC, on the southern side of the Gila River, in the Casa Blanca area (Figure 39). Two hundred and four features, including 103 *ke'* (i.e., traditional round house) depressions, 3 cemeteries, numerous middens, and other areas with structural remains, were identified on the surface.

Diagnostic artifacts from the site were largely from the Historic period (Randolph et al. 2002). The site therefore provides an opportunity to consider diachronic variation during the Historic period in a context in which earlier remains are largely not intermixed. Nearly 120 projectile points and preforms were recovered from GR-909. Projectile points from the site are almost exclusively small, triangular forms that lack notching or serration (Figure 40). In fact, no side-notched points were recovered from the site, which suggests, by inference, that these people did not commonly practice big-game hunting. This possibility is consistent

with ethnographic documentation (see Chapter 5) and with analyses presented below.

Darling (2011) described a process whereby village locations drift over time, resulting in horizontal stratigraphy, and analyses of nonindigenous artifacts from the Sacate site support that model (Randolph et al. 2002:13). Preliminary examination of indigenously produced artifacts, however, failed to identify spatial patterning in these data (Randolph et al. 2002). Nonindigenous-artifact data suggest that the initial area of habitation at the Sacate site occurred in the central section of the site, and that portion of the site was occupied for the longest period of time (Figure 41). The area of occupation then extended to the east and west, in the locations designated as the expansion area on Figure 41. The most recent habitation occurred in the western portion of the site.

Because Euroamerican goods were rare in the area until the mid-1800s, it is difficult to establish when the site was first occupied based on this evidence alone (Figure 42), and Wilson (forthcoming) suggested that Sacate was visited by Kino in the late 1600s. It is unlikely that the village was settled immediately before his visit, and Classic period Salado Polychrome ceramics were collected. The oldest nonindigenous artifacts were recovered from the central area and consist of one-piece metal buttons manufactured between 1750 and 1812. Other nonindigenous artifacts suggest that the area was occupied through at least the late 1800s. In contrast to the central area, *ke'* depressions are less common in the expansion area. A shift in structure types occurred the late 1800s, but there is evidence that *ke' ke'* (plural of *ke'*) were used until at least 1910. The low incidence of *ke' ke'* in the expansion area suggests that it was first inhabited more recently than was the central portion of the site. Nonindigenous artifacts from the expansion area include military buttons and black glass, including one example with an "improved" pontil scar, suggesting that the area was used prior to the 1880s. The nonindigenous collection from the western area differs substantially from the collections from the rest of the site, and the percentages of glass, ceramics, and metal items are higher, suggesting that this area had the most recent occupation (Randolph et al. 2002). Shifts in the occupied area at the site were argued to have resulted from historical and environmental events, including Apache raiding, movement of the Gila River channel, flooding episodes, Euroamerican interaction, and the construction of the railroad and other transportation routes (Randolph et al. 2002).

Figure 43 shows box plots of weights for complete small projectile points by area of the site. The smallest points, on average, are from the western portion of the site, where the most recent occupation appears to have occurred, based on the nonindigenous-artifact assemblage. Statistically significant differences exist between the western and central areas (t-test: $p = .002$; equal variances not assumed) and the western and expansion portions (t-test: $p = .003$; equal variances not assumed), but greater similarity exists between

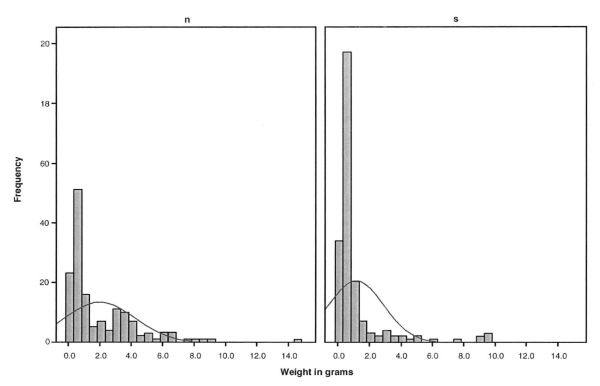

Figure 37. Histograms for all complete projectile point weights (n = 311), by side of the Middle Gila River, Pima-Maricopa Irrigation Project collection. n = northern side of the river; s = southern side of river (excludes isolated occurrences, preforms, and broken points).

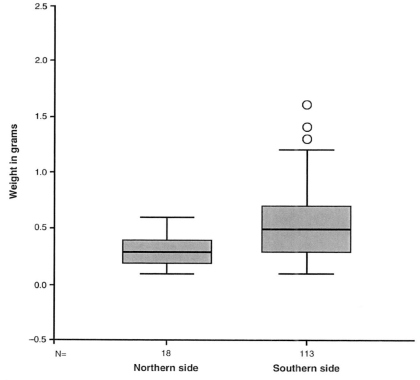

Figure 38. Historic period point weights by side of the Gila River, Pima-Maricopa Irrigation Project collection (excludes isolated occurrences, preforms, and broken points).

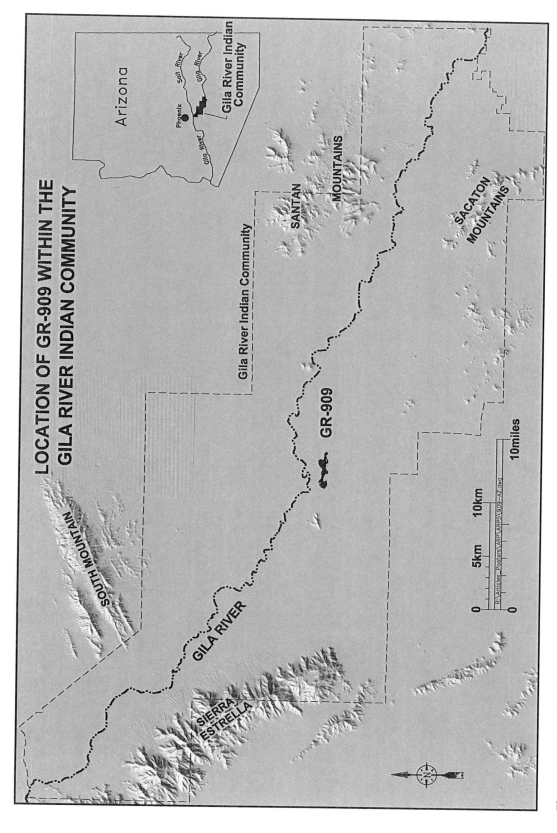

Figure 39. Map showing the location of the Sacate Site (GR-909), Gila River Indian Community.

Figure 40. Historic period projectile points collected from the Sacate site (GR-909), Gila River Indian Community. The point in the center is human-made glass.

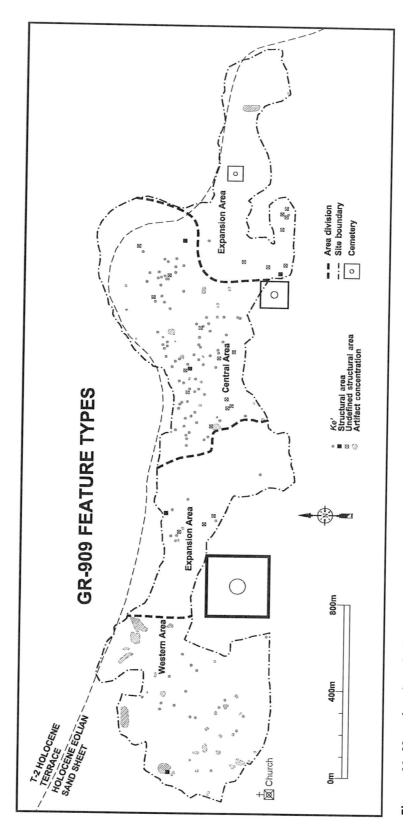

Figure 41. Map showing the locations of architectural features, cemeteries, and site areas at GR-909, Gila River Indian Community.

Figure 42. Nonindigenous artifacts from the Sacate site, including glass-container fragments (*top left* and *right*), a ceramic pipe (*top center*), metal buttons (*bottom two on left*), metal crucifixes (*bottom two in center*), and a center-fire-cartridge casing (*bottom right*).

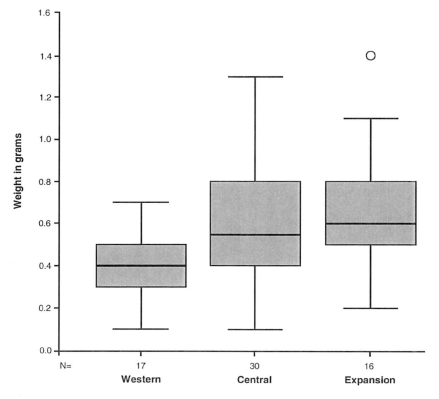

Figure 43. Box plots of point weight at the Sacate site, by site area (excludes broken points, preforms, and large projectile points).

the central-area and expansion-area point weights. These data are consistent with a general drift of the settlement location over time, as modeled by Darling (2011), and with patterning in the nonindigenous-artifact assemblage from the site (Randolph et al. 2002).

Cienega Creek Burial Data

A range of variation in point design is expected at any moment in time, and one way to assess this variance is to consider large collections of artifacts recovered from contexts that suggest that they are contemporaneous—for example, points from burial facilities. Historic period interments associated with large numbers of projectile points have not as yet been reported for the GRIC, but weight data are available for two inhumations recently excavated along Cienega Creek, which is located between the Santa Cruz and San Pedro Rivers, to the southeast of the GRIC (Vint 2005). Over 150 Huachuca projectile points (Figure 44) were recovered from the body cavities of two old-adult males who were covered with rocks; at least one of them was partially dismembered (Vint 2005). All of the points were unnotched, which is consistent with test expectations for points designed for use against people. Nearly half of the points were serrated, and all of the points had irregular edge margins that were, to some extent, uneven (Vint 2005:17).

Although the precise temporal association of the burials is uncertain, a domestic-cow vertebra was found with Feature 1, and that interment must have occurred after the arrival of European livestock in the area. The earliest mention of cattle in the region occurred in 1696, when Father Kino took livestock to San Xavier del Bac, near modern Tucson, Arizona (Wilson forthcoming). This suggests that the burials postdate the late 1600s (Vint 2005:11); however, cattle were rare in the region until after the gold discoveries in 1849, when large stock drives were undertaken along the Gila River (Wilson forthcoming): "One drover estimated that in 1854 alone some 3,000 head of cattle were lost along the trails south of the Gila [River], mostly to Indians" (Wilson forthcoming).

Figure 45 is a histogram of weights for complete or nearly complete projectile points recovered from the two bodies. The mean, median, and mode for the assemblage are each 0.3 g. The distribution is nonnormal, with a skewness of 1.3 and a kurtosis of 3.1, indicating that the weight values are more clustered than a normal distribution and are skewed right. Over 75 percent of the points weighed within just 0.1 g of the mean/median/mode of 0.3 g, which is consistent with the suggestion that Historic period points were generally small. In addition, over half of the points were broken, which supports the observation that points were likely to catastrophically break when used. At the same time, the large number of projectile points found within the two bodies is consistent with the suggestion that warfare points were not generally recovered for reuse or reworking.

Interestingly, comparison of the point assemblages from the two burials suggests that it is possible that they were not precisely contemporaneous, which has implications for understanding the cultural practices that resulted in the interment of the individuals. Figure 46 shows box plots of point weights for the two burials. Point weights associated with Features 1 and 2 are significantly different (t-test: $p = .04$; equal variances not assumed). Other observations also support the possibility that the two burials may not have been interred together.

First, breakage patterns vary significantly between the two burials at the 90 percent confidence interval (Yates corrected $\chi^2 = 3.6$; $p = .06$); points associated with Feature 2 are more likely to be broken, suggesting that the exact conditions under which the points were shot into the bodies varied. Second, raw-material frequencies vary between the two assemblages. Although the proportion of jasper points is roughly similar, a significant difference at the 90 percent confidence level exists between the proportions of chert and chalcedony in the two assemblages (Yates corrected $\chi^2 = 3.0$; $p = .08$).

Independent Age Estimates

The most rigorous way to test the point-size hypothesis is to examine projectile points from controlled contexts with independent age estimates. Although he does not appear to have considered weight, Shott (1996) compared radiocarbon-age estimates for occupational levels at seven Woodland and later sites in the American Bottom. These components ranged in age from 1620 to 883 B.P. When ordered by site, the correlations between metric attributes and age ranged between 0.5 and 0.97. Shott (1996:294–297) identified a gap in the size distribution that he suggested was possibly associated with the introduction of the bow and arrow, but he also found that probable arrow tips decreased in size over time. Furthermore, he observed that "time-dependant trends in the size of probable arrows are found in other areas" (Shott 1996:297). For example, correlations between age-estimate midpoints and metric attributes ranged between 0.36 and 0.72 for a collection of 126 Paleo-Indian through Historic period points from southeastern Colorado (Owens et al. 2000:275–281). Shott (1996) used Optimal Foraging Theory to explain continuous variation in point size and suggested, "If projectile length and shaft diameter must decline to achieve improvements in accuracy and range, then projectile point width, especially neck and base width, also should decline" (Shott 1996:301). This investigation suggests that weight is the best single measurement of this relationship and has further explored the association between point size and performance.

Historic period Akimel O'odham habitation within the Phoenix Basin was largely restricted to the location of the modern GRIC, and until recently, little research had been done in the area. As a result, the only Historic

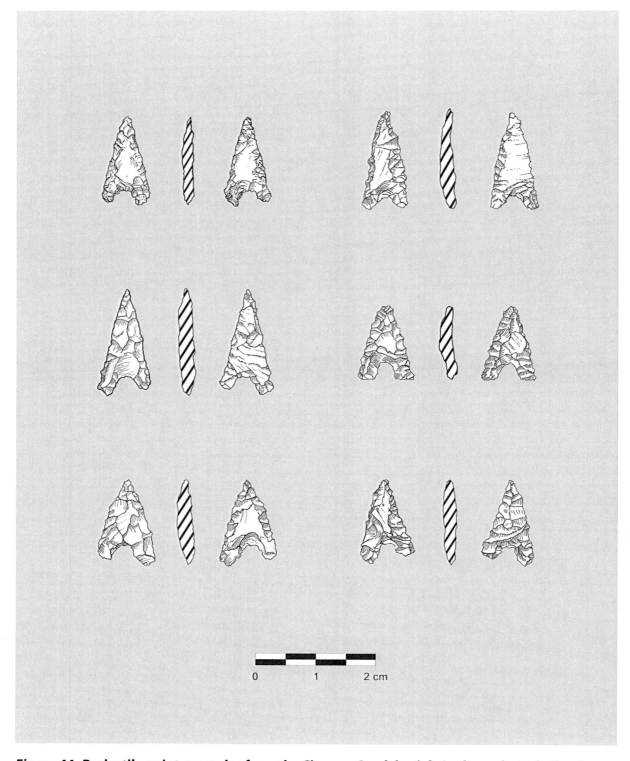

Figure 44. Projectile point examples from the Cienega Creek burials (redrawn by Rob Ciaccio after Vint [2005]).

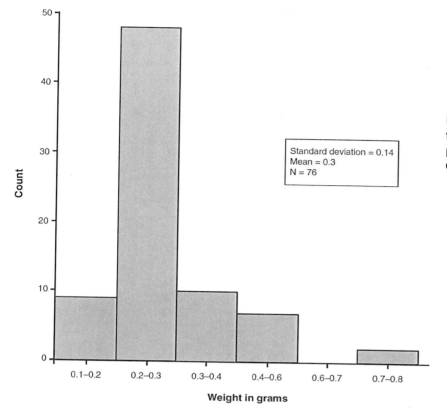

Standard deviation = 0.14
Mean = 0.3
N = 76

Figure 45. Histogram of weights for 76 complete or nearly complete projectile points from the Cienega Creek burials.

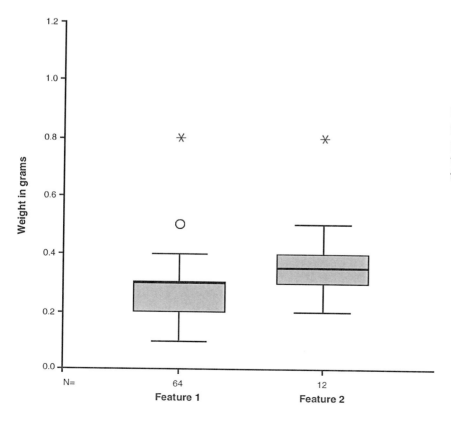

Figure 46. Box plots of weights for complete and nearly complete projectile points from the Cienega Creek burials, by feature.

period projectile point from a controlled excavation context within the study area is an artifact from a feature at the Sweetwater site (Woodson 2003). This projectile point was found in a nonthermal pit (Feature 58), and a Thermal Luminance (TL) age estimate of 1808 ± 21 was obtained for a sherd in a deeper portion of the feature. One of the two coins found at the site was minted between 1832 and 1838 and was recovered from another pit (Feature 51) located 8 m south of Feature 58. A TL estimate of 1836 ± 49 obtained for this feature falls within the range of manufacture for the coin. The point is a Straight Base type, and the age estimates from the site support the association of this variety with the late Historic period. The weight of the point is 0.4 g, which is close to the mean/median/mode of 0.3 g for the Cienega Creek Historic period points.

Although Historic period burial data from excavation contexts within the study area are not available, it is possible to compare points from Classic period contexts to the collections from Cienega Creek. Figure 47 graphs the data for the Cienega Creek Historic period points and all of the complete or nearly complete projectile points from Classic period room floors or pits at GR-140 and GR-522 in the GRIC (Fertelmes 2010). Both sites are located at the edge of the Santan Mountains *bajada*, and both of these habitation areas have surface structures with enclosing compound walls. GR-140 is predominantly early Classic period, and GR-522 includes both early Classic and late Classic period rooms. The Classic period points are significantly heavier than the Historic period points (t-test: p = .01; equal variances not assumed), which supports the possibility that Historic period points are, on average, smaller than Classic period artifacts.

In order to increase the Classic period sample size, it is necessary to include additional excavation data from outside the study area. Figure 48 shows box plots for Classic period inhumation data from the Roosevelt Platform Mound Study (RPMS). The box plot labeled "Feature 22" includes all complete projectile points from an early Classic period inhumation at AZ U:4:75 (ASM). This individual had the largest assemblage of projectile points identified during the RPMS (Loendorf 1996). The "All RPMS" plot includes all complete projectile points recovered from all Classic period inhumations excavated during the project. The Classic period Feature 22 assemblage from Tonto Basin is significantly heavier than the Cienega Creek Historic period points (t-test: p <.001; equal variances not assumed), as are all of the RPMS inhumation points (t-test: p <.001; equal variances not assumed).

Point-Weight Data: Discussion

Analyses presented here support the suggestion that points generally decreased in size over time within the study area. This does not mean that points can be used to date sites, and these data appear to have a limited resolution. However, in at least some cases, it is possible to identify significant temporal patterning with sufficiently large projectile point assemblages. At the same time, considerable overlap occurs among different contexts, and the weights for individual artifacts cannot be used alone to suggest temporal estimates. Furthermore, because culturally contingent technological factors are suggested to have driven the change in size over time, points are not expected to have decreased uniformly in size among different regions, and any comparisons across technological traditions may produce spurious results. For example, if the Apache did indeed introduce recurved bow technology, it is expected that they made smaller points earlier in time than did existing southwestern populations. As a result, smaller points are expected to occur earlier in time within the areas that they occupied. The rate of adoption for recurved bow technology (e.g., because some groups lacked access to the necessary wood and manufacturing techniques) may also have varied among cultural traditions, and some people therefore may have continued to produce large points later in time than did others.

Although the exact ages of the Cienega Creek and Sacate loci remain unclear, these data suggest that it may be impossible to separate late Classic period points from early Historic period artifacts from the study area based on weight alone, and it is also necessary to consider shape. Furthermore, it is probable that at a given time, hunting points were smaller than warfare points (Cotterell and Kamminga 1992:181; Ellis 1997:45), which suggests that it is necessary to control for point design factors. Although the resolution of the size data may be limited, previous researchers have had little success in seriating points from the Ceramic term, and there is consequently considerable room for improvement. In addition, lithic analysts have long used point size to separate atlatl darts from arrow points, and the design theory presented here attempts to more clearly define the underlying performance factors associated with this change.

Analyses in this section do not prove that the projectile-point-size hypothesis is correct, but they do suggest that it merits further investigation and may have heuristic value. Although other lines of evidence (largely ceramics) can be used in some instances to suggest temporal associations for nondiagnostic artifacts, that is not the case for assemblages produced by late Prehistoric and Historic period populations who did not commonly make temporally diagnostic decorated ceramics (e.g., the Apache). Ethnohistorical observations presented in Chapter 5 suggest that these highly mobile peoples had considerable effects on the Historic period sedentary agriculturalists who lived in the Southwest and that the identification of any temporally diagnostic artifacts they may have produced is therefore of importance. The next section examines the relationship between notching and the performance of triangular projectile points.

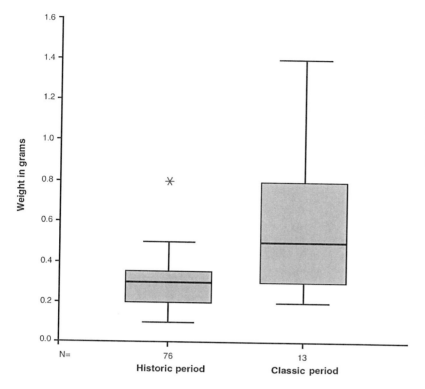

Figure 47. Box plots of Historic period Cienega Creek burial data and Classic period projectile points from the Gila River Indian Community.

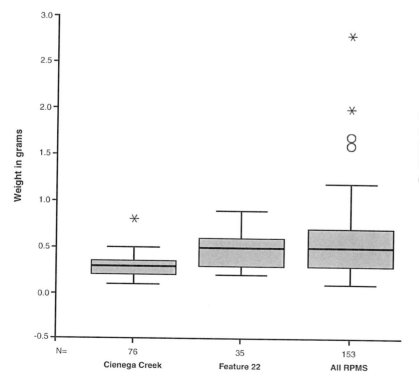

Figure 48. Box plots of Historic period Cienega Creek burial data and Classic period projectile points from inhumations excavated during the Roosevelt Platform Mound Study (RMPS).

Warfare- and Hunting-Point Designs

The following analyses test expectations for warfare- and hunting-point designs that are based on ethnographic descriptions and performance requirements: (1) hunting points should generally have rounded tangs, whereas warfare points may more frequently have pointed tangs that resist backing out of wounds; (2) where defensive armor was present, as was the case along the Middle Gila River in the Historic period (Shaw 1994:35–46; Webb 1959:25), warfare points are expected to have narrower bases than hunting-arrow points (Bergman and McEwen 1997:153; Cotterell and Kamminga 1992:181); (3) because arrows with broken points attached were recovered for reuse, hunting points are expected to have higher fragmentation rates, and warfare points are anticipated to more commonly be whole (see Rea 1998:74).

Table 14 presents basal-corner (i.e., tang) shape for side-notched and unnotched points. Expectations based on ethnographic research presented in Chapter 4 suggest that rounded tangs should be more common on hunting points, whereas pointed tangs should be more common for points designed for use in warfare. As hypothesized, pointed tangs are most common for unnotched specimens, and side-notched points are more likely to have rounded tangs. A significant difference exists in basal-corner treatment for notched and unnotched points, supporting the postulated expectation for variation between these designs (Yates Corrected χ^2 = 91.8; p <.001).

Similarly, side-notched arrow points are also significantly more likely to have straight bases, whereas unnotched points more commonly have concave bases (Table 15) (Yates Corrected χ^2 = 6.41; p = .01). Highly concave bases create two basal points (i.e., barbs) at different angles from each other that would resist backing out of wounds.

Because shielding was employed in the study area, it is expected that warfare-point designs should be narrow types that were intended to pierce those defenses (Bergman and McEwen 1997:153; Cotterell and Kamminga 1992:181). Narrow, armor-penetrating designs have been referred to as "bodkin" points, and wider hunting points are termed "broadheads," based on analogy with Medieval European metal-point designs (Harlan 2009). Similarly, Rice and Simon (1994) identified a tendency for points from the Tonto Basin to be long and narrow or short and wide. Figure 49 shows box plots of basal widths for unnotched and side-notched points from the study area (see Figure 12 for measurement locations). Although considerable overlap occurs, a significant difference exists in the basal widths of these designs, as postulated (t-test: p <.001; equal variances not assumed).

In order to haft a projectile point, the width of the neck (i.e., stem) is constrained by the shaft diameter. When attempting to securely fasten a point, several problems occur if the stem is wider than the shaft (Christenson 1997:134–135; Geneste and Maury 1997:183). As shown in Figure 50, it does not appear to be the case, however, that narrow points were left unnotched because the points were already narrower than the shaft diameters. In fact, the neck (i.e., stem or haft element) widths for unnotched projectile points are significantly larger than the widths of side-notched points (t-test: p <.001; equal variances not assumed).

Comparison of breakage patterns for unnotched and side-notched points also suggests that these point types

Table 14. Tang Treatment for Small Projectile Points, by Notch Design

Basal Corners (Tang)	Unnotched Points		Low-Side-Notched Points	
	n	%	n	%
Rounded	10	3.4	40	41.7
Pointed	285	96.6	56	58.3
Total	295	100.0	96	100.0

Table 15. Base Treatment for Small Projectile Points, by Notch Design

Base Shape	Unnotched Points		Low-Side-Notched Points	
	n	%	n	%
Straight	88	30.0	43	44.8
Concave	205	70.0	53	55.2
Total	293	100.0	96	100.0

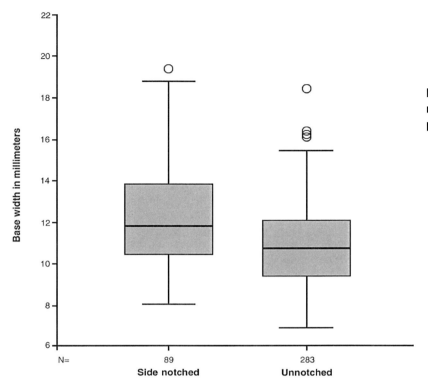

Figure 49. Base widths for side-notched and unnotched small projectile points.

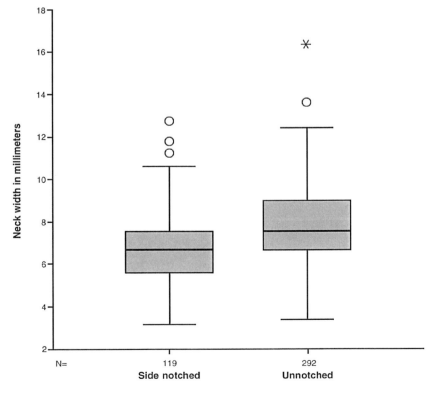

Figure 50. Neck widths for side-notched and unnotched small projectile points.

were used differently. Points that lack notches are significantly more likely to be whole than are side-notched points (Table 16) (Yates corrected $\chi^2 = 59.1$; $p <.001$). The circumstances of warfare are expected to have resulted in a lower recovery rate for these arrows, whereas hunting arrows (with broken points securely attached) were more commonly retrieved for reuse of the shaft. Even if the warfare arrows were recovered after use, the points are likely to have been detached, because they were intentionally loosely secured. In contrast, the bases of side-notched points would be more readily retrieved, because they were firmly attached to shafts. These points were then removed and discarded at habitation sites.

Finally, variation in the material types used to make the points also supports the suggestion that notching patterns are related to differences in the intended functions of projectile points (Table 17). For example, the incidences of basalt and obsidian vary significantly by notch type; side-notched points were only rarely made from basalt (Yates corrected $\chi^2 = 27.1$; $p <.001$). Obsidian has the lowest fracture toughness of all flaked stone materials; basalt

has a higher fracture toughness and is therefore less likely to shatter on impact (Whittaker 1994). One possibility is that less-brittle basalt points were employed on war arrows in an attempt to more effectively penetrate shielding employed by opponents.

In summary, patterns in base width and shape, point completeness, and basal-corner design are all consistent with expectations for variation between warfare- and hunting-point design features. These data support the hypothesis that triangular projectile points with side notches in the lower one-third of each blade were designed for big-game hunting, and unnotched triangular points were designed for use against other people. The following section explores patterning in the spatial and temporal distributions of warfare- and hunting-design projectile points. These data are consistent with independent lines of evidence, including faunal remains and ethnohistoric as well as ethnographic descriptions of cultural practices in the study area. These correspondences further support the hypothesis that projectile points in the study area were designed differently for hunting and for warfare.

Table 16. Point Completeness for Projectile Points, by Notch Design

Point Portion	Unnotched Points		Low-Side-Notched Points	
	n	%	n	%
Broken				
Nearly complete	69	14.3	42	27.8
Midsection	5	1.0	14	9.3
Base	83	17.3	33	21.9
Longitudinal fragment	2	0.4	15	9.9
Small fragment	3	0.6	1	0.7
Total, broken	162	33.7	105	69.5
Complete	319	66.3	46	30.5
Total	481	100.0	151	100.0

Table 17. Material Type for Projectile Points, by Notch Design

Material Type	Unnotched Points		Low-Side-Notched Points	
	n	%	n	%
Chert	197	41.0	42	27.8
Obsidian	132	27.4	82	54.3
Basalt	83	17.3	7	4.6
Chalcedony	33	6.9	8	5.3
Other	17	3.5	4	2.6
Rhyolite	11	2.3	8	5.3
Glass	8	1.7	—	—
Total	481	100.0	151	100.0

Projectile Point Functional Attributes

The first portion of this section examines the spatial distribution of projectile points that may have been designed for hunting. Next, patterning in the distribution of points with features that suggest that they were designed for warfare is presented. Finally, temporal variation in the incidence of these two types is considered.

Hunting Design Projectile Points

Table 18 lists the counts and densities for projectile points with design attributes that suggest that they were intended to be securely attached to arrow shafts (i.e., points designed for big-game hunting), and Figure 51 shows the overall densities of these points by portion of the study area. This category includes all side-notched, corner-notched, and stemmed points. Although the ethnographic literature presented in Chapter 4 suggests that some warfare-point designs may have had thick, narrow stems that were designed to split their shafts, points with that design feature are rare in the collection (Loendorf and Rice 2004), and all stemmed points are included as possible hunting designs. The point data are organized based on temporal estimates for the types, and Archaic and pre-Classic period artifacts are included for comparison with the Classic and Historic period distributions.

Overall, points that may have been designed for hunting are most concentrated in the Snaketown and Santa Cruz areas. The densities for those two areas are over twice as high as the next-highest overall density. Points from different periods are most concentrated in those areas, suggesting that hunting was more important for people in those areas through time. This patterning by type suggests long-term continuity in practices within the study area. Although 7,500 ha were surveyed in the Santan and Sacaton Mountains as part of P-MIP investigations, no projectile points were collected from either of those locations (see Table 5; Figure 10). These observations are consistent with diachronic and synchronic patterns of big-game-hunting practices in the Southwest based on faunal remains.

Dean (2003:179), in an analysis of faunal data from throughout the American Southwest, argued that large "prey species, including mule deer (*Odocoileus humionus*), bighorn sheep (*Ovis canadensis*), pronghorn antelope (*Antilocapra americana*), and white-tail deer (*Odocoileus virginianus*), were only a minor part of most prehistoric diets." She further argued that "it is clear that ungulate hunting was not sufficient to meet protein needs of populations

in Southern Arizona from at least the Middle Archaic" through the Classic period (Dean 2003:179). Szuter (1991) developed the Artiodactyl Index (the number of individual specimens [NISP] of artiodactyls divided by the sum of the NISP of lagomorphs and artiodactyls) and used it to compare Archaic period and Hohokam sites. She observed that big-game acquisition was primarily related to elevation and site size.

Similarly, Dean (2003) found that sites below 800 m usually have low Artiodactyl Indexes and found similar patterning based on site type. For low-elevation sites, villages have higher values than farmsteads, field houses, or camps. She argued that low-elevation villages probably had more artiodactyl remains because hunting groups brought resources from upland environments down to the community for redistribution and that "this distribution would have taken place in villages, rather than small farmsteads, and the logistic camps associated with floodplain and river terrace occupations would have focused on plant resource extraction, rather than large game hunting" (Dean 2003:198). She also argued that faunal analysts may be underestimating the importance of large mammals in the diet of villagers, because many of the bones were left in upland logistic camps (Dean 2003:211). One way to examine this possibility is to consider projectile point data.

Hunting design points are concentrated in the areas in which Hohokam and Akimel O'odham villages were located, rather than in peripheral areas, such as the Santan and Sacaton Mountains, where lowland specialized-activity sites and logistical camps were located (Wells, Rice, et al. 2004). Figure 52 shows areas in the vicinity of the study area that are above 800 m. All P-MIP survey data are from below 800 m (including the survey areas in the Santan and Sacaton Mountains), and with the exception of small portions of the South and Sacaton Mountains, only the Sierra Estrella have areas above 800 m.

The nearest extensive upland areas are roughly 30 km away, in the Superstition Mountains to the east and north, locations that were occupied by hunter-gatherers during the Historic period, which limited access to these areas for the Akimel O'odham. This would have reduced big-game-hunting opportunities during the Historic period. These data suggest that hunting points were collected from habitation areas and that locations in which big-game hunting actually occurred are not present in the surveyed area. The greater importance of hunting in the Sierra Estrella communities is consistent with the observation that Anna Shaw's (1994:95) father, who lived at the base of the Sierra Estrella, hunted big-game animals. These arguments are also supported by ethnographic data assembled by Rea (1998:61–63), who argued that Historic period big-game hunters who lived in the GRIC traveled between 30 and 160 km in order to hunt. The only areas he identified as Historic period large-game-hunting locations are to the south and east of the community, toward where allied Tohono O'odham groups lived. He also suggested that

Table 18. Hunting Design Projectile Points, by Study Unit within the Gila River Indian Community, Pima-Maricopa Irrigation Project Collection

Site Group	Map Unit	Survey Area (ha)	Archaic Period		Pre-Classic Period		Classic Period		Historic Period		Total	
			n	Points/ 1,000 ha	n	Points/ 1,000 ha	n	Points/ 1,000 ha	n	Points/ 1,000 ha	n	Points/ 1,000 ha
Northern side												
Maricopa	12	5,223	2	0.4	6	1.1	1	0.2	—	—	9	1.7
Borderlands	9	13,752	45	3.3	3	0.2	1	0.1	—	—	49	3.6
Blackwater	1	1,778	—	—	—	—	—	—	—	—	—	—
Santan	4	3,052	3	1.0	1	0.3	2	0.7	—	—	6	2.0
Lone Butte	10	3,432	5	1.5	1	0.3	1	0.3	—	—	7	2.0
Snaketown	7	8,267	26	3.1	32	3.9	19	2.3	—	—	77	9.3
Total, northern side		35,504	81	2.3	43	1.2	24	0.7	—	—	148	4.2
Southern side												
Sacaton	5	1,535	—	—	2	1.3	1	0.7	—	—	3	2.0
Santa Rosa	2	5,449	15	2.8	1	0.2	0	0.0	—	—	16	2.9
Santa Cruz	11	3,047	14	4.6	2	0.7	13	4.3	—	—	29	9.5
Casa Blanca	8	5,325	7	1.3	5	0.9	9	1.7	—	—	21	3.9
Total, southern side		15,356	36	2.3	10	0.7	23	1.5	—	—	69	4.5
Total		50,860	117	2.3	53	1.0	47	0.9	—	—	217	4.3
Southern-to-northern ratio		0.4	0.4	1.0	0.2	0.5	1.0	2.2	—	—	0.5	1.1

Note: Excludes points collected as isolated occurrences.

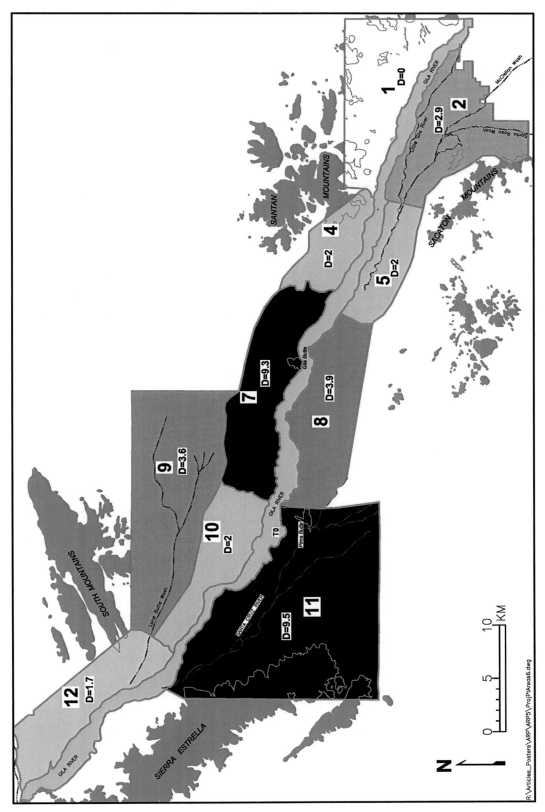

Figure 51. Density of hunting design projectile points, by study unit within the Gila River Indian Community, Pima-Maricopa Irrigation Project collection. Units are shaded based on density, and black represents the greatest. D = point density for the unit.

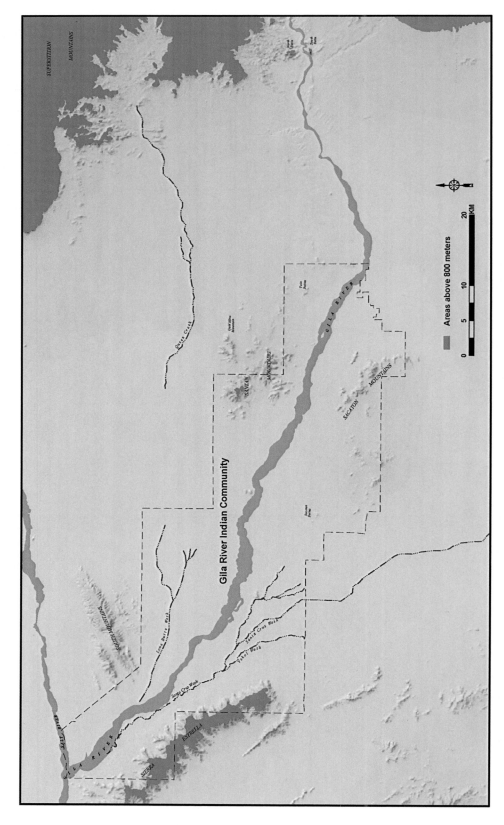

Figure 52. Upland areas in the vicinity of the study area with elevations greater than 800 m above mean sea level.

desert bighorn, mule deer, and white-tailed deer were hunted in the Sierra Estrella, where hunting design points are most concentrated.

Warfare Design Projectile Points

Table 19 shows the distribution of projectile points that may have been designed for warfare, by portion of the GRIC and temporal assignments for artifacts. Figure 53 shows the overall densities for these points. This category includes all completed projectile points that lack notches. The highest densities of that design occur in the areas along the river where villages were concentrated, which is consistent with patterning observed for big-game-hunting points. There are a number of differences, however, in the distributions of these two designs. In general, warfare points occur at higher overall densities than hunting-point designs, which is consistent with the limited opportunities for large-game hunting in the study area.

Although projectile point densities are low throughout the GRIC, nearly 400 warfare points were collected, because 50,860 ha were surveyed. All of the points considered here were recovered from locations with extensive evidence of habitation, and it appears that warfare points were rarely, if ever, recovered from contexts of use away from habitation areas (e.g., battlefields). In contrast to hunting designs, the overall density of all warfare design points on the southern side of the river is three times higher than that of warfare-design points on the northern side—a ratio that includes Middle Archaic through late Historic period artifacts. The highest densities for pre-Classic and Classic period types, however, occur in the Snaketown area, on the northern side, where the population was concentrated at that time. During the Historic period, people aggregated on the southern side of the river for protection from hunter-gatherers who regularly raided the Akimel O'odham villages, and all points from that time period are therefore expected to be concentrated in that area. The following section explores temporal variation in the incidence of warfare- and hunting point designs.

Diachronic Variation in Warfare- and Hunting-Point Designs

All three of the Historic period types have warfare design features, whereas both hunting and warfare types are present in the Archaic, pre-Classic, and Classic period point categories (Loendorf and Rice 2004; Sliva 1997, 2006). This suggests that big-game hunting was only rarely practiced during the Historic period, a possibility that is supported by extensive ethnographic research (see Chapter 5).

Figure 54 shows bar charts of the incidences of projectile points with hunting- and warfare-design features, by time period for the types. The incidence of warfare points tended to increase over time, and the frequency of hunting design points tended to decrease over time. Because extensive large-game-hunting areas do not occur in the survey area, increased conflict may have resulted in limited access to suitable hunting locations in higher elevations, away from the villages along the Middle Gila River. The diachronic patterning in point design is also supported by faunal data from the study area. Based on faunal remains from the Santa Cruz area, Clark (2007:18.23) argued that the incidence of large-game hunting decreased over time from the pre-Classic period to the Classic period. Similarly, James (2003:76–77) argued that the Pueblo Grande Artiodactyl Index values suggested that there was a general decrease in the incidence of large game over time from the pre-Classic period to the Classic period.

Projectile Point Stylistic Attributes

Based on an analysis that employed the Unified Theory of Stylistic Design (Carr 1995), Hoffman (1997) argued that the Hohokam used projectile point blade-margin treatment, including serration, to signal group affiliations. Hoffman (1997:95) recognized that the shaft and the fletching were the most visible portions of arrows and, therefore, that those elements "were commonly decorated or designed to reflect individual ownership or tribal affiliation" (see also Mason 1894:662). He focused on points because data from the shafts are not available. He argued that because the haft element was not visible when the points were used (i.e., when they were attached to arrows), the blade margins were the most visible aspects of the points and therefore the most likely to exhibit intentional expressions of cultural affiliation.

Characteristics employed as active symbols of social-group membership are generally associated with highly visible artifacts used in public contexts (Carr 1995; Hodder 1982; Wobst 1977). Small stone points would seem to fit this definition poorly; however, those artifacts were designed for use in warfare, which is a public setting that was possibly the primary context of interaction for some social groups. Although small points may not have been visible from a distance, they were shot at the enemy, thereby increasing the proximity of observation by other groups. Furthermore, stone points were designed to detach within wounds, leaving behind a potent symbol of the maker's cultural affiliation.

Table 19. Warfare Design Projectile Points, by Study Unit within the Gila River Indian Community, Pima-Maricopa Irrigation Project Collection

Site Group	Map Unit	Survey Area (ha)	Archaic Period		Pre-Classic Period		Classic Period		Historic Period		Total	
			n	Points/ 1,000 ha	n	Points/ 1,000 ha	n	Points/ 1,000 ha	n	Points/ 1,000 ha	n	Points/ 1,000 ha
Northern side												
Maricopa	12	5,223	—	—	8	1.5	4	0.8	—	—	12	2.3
Borderlands	9	13,752	18	1.3	3	0.2	4	0.3	4	0.3	29	2.1
Blackwater	1	1,778	—	—	—	—	1	0.6	1	0.6	2	1.1
Santan	4	3,052	1	0.3	4	1.3	4	1.3	3	1.0	12	3.9
Lone Butte	10	3,432	—	—	3	0.9	7	2.0	3	0.9	13	3.8
Snaketown	7	8,267	6	0.7	25	3.0	34	4.1	32	3.9	97	11.7
Total, northern side		35,504	25	0.7	43	1.2	54	1.5	43	1.2	165	4.6
Southern side												
Sacaton	5	1,535	5	3.3	1	0.7	1	0.7	4	2.6	11	7.2
Santa Rosa	2	5,449	9	1.7	1	0.2	4	0.7	20	3.7	34	6.2
Santa Cruz	11	3,047	5	1.6	3	1.0	7	2.3	37	12.1	52	17.1
Casa Blanca	8	5,325	3	0.6	5	0.9	20	3.8	100	18.8	128	24.0
Total, southern side		15,356	22	1.4	10	0.7	32	2.1	161	10.5	225	14.7
Total		50,860	47	0.9	53	1.0	86	1.7	204	4.0	390	7.7
Southern-to-northern ratio		0.4	0.9	2.0	0.2	0.5	0.6	1.4	3.7	8.7	1.4	3.2

Note: Excludes points collected as isolated occurrences.

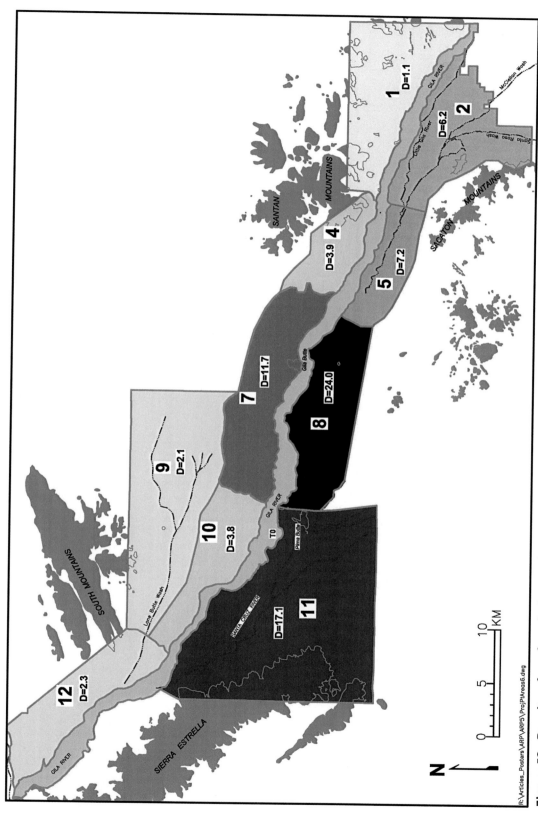

Figure 53. Density of warfare design projectile points, by study unit within the Gila River Indian Community, Pima-Maricopa Irrigation Project collection. Units are shaded based on serration proportion, and black represents the greatest. D = point density for the unit.

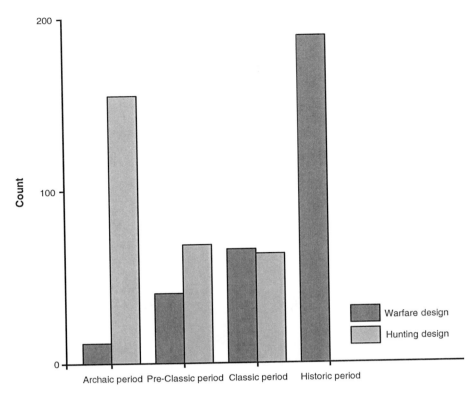

Figure 54. Bar chart of all classified projectile points in the collection, by time period and point design.

Point-Serration Data

Points with serrated blades are unequally distributed across the study area (Table 20; Figure 55). The data are organized based on the time periods assigned to the artifacts, following the typological classifications. Only 6 percent of all points from the Casa Blanca area were serrated, whereas over a third of points from other locations had that form of edge treatment (Yates corrected χ^2 = 45.4; p <.001). This total includes artifacts classified as Middle Archaic through Historic period remains.

This patterning by point type suggests that serration was rarely practiced in the Casa Blanca area throughout the archaeological sequence, whereas more substantial percentages of points from other locations were serrated. The lowest incidence of serration for Casa Blanca points occurred during the Historic period, a time when almost 40 percent of the points from elsewhere in the community were serrated (Yates corrected χ^2 = 40.06; p <.001). As shown in Figure 58, the overall density of serrated points tends to increase with distance from the Casa Blanca area. Furthermore, serration occurs on only 2 of the 22 Archaic period points from Casa Blanca, whereas 34 percent of the Archaic period types from elsewhere in the community

have serrated blade margins (Fisher's exact test: p = .03). These data therefore suggest that long-term cultural traditions in the Casa Blanca area were maintained through time into the Historic period.

Other researchers have also noted regional and temporal variation in projectile point serration data from the Southwest. For example, in her overview of stone points from Arizona, Sliva (2006:60) argued that although serrated points were common during the pre-Classic period Hohokam sequence, "serrated Puebloan points are rare in any time period." Marshall (2001b) argued that serration was most frequent during the Santa Cruz and Sacaton phases and was less common for earlier and later points from Grewe.

This continuation of practices over time provides another example of cultural continuity and is inconsistent with the argument that the Akimel O'odham were recent migrants to the area. The temporal and spatial variability in serration data also suggest that different social segments lived within the study area, and it appears that these people were not highly politically integrated. The following discussion analyzes obsidian data in order to further explore synchronic and diachronic variation among these social groups as well as those in surrounding locations.

Table 20. Serrated Projectile Points, by Study Unit within the Gila River Indian Community, Pima-Maricopa Irrigation Project Collection

Site Group	Archaic Period			Pre-Classic Period			Classic Period			Historic Period			Total		
	Absent	Present	% Present	Absent	Present	% Present	Absent	Present	% Present	Absent	Present	% Present	Serration Absent	Serration Present	% Present
Maricopa (12)	2	1	33	6	8	57	3	2	40	—	—	—	11	11	50
Borderlands (9)	55	25	31	2	2	50	3	2	40	4	—	0.0	64	29	31
Blackwater (1)	—	—	—	—	—	—	—	1	100	—	1	100	—	2	100
Santan (4)	2	3	60	1	4	80	6	—	0.0	3	—	0.0	12	7	37
Lone Butte (10)	4	2	33	2	3	60	5	3	38	2	1	33	13	9	41
Snaketown (7)	28	12	30	35	25	42	43	9	17	12	20	63	118	66	36
Sacaton (5)	8	—	0.0	2	1	33	2	—	0.0	1	3	75	13	4	24
Santa Rosa (2)	33	7	18	1	—	0.0	2	2	50	12	8	40	48	17	26
Santa Cruz (11)	27	2	7	4	4	50	17	3	15	19	17	47	67	26	28
Subtotal	159	52	25	53	47	47	81	22	21	53	50	49	346	171	33
Casa Blanca (8)	20	2	9	7	2	22	25	3	11	98	2	2	150	9	6
Total	64	25	28	25	11	31	69	36	34	204	67	25	496	180	27

Note: Excludes isolated occurrences. Numbers in parentheses are associated map-unit numbers. Percentages are rounded to the nearest whole numbers. Overall total includes fragmentary points for which age estimates could not be given.

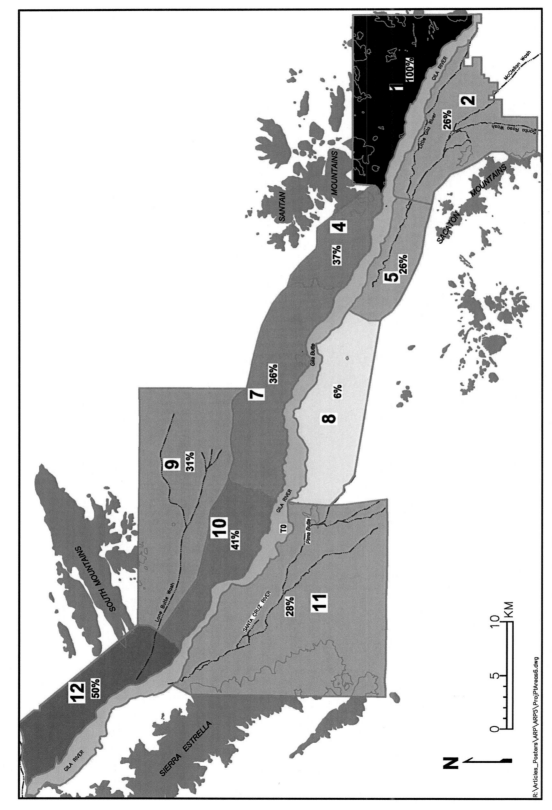

Figure 55. Proportions of serrated projectile points, by study unit within the Gila River Indian Community, Pima-Maricopa Irrigation Project collection. Units are shaded based on serration proportion, and black represents the greatest. Percentages are the serrated proportions in the collection.

Socioeconomic Interaction Patterns

The final portion of this analysis considers variation among the raw materials that were employed to manufacture stone points. A projectile point is a small part of a comparatively complex system that includes the archer, the arrow, and the bow. In order to function effectively, all parts of the system have to operate in concert, which places considerable constraints on the design of projectile points. Unless the manufacturing process is standardized, components of the system are not freely interchangeable between archers. As a result, it is improbable that finished projectile points or arrows were commonly exchanged among groups. Instead, it is more likely that raw materials were traded between different people.

Furthermore, the use of these artifacts in warfare is expected to have affected patterns of exchange for the raw materials necessary for point manufacture. This section considers patterning in projectile point raw-material data to further explore social and economic interactions among people within the study area as well as in the surrounding regions. This analysis focuses on obsidian source data, which have ideal properties for studying socioeconomic interactions in southern Arizona (see Chapter 3). Table 21 presents obsidian proportions for collections with more than 40 artifacts from the Hohokam area (data derived from Loendorf et al. [2004]; Marshall [2002]; Mitchell and Shackley [1995]; Peterson et al. [1997]; Rice et al. [1998]; Shackley and Bayman [2001]). As a geographical reference point, the sites are ordered based on distance from Snaketown, which is located near the center of the study area. The sources are arranged from west to east with respect to the study area (Figure 56). The results of a nonhierarchical K-means cluster analysis are also reported.

Examination of the cluster assignments and the underlying obsidian proportions suggested that site proximity to sources alone is a poor predictor of assemblages. For example, although Loci A and D from GR-522 are immediately adjacent to each other, they have different cluster assignments. Instead, temporal and regional differences are apparent within these data.

Cooperation within the Hohokam Core Area

With the exception of Sand Tanks, the closest obsidian sources to the core were the most commonly used by the Hohokam (Shackley 2005). These include the Sauceda, Superior, and Vulture sources (Figure 57). The use of these source materials, however, varied substantially over time

and space. Although Sand Tanks is geographically closest, obsidian from that source rarely occurs. The Sand Tanks source does not appear to have been extensively utilized throughout the Hohokam region, but the reasons for that remain unclear (Shackley and Tucker 2001).

Sauceda obsidian was one of the most common sources used by the Hohokam throughout the archaeological sequence, and its proportion in assemblages is very weakly correlated (Pearson's correlation = −0.03) to distance from the source (Figure 58). These data are not consistent with direct-access models for obsidian acquisition that assume that the end user of the obsidian personally traveled to the source to collect the material.

Peterson et al. (1997) referred to this category as the Opportunistic Model, in part because some researchers have argued that obsidian procurement strategies were embedded within the acquisition of other goods. It is assumed that obsidian was a comparatively low-value item that was obtained when possible in the context of other activities. This model holds that distance to the source should be a primary factor that determines obsidian frequencies at sites, but temporal variation in obsidian utilization and the lack of distance-decay relationships for common types suggest that this model is not the most parsimonious explanation for obsidian acquisition in the Hohokam region.

Nonetheless, distance-decay relationships are apparent in the obsidian frequencies for the P-MIP survey data. Figure 59 graphs obsidian proportions for the three most common source areas within different portions of the community, by distance to the sources. A rapid falloff with distance is apparent for the proportions of Superior and Vulture obsidians; however, the two types have opposite falloff patterns. Superior obsidian, which is located to the east, demonstrates proportion falloff from east to west. In contrast, Vulture obsidian, which is located to the west, demonstrates proportion falloff from west to east. Excluding the Sauceda source, a negative linear relationship exists between the log transformations of source proportion and distance. The Pearson's correlation coefficient for this relationship is −0.87, with a significance of 0.02. Distance to the source appears to be the primary barrier for the movement of these two obsidian types within the study area, and the steep falloff curve is consistent with down-the-line exchange within the community (Kooyman 2000:139). These data provide evidence for socioeconomic cooperation within the study area.

Classic Period Regional Obsidian Source Patterns

In order to further examine patterning in social interactions at a given time, this section focuses only on the Classic period data. Figure 60 is a cluster-analysis dendrogram for Classic period obsidian frequencies. The analysis employed

Table 21. Obsidian Source Proportions for Collections with More Than 40 Sourced Artifacts

Collection	Period	Obsidian Source Percentages (West to East)													K-Means Cluster	Sample Size
		Tank Mountains	Burro Creek	Partridge Creek	Los Vidrios	Vulture	Government Mountain	R. S. Hill/ Sitgreaves	Sauceda Mountains	Sand Tanks	Superior	Cow Canyon	Mule/Antelope Creek	Unknown/ Other		
Snaketown	pre-Classic	—	—	—	—	5.0	2.0	2.0	22.0	1.0	60.0	2.0	1.0	—	3	299
GR-522, Locus D	pre-Classic	—	—	—	—	3.0	13.0	—	15.0	—	51.0	—	—	18.0	3	39
GR-522, Locus A	Classic	—	—	—	2.0	—	4.0	—	61.0	—	20.0	—	2.0	12.0	1	51
ELXP	Classic?	—	1.0	—	7.0	5.0	3.0	4.0	63.0	5.0	8.0	—	—	1.0	1	76
Rowley	Classic	—	—	—	—	47.0	—	—	30.0	—	23.0	—	—	—	5	43
Pueblo Grande	Classic	—	—	4.0	4.0	27.0	22.0	—	30.0	—	10.0	—	—	3.0	5	220
Los Colinas	pre-Classic	4.0	—	2.0	4.0	26.0	38.0	10.0	10.0	—	2.0	—	—	4.0	2	50
Casa Grande	Classic	—	—	—	—	1.0	29.0	—	46.0	—	7.0	—	14.0	2.0	4	137
Grewe	pre-Classic	—	—	—	—	1.0	—	—	1.0	—	95.0	—	1.0	2.0	3	137
Palo Verde	pre-Classic	—	—	2.0	—	55.0	31.0	11.0	—	—	—	1.0	—	—	2	122
Gatlin	pre-Classic	—	3.0	—	1.0	4.0	—	—	85.0	—	—	—	—	7.0	1	75
Brady Wash	Classic	—	—	—	3.0	7.0	4.0	—	79.0	—	3.0	—	1.0	1.0	1	67
Tonto River portion, early	Classic	—	—	—	—	—	5.0	—	—	—	90.0	2.0	—	3.0	3	11
Tonto River portion, late	Classic	—	—	—	—	—	38.0	—	20.0	—	6.0	4.0	32.0	—	4	80
Salt River portion, early	Classic	—	—	—	—	—	13.0	13.0	13.0	—	64.0	—	—	—	3	54
Salt River portion, late	Classic	—	—	—	—	3.0	33.0	—	11.0	—	15.0	9.0	26.0	3.0	4	45
Marana	Classic	—	—	—	—	6.0	—	—	85.0	—	4.0	1.0	3.0	1.0	1	152

continued on next page

Table 21. Obsidian Source Proportions for Collections with More Than 40 Sourced Artifacts (*continued*)

Collection	Period	Obsidian Source Percentages (West to East)														K-Means Cluster	Sample Size
		Tank Mountains	Burro Creek	Partridge Creek	Los Vidrios	Vulture	Government Mountain	R. S. Hill/ Sitgreaves	Sauceda Mountains	Sand Tanks	Superior	Cow Canyon	Mule/Antelope Creek	Unknown/ Other		
P-MIP survey data																
Pre-Classic period GRIC	pre-Classic	—	—	—	—	—	11.0	—	55.0	—	33.0	—	—	—	—	9
Classic period GRIC	Classic	—	—	—	—	8.0	—	—	67.0	—	8.0	—	8.0	8.0	—	12
Historic period GRIC	Historic	—	—	—	5.0	9.0	—	—	76.0	—	9.0	—	—	—	—	21
All data																
Pre-Classic period average	pre-Classic	0.6	0.4	0.6	0.7	13.5	13.5	3.3	26.8	0.2	34.4	0.4	0.2	4.4	—	731
Classic period average	Classic	0.1	0.1	0.3	1.3	8.7	12.6	1.4	42.1	0.4	21.5	1.4	7.2	2.8	—	948
Total, all data		0.3	0.3	0.5	1.0	11.1	13.0	2.4	34.5	0.3	28.0	0.9	3.7	3.6	—	1,679

Key: ELXP = East Line Expansion Project; GRIC = Gila River Indian Community; P-MIP = Pima–Maricopa Irrigation Project.

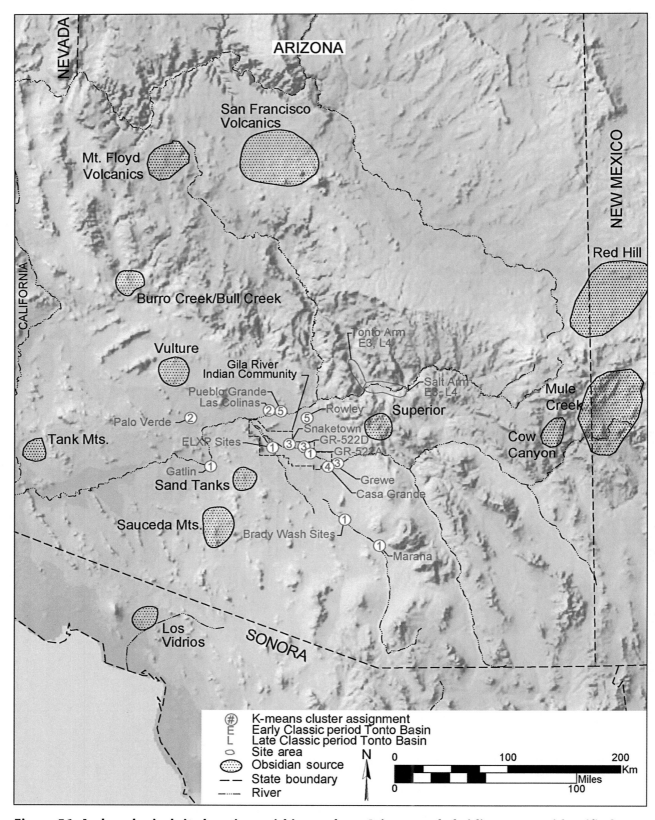

Figure 56. Archaeological site locations within southern Arizona and obsidian sources identified at these sites.

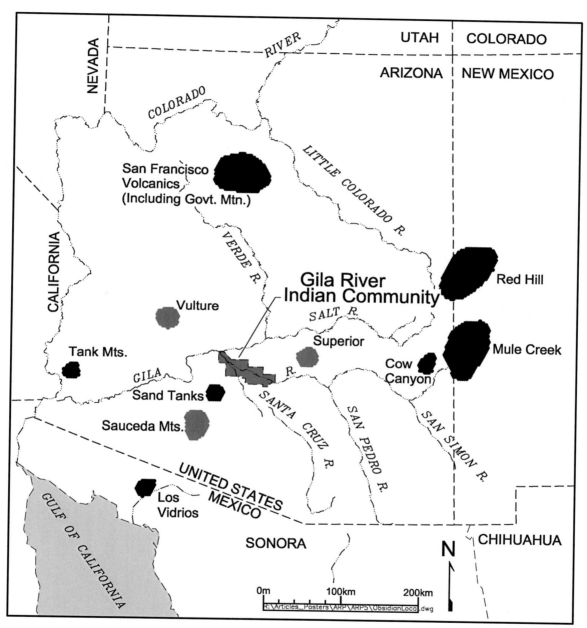

Figure 57. Obsidian sources identified in the Pima-Maricopa Irrigation Project survey collection. The most common sources are shown in red.

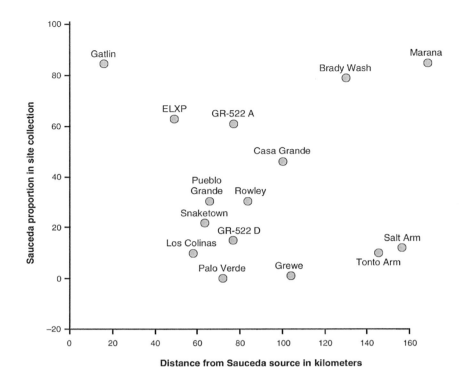

Figure 58. Scatter plot of Sauceda obsidian proportions, by straight-line distance (in kilometers) from the source location.

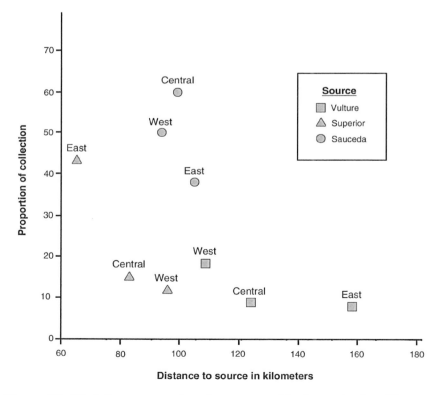

Figure 59. Obsidian proportion, by geographical area in the Gila River Indian Community (east, central, and west) and distance to the source, Pima-Maricopa Irrigation Project collection.

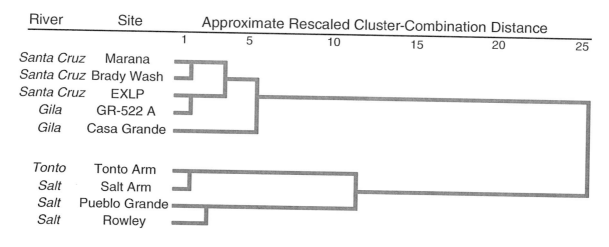

Figure 60. Cluster-analysis dendrogram (squared Euclidean distance measure and Ward's method) for Classic period obsidian data.

a squared Euclidian distance measure and Ward's method. At the two-cluster solution level, all Salt River Basin sites are in one cluster, and all sites in the Gila River Basin are in the second. Although some GRIC sites occur in close proximity to the lower Salt River sites, obsidian proportions differ substantially between sites along the two rivers (Loendorf 2008). At the same time, the Tonto Basin is more than 80 km away from the lower Salt River, over difficult terrain, yet it has similar obsidian proportions. These data suggest that socioeconomic ties among communities were strongest among people who were dependent on the same water sources.

Episodes of low stream flows may cause conflicts to arise between upstream and downstream users of water (Rice 1998b). One way to avoid disagreements that result from disputes over limited resources is to develop social institutions that mitigate these stresses. For example, regular social activities, such as ballgames or gatherings for important ceremonies, can be used to bring people from different communities together and relieve stress through nonviolent competition or communal involvement in rituals (Wilcox and Sternberg 1983:184). These events also create opportunities for social and economic interactions among communities (Abbott et al. 2003:13; Abbott et al. 2007; Bayman 1994). Exchanging food for other items provides a mechanism for redistributing water-dependent resources, which further ameliorates stresses caused by water shortages.

Regional Diachronic Trends in Obsidian Utilization

Several temporal trends are also apparent in the obsidian source data. P-MIP survey artifacts suggest that the

dependence on Sauceda obsidian increased over time and that the highest incidence occurred in the Historic period (Loendorf et al. 2004). This possibility is also supported by the observation that obsidian artifacts in the sample from the Historic period Sacate site are almost exclusively from the Sauceda source: 13 of the 14 analyzed samples are Sauceda obsidian, and the remaining artifact is from Los Vidrios, which is located farther to the south, in Mexico. The proportion of Sauceda obsidian along the lower Salt River also increased over time, and that trend toward greater reliance on southern sources appears to have occurred throughout the Hohokam core area in the Phoenix Basin (Marshall 2002:132–133).

At the same time, use of obsidian from the Superior source declined after the pre-Classic period. For example, data from Grewe (a large pre-Classic period village) and Casa Grande (a nearby Classic period site) show that a dramatic decline occurred in the use of Superior obsidian during the Classic period (Bayman and Shackley 1999). At 60 percent, Superior obsidian was also the most common material identified at the pre-Classic period Snaketown site, located within the GRIC (Shackley and Bayman 2001). A similar pattern occurs in the Tonto Basin, where the use of Superior obsidian also declined between the early and late Classic periods (Rice et al. 1998).

The tendency for reliance on obsidian sources located to the southwest of the Middle Gila River is consistent with Historic period socioeconomic interaction patterns that were summarized in Chapter 5. During that time, the movement of Apache and Yavapai populations cut off access to northern, western, and eastern sources, including the San Francisco Volcanics, Vulture, and Superior obsidian. Meanwhile, alliances between the Tohono O'odham and the Pee Posh allowed continuing access to raw materials to the southwest of the GRIC.

Figure 61 shows Historic period Native American territories and obsidian locations. Sauceda is the only obsidian source located within an area occupied by speakers of the same language as the Akimel O'odham. The observation that the decline in the use of obsidian from northern, western, and eastern sources began during the Classic period suggests the possibility that highly mobile foragers, such as the Apache, moved into southern Arizona earlier than has traditionally been assumed.

Most previous researchers have argued that the Apache did not arrive in southern Arizona until after the end of the Classic period, around roughly A.D. 1450. For example, Hodge (1895) analyzed ethnohistorical population descriptions, Historic period settlement patterns, and Navajo and Akimel O'odham creation stories and concluded that the Apache were not in southern Arizona before the late 1600s. More recently, Doyel (1978:201) wrote that the "feeling is that the Apache were probably not in the area [in the vicinity of the Superior obsidian source] before A.D. 1500." Whittlesey et al. (1997:185) completed a review of the archaeological data and concluded that Athapaskan, Yuman, and Numic speakers established themselves in the Southwest after A.D. 1450. In a recent review of archaeological data from the area, Pinter and Stokes (2009:51) placed the arrival of the Apache in the Superior area somewhere around A.D. 1550. Based on analyses of multiple cultural traits thought to be associated with the Athapaskan populations, Baldwin (1997) argued that Apache moved into the Pueblo area of the Southwest after A.D. 1400, which is one of the earliest dates previously suggested for the arrival of Apache populations in Arizona. Most recently, Seymour (2011:74) completed a comprehensive review of archaeological, ethnographic, and ethnohistoric information and concluded that "proto-Apache" (so termed by Seymour) "were present in Southern Arizona from at least the A.D. 1400s, if not earlier."

Western Apache oral traditions also describe their arrival prior to the abandonment of the Classic period sites in the Tonto Basin and elsewhere (Goodwin 1942). For example, Goodwin (1942:63) observed that the White Mountain and San Carlos Apache have stories regarding conflicts with the inhabitants of an abandoned prehistoric site at Dewey Flat, on the Gila River, east of the study area. Another story refers to a time when the Tonto National Monument dwellings in the Tonto Basin were still inhabited by a people the Apache called *sáikìné* ("sand house people"). Initially some Apache peacefully moved to the area and lived nearby, but conflict soon arose with the *sáikìné*. As a result of the fighting, the *sáikìné* were eventually forced to abandon the area and migrate to the Salt River Valley, where they became the Akimel O'odham (Goodwin 1942:64). Similarly, Hodge (1910:252) observed that "the names applied to the Pima by the Apache and some other tribes furnish evidence that they formerly dwelt in adobe houses," which suggests that the Apache first encountered the Akimel O'odham when they were still living in Classic period–style adobe architecture.

Chapter Summary

The spatial distribution of Historic period projectile point types closely corresponds to independent lines of evidence for settlement patterns at that time, including ceramics and ethnohistorical descriptions of Akimel O'odham village locations. These data indicate that the Casa Blanca area was a focal point for the coalescence of populations that formerly lived throughout much of the Sonoran Desert. Casa Blanca is located on the southern side of the Middle Gila River, at the center of the study area, a location that is immediately opposite Snaketown, which is one of the largest pre-Classic period sites in the region. These data also suggest that Sobaipuri groups, probably from the San Pedro and Santa Cruz Rivers, were among the peoples who immigrated to the study area during the Historic period.

Classic period platform-mound and ceramic data suggest that habitation was most densely concentrated on the northern side of the river at that time. Highly similar point types were made during the Classic and Historic periods, and as Ravesloot and Whittlesey (1987) recognized, that has complicated the identification of distinctive Historic period types. At the same time, the continuity in point design is also an example of the continuation of material-cultural traditions from the Prehistoric to the Historic period.

Point-data patterning at a range of scales from study-region-wide patterns, intrasite differences, and variation within individual features are consistent with the hypothesis that stone points generally became smaller over time (Shott 1996). These data suggest that in addition to shape, point size may be a useful indicator of age for these artifacts. This hypothesis is of particular importance in regions where some point shapes were produced for thousands of years, such as the study area. Furthermore, the ability to recognize any remains left behind by highly mobile hunter-gatherer groups who only rarely produced diagnostic ceramics is of considerable importance. These analyses suggest that although it is not possible to precisely suggest ages for individual artifacts using size alone, significant variation in point weight is present between the Classic and Historic period assemblages considered here. Although these investigations do not prove that the projectile point size hypothesis is correct, they do suggest that it warrants further testing.

Projectile point metric data from the study area are consistent with expectations for the warfare- and hunting-point designs that were presented in Chapters 4 and 5. Furthermore, the spatial and temporal distributions of warfare- and hunting-point designs are coherent with other lines of evidence, including faunal data as well as the ethnohistorical descriptions of conflict along the Middle Gila River that were presented in Chapter 5. These data suggest

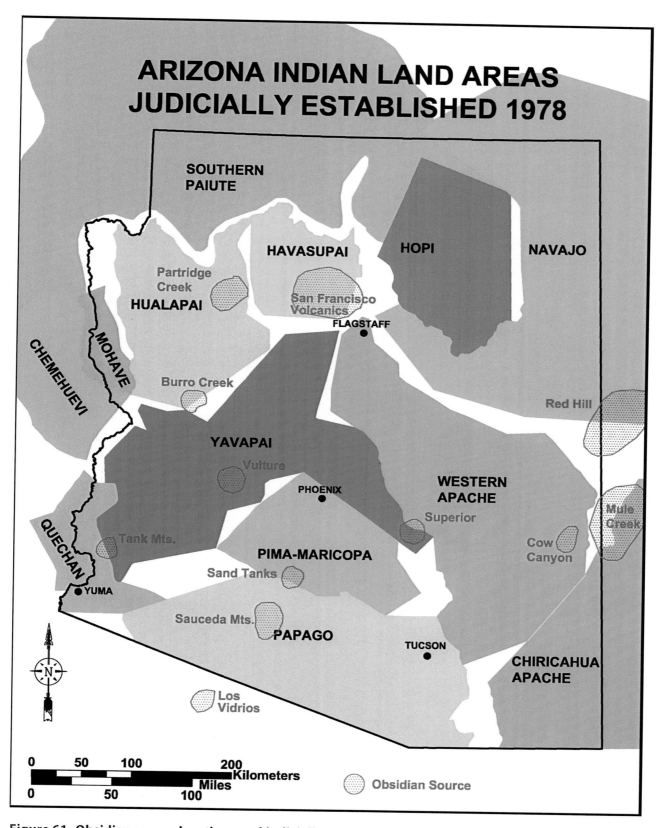

ARIZONA INDIAN LAND AREAS JUDICIALLY ESTABLISHED 1978

SOUTHERN PAIUTE

HAVASUPAI

HOPI

NAVAJO

Partridge Creek

HUALAPAI

San Francisco Volcanics

FLAGSTAFF

CHEMEHUEVI

MOHAVE

Burro Creek

Red Hill

YAVAPAI

Vulture

PHOENIX

WESTERN APACHE

Superior

Mule Creek

QUECHAN

Tank Mts.

Cow Canyon

PIMA-MARICOPA

Sand Tanks

YUMA

Sauceda Mts.

PAPAGO

TUCSON

CHIRICAHUA APACHE

Los Vidrios

0   50   100   200 Kilometers
                    Miles
0   50   100

○ Obsidian Source

Figure 61. Obsidian source locations and judicially established tribal territories.

that the intensity of conflict generally increased over time along the Middle Gila River and that rather than reflecting population migrations, the complete disappearance of side-notched points at some Historic period sites, such as Sacate, is the result of a decrease in big-game-hunting opportunities at that time.

These diachronic changes in projectile point design suggest that the incidence of big-game hunting generally decreased over time in the study area and that by the end of the Historic period, people only occasionally hunted large animals. This is consistent with the observations that Classic period side-notched projectile point types are present within the classification scheme and that the types thought to be from the Historic period are all un-notched. Both the decline in points designed for hunting (suggesting greater circumscription of populations with less access to favorable big-game habitats away from villages) (Kozak and Lopez 1999:43) and the increased incidence of warfare-point designs suggest that the intensity in conflict increased over time from the Classic period to the Historic period along the Middle Gila River.

Projectile points from the Casa Blanca area that were made throughout the archaeological sequence were rarely serrated. In contrast, projectile points from the north, east, and west of Casa Blanca more commonly had that form of edge treatment. This variation suggests that different social groups existed in the study area and that these people were not a politically centralized entity. Because Casa Blanca–area projectile points, regardless of type or size, have a lower incidence of serration, these data suggest long-term continuity in the cultural traditions of people who lived in the area, which is another example of the link between Hohokam and Historic period populations.

Within the study area, direction of the source has a substantially greater effect on raw-material utilization than does absolute distance. If people traveled to sources themselves in order to obtain obsidian, then distance should be the primary barrier for the acquisition of the material; however, obsidian proportions for the most common source are very weakly correlated to distance. Observations also suggest that prehistoric people in the lower Salt Basin, Middle Gila River, and Casa Grande areas as well as the Tonto and Salt River portions of the Tonto Basin maintained different trade contacts. Data suggest that by the late Classic period, little obsidian was transferred between adjacent subregions. Instead, communities of sites received most of this raw material from distant areas in different directions. Patterning in obsidian acquisition suggests that the strongest socioeconomic ties among communities were those between sites located on the same rivers, and exchanging food for such items as obsidian may have provided a mechanism for redistributing water-dependent resources.

Use of the closest source, Superior, decreased dramatically over time from the pre-Classic period to the Classic period. Sauceda obsidian, which is located to the southwest of the core area, became the main supply of obsidian by the late Classic period, and that trend continued into the Historic period. This continuity of trends between the Classic and Historic periods provides another example of the link between the Hohokam and the Akimel O'odham. Decline in the use of obsidian from sources located in Yavapai and Apache Historic period territories began during the Classic period, which suggests that these people may have moved into those areas prior to the Historic period. The next chapter explores broader implications of this possibility as well as other patterns identified in this chapter.

CHAPTER 7

Corporate-Network Political Strategies

The previous chapters presented several lines of ethnohistorical and archaeological data that suggest that cultural continuity existed between the Classic and Historic periods along the Middle Gila River. At the same time, substantial alterations in material culture occurred between these two periods, and similar episodic transitions in archaeological remains have been documented as having occurred earlier in time. Indeed, researchers have long used these punctuated differences in material culture to define "periods" (i.e., Paleo-Indian, Archaic, pre-Classic, and Classic) in the prehistoric archaeological record. However, why these episodic alterations occurred remains less understood.

This chapter explores the possibility that these periodic changes reflect human economic, political, social, religious, and technological responses to constraints that resulted from climatic oscillations between warmer and colder regimes. The focus of this discussion is on political changes, which are described using the concept of corporate-network strategies developed by Blanton et al. (1996). This model provides insight into dimensions of social organization that depart in fundamental ways from the traditional anthropological classifications of egalitarian vs. hierarchical. After the Blanton et al. (1996) model is summarized, this theory is applied to pre-Classic, Classic, and Historic period material-culture records from the Phoenix and Tonto Basins of Central Arizona.

Corporate-Network Conceptual Model

Social complexity remains one of the most acrimoniously contested topics among southwestern archaeologists (Craig 2004:287). Until the 1980s, most of the dispute revolved around the existence of complexity, one group arguing that southwestern societies were egalitarian and another arguing that they were hierarchical. Feinman et al. (2000:450) observed, "This debate regrettably became adversarial and was characterized by arguments that presumed a polar dichotomy between hierarchical and nonhierarchical political formations."

After that time, archaeologists recognized that social organization is a multidimensional phenomenon with multiple aspects that do not necessarily vary in concert (Nelson 1995). By the late 1990s, a certain measure of consensus was reached that status and ranking were largely related to ceremonial authority; however, like most things in archaeology, the argument was not fully resolved (Kintigh 1998).

Feinman et al. (2000) introduced the concept of corporate-network strategies into the debate. Blanton et al. (1996) developed this conceptual model through the study of Mesoamerican societies. According to Feinman et al. (2000:453), "[t]he network strategy of political action is associated with heavily personalized or centralized forms of leadership. Wealth is concentrated in the hands of a few, who use their network of personal connections to enhance and expand their individualized power and authority." In contrast, the corporate conception shares similarities with Johnson's (1989) characterization of sequential hierarchies, and "[i]n corporate organizations, economic resources are more dispersed, leadership is less personalized, and ostentatious displays and individual aggrandizement are less apt to be found" (Feinman et al. 2000:453).

These two forms of organization are not replacements for the concepts of "egalitarian" and "hierarchical" but, instead, are orthogonal to the dimension of hierarchal organization such that stratified societies can have network or corporate organizational strategies. Rather than binary variables, corporate and network forms are recognized within a continuum, and it is unlikely that either of the two extremes would ever occur in a society. Feinman et al. (2000:465) concluded that southwestern political formations varied through time along the two dimensions of corporate-network strategies and hierarchical differentiation. They also identified at least two major episodes of political change in the Puebloan Southwest.

Corporate-Network Strategies in the Sonoran Desert

Discussing political organization in the Hohokam region of southern Arizona requires addressing a number of interrelated issues; however, the primary data that archaeologists have to analyze are from nonperishable material culture, and furthermore, most of these remains are items that were discarded. The relationship between material culture and social organization is a complicated one, in part because multiple factors in addition to the many facets of social complexity may condition diachronic or synchronic variation in the limited data preserved at sites. In the following discussion, I marshal as much of the ethnographic, ethnohistorical, and archaeological information as possible.

I begin with what the people who were living along the Middle Gila River at the time of Spanish contact have said about themselves. The Akimel O'odham worldview involves an inception, overpopulation, and a breakdown of traditional practices and subsequent destruction; the cycle then repeats (Bahr 1975:77). This paradigm differs fundamentally from the assumption that prehistoric populations increased slowly and steadily over time. The Akimel O'odham story says, instead, that the population fluctuated dramatically over time. This possibility has important implications for the interpretation of variation in material culture and social organization in Central Arizona.

The O'odham conception is similar to Hopi traditions, which also describe a cycle of creation and destruction, but there are many substantial differences. One fundamental distinction is that the cycle in Hopi reasoning involves the creation of different worlds and the continuation of essentially the same creatures through time, whereas the O'odham beliefs emphasize the creation and destruction of people and the continuation of essentially the same world through time. The Hopi believe that the cycle involves the movement between "worlds": people physically leave one world and travel to the next. In each cycle, the creator of the world becomes unhappy with the transgressions of some people; so, he creates a new world for the few righteous beings from the previous land (see Waters 1963). Basically, the continuity of place is emphasized in the O'odham story, and the continuity of people and migration are more important in the Hopi traditions.

Akimel O'odham Creation Story

Rather than a narrative that has historical meaning, the Akimel O'odham creation story has been regarded as an

invention or myth that these people made up to explain the existence of the world (Russell 1908:206). For example, Curtis (1909:284) wrote:

The Pima claim to have lived always in the Gila valley, their lands stretching along some sixty miles of its length. They farm by irrigation and likely had canals larger and longer than other tribes. The very large prehistoric canals which formed a part of the development, with the building and occupancy of the Casa Grande and other like large prehistoric ruins, are in the country of the Pima. In their legends they account for these ruins and ditches and claim them as the work of Pima. There is, however, little to encourage this claim.

Examination of the creation story, however, suggests that it has close parallels with the archaeological record that are unlikely to have occurred by coincidence (Lewis and Rice 2009; Teague 1993). McIntosh (2000) introduced the term "social memory" to describe the communal, multigenerational knowledge of the environmental and biocultural dynamics possessed by a society and argued that deep-time motivations based on social memory are potentially verifiable by archaeologists. He maintained that it is irrelevant whether social memory is correct in all particulars, and it is clear that such knowledge "is integral to an ancient social construction, or social perception, of the dynamics of the physical environment" (McIntosh 2000:173).

The Akimel O'odham social memory describes a cycle in which humans are created and destroyed by their paramount deity. Although there are many recorded versions of the creation story, they all share the same basic structural elements (Bahr 1975, 2007; Bahr 2001; Bahr et al. 1994; Baker 1973; Farish 1916; Fewkes 1912; Grossman 1873; Lloyd 1911; Russell 1908; Shaw 1995; Thomas 1917; Webb 1959:90–126). For this discussion, I refer to the version written by Russell (1908:206–230).

The story begins with Earth Doctor's creating the world and humankind, but the people rapidly became too numerous and started eating each other; so, Earth Doctor destroyed his creations. He then made different people, but in contrast to the previous cycle, a new supernatural being (Elder Brother) entered the picture at that time. "The people increased in numbers, but Elder Brother shortened their lives, and they did not overrun the earth as they had done before" (Russell 1908:209). This, however, did not satisfy Elder Brother, and he decided to destroy the people that Earth Doctor had made. The story specifies that this act of destruction was a flood. Before the flood, Earth Doctor helped some people escape through a hole in the earth, and he directed others to a high place above the floodwaters.

After traveling back from the distant locations to which the water had carried them, Coyote, Earth Doctor, and Elder Brother reunited. They agreed that Elder Brother was first to emerge and that he was therefore "the ruler of the world" (Russell 1908:213). They traveled again until they found the center of the world, and the three of them made new people and animals. Coyote created web-footed animals, snakes, and birds that Elder Brother said to throw into the water. Earth Doctor made creatures resembling human beings, but they were deformed. Elder Brother told Earth Doctor to put his creations in the west, after which Earth Doctor sank into the ground, leaving sickness behind him. Elder Brother then made four groups of people, the second of which became the Apache.

After a series of more-detailed events, the people decided to kill Elder Brother because he had become mischievous. After three attempts (he revived each time), they enlisted the help of Vulture for a fourth try, but Elder Brother still was not destroyed. In retaliation, he sank into the ground and resurrected the people Earth Doctor had previously helped escape (i.e., people from before the flood), who proceeded to attack and defeat, one by one, the platform-mound villages along the Salt and Gila Rivers.

Each village is associated with a specific, named individual, such as Morning-Blue for Casa Grande, and Elder Brother himself is connected with a particular platform mound. During the conquest, the mound leaders tried to defend themselves by causing windstorms and other, mostly weather-related, phenomena. After completing the destruction, the people from before the flood continued moving with Elder Brother and then eventually returned to the Middle Gila River.

So what do we have? This version of the creation story (others have more or fewer cycles of creation and destruction) indicates the following: (1) a creation and vague destruction, (2) a re-creation and subsequent destruction by flood, (3) a third creation followed by a conquest by people who lived there before the flood, (4) the creation of the Apache and other non-O'odham peoples after the flood but before the conquest, (5) the association of named leaders with specific communally constructed architecture, (6) leaders who lived at the platform mounds and were believed to control the weather and other forces, and (7) people who moved across the landscape during episodes of destruction.

Prehistoric Climate

Some anthropologists reject the kinds of arguments presented in the following discussion as "ecological determinism." This is in part because human beings can (and are likely to) respond to the same natural events in different ways (Ingram 2010). For example, some people might react to a catastrophic flood by moving, others could change their social organization to facilitate the increased labor necessary to maintain previous agricultural practices (Waters and Ravesloot 2001:292), and many might simply die. I argue that all of these responses (and others) may

have occurred, and I agree that environmental conditions do not cause cultural practices. Environmental factors, however, constrain human behavior, and we can see the responses of individuals to those changing limits in the archaeological record.

The study area lies at the junction of the Salt and Gila Rivers. Graybill et al. (2006:82) noted that "[o]wing to differences in the topography and elevation of the two drainage basins, and thus to the manner in which climate affects precipitation and discharge, the Salt and Gila differ markedly in discharge volume" (see also Graybill 1989) and that "[a]nnual discharge of the Salt River is determined primarily by winter precipitation in the upper reaches of the watershed" (Graybill et al. 2006:83). "By contrast," Graybill et al. (2005:85) also noted, "Gila River discharge reflects a much more substantial contribution from the summer convective rainfall (monsoonal) component than Salt River discharge." Based on differences in reconstructed stream-flow patterns between the rivers, Graybill et al. (2006:107) argued that "there may have been substantial long-term differences in the timing and magnitude of labor requirements and in the reliability of foodstuffs derived from irrigation farming" along the two rivers.

These stream-flow data are based on dendroclimatology records that are largely derived from trees that grow in the upper portions of the watersheds for the streams, and consequently, these reconstructions do not accurately reflect the contribution of flows from summer convective rainfall (Graybill et al. 2006). Another major weakness of the stream-flow data is that it is not possible to determine the configuration and discharge capacities of the river channels (Ravesloot et al. 2009:239). However, geoarchaeological investigations undertaken along the Middle Gila River have reconstructed the alluvial history of the river (Waters and Ravesloot 2000, 2001, 2003) and have provided data that are critical to understanding the development and organization of irrigation communities that were dependent on the two rivers (Ravesloot et al. 2009:238). The studies demonstrated "that after 750 years of floodplain stability and a predictable stream-flow regime, Hohokam farmers had to contend with a major environmental catastrophe" (Ravesloot et al. 2009:238). This major sedimentological change (i.e., down-cutting event) occurred sometime between A.D. 1020 and 1160.

LeBlanc (1999:32–36, 2003:147–149, 2006) argued that a long-term, worldwide climatic cycle between warmer and colder conditions over the last 2,000 years affected southwestern agricultural populations. Although the exact timing and local effects of these oscillations remain uncertain, LeBlanc (1999:33) suggested that "any change in temperature could have had major effects in Southwestern crop yields, not only in higher elevations but also in lower ones." Dean (2000:97–101) synthesized paleoclimatic data that show low-frequency and high-frequency climatic change over the last 2,000 years on the Colorado Plateau

(Coconino Plateau) in Arizona and identified intervals of potential environmental stress. He argued that the period between A.D. 900 and 1130 was the most favorable interval for irrigation agriculture in the last 2,000 years (Dean 2000:101). This long period of stability roughly coincides with the Hohokam Sedentary period. These extended favorable conditions may have resulted in population increases, which may have made groups more susceptible to subsequent climatic events. Following Dean (2000), Lekson (2002) examined dendroclimatology records for the Southwest and identified patterns of high temporal variability in resource availability that he associated with cycles of conflict and variation in settlement patterns. Based on his analysis, Lekson (2002) concluded that war in prestate societies is predicated by resource unpredictability and socialization for fear.

More recently, Mayewskia et al. (2004) examined nearly 50 globally distributed paleoclimate records and identified as many as six episodes of rapid climate change during the Holocene. Most of these climate-change events were characterized by polar cooling, tropical aridity, and major atmospheric-circulation changes. However, during the most recent interval (600–150 cal yr B.P.), polar cooling was accompanied by increased moisture in some parts of the tropics. They found that several of these intervals coincided with major cultural disruptions and argued that Holocene climate variability had substantial effects on human populations. They concluded that the periods of rapid climate change were generally characterized by bipolar cooling and intensification of atmospheric circulation in high latitudes and aridity in low latitudes. When the poles cool and polar atmospheric circulation intensifies, the low-latitude band of atmospheric circulation may be compressed. This may dramatically alter the distribution of moisture-bearing winds in the monsoon regions of the world and the carrying capacity for moisture in the atmosphere.

If the climatic oscillations suggested by Mayewskia et al. (2004) affected summer and winter precipitation patterns in southern Arizona, then given the differences in the hydrology of the two streams, periods of good conditions for agriculture on the lower Salt River would have alternated with more-favorable conditions for irrigation along the Middle Gila River. This possibility may have affected the cultural practices of the irrigation agriculturalists that lived along these streams in the Hohokam core area (cf. Grebinger 1976).

Pre-Classic to Classic Period Transition

The down-cutting event identified by Ravesloot and Waters (2004) that occurred between A.D. 1020 and 1160

corresponds roughly with the pre-Classic to Classic period transition, and the "duration of this event was probably less than the 80-year-error range of the associated radiocarbon dates" (Ravesloot and Rice 2004). This event occurred close to when, as LeBlanc (1999:35, 2003:147–149), Dean (2000:102), and Lekson (2002) suggested, a major change in climatic patterns occurred. Material-cultural changes that happened around that time within the Hohokam core area include the following: a shift in settlement patterns occurred, pit houses were replaced by surface structures, red-on-buff ceramics became less common (Figure 62), Salado polychromes appeared (Figure 63), ball courts were no longer built, platform mounds were constructed, and production of some items (e.g., palettes and censers) (Figures 64 and 65) that appear to have been associated with religious activities (Haury 1976:286–289) stopped.

The down-cutting event would have made irrigation more difficult (Craig 2004:280; Waters and Ravesloot 2001), which, when combined with a shift in regional precipitation patterns, may have made some people respond by moving to locations along the Salt River and possibly other areas. Comparatively few researchers have considered the possibility of migration away from the Hohokam core area, but the Zuni area is one possible location to which people traveled. Based on linguistic research, Shaul and Hill (1998:377) argued that "Zuni speakers may have been part of the Hohokam system during the Classic period in the fourteenth century." Similarly, Teague (1993) identified communalities in both the languages and the ceremonial practices of the Zuni and the O'odham (see also Fewkes 1912:46 [footnote]).

Movement away from the Gila River is considered likely, because during the pre-Classic period, conditions were less favorable along the Salt River, and population densities would consequently have been lower, providing a "pull." Furthermore, Waters and Ravesloot (2001) argued that aggregation occurred in response to the down-cutting event because of the increased labor necessary for irrigation (Ravesloot 2007; Ravesloot et al. 2009). Similarly, Ingram (2008:137), in his study of Canal System 2 along the lower Salt River, found that "population growth rates generally increased as the frequency, magnitude, and duration of inferred flooding, drought, and variability increased." He later noted, "This relationship suggests that the Lower Salt may have been a refuge for people moving away from other areas" (Ingram 2010:65).

Haury (1976) argued that the largest Sedentary period site (i.e., Snaketown) in the study area was abandoned at the end of the pre-Classic period (Craig 2004; Woodson 2010). Wilcox and Sternberg (1983:198–203) suggested that Snaketown was the paramount regional center within the Phoenix Basin during the pre-Classic period, and they thought that the population declined along the Middle Gila River during the Classic period while it increased along the lower Salt River.

Figure 62. Pre-Classic period red-on-buff bowl collected from GR-915 (photograph by Melissa Altamirano).

Figure 63. Gila Polychrome bowl collected from the Tonto Basin, Roosevelt Platform Mound Study, Arizona State University (photograph by Brenda Shears).

Figure 64. Palettes from pre-Classic period components at GR-441, Locus A, Gila River Indian Community (photograph by Melissa Altamirano).

Figure 65. Greenstone effigy censer collected from GR-520, Gila River Indian Community (photograph by Melissa Altamirano).

Based on his comprehensive analysis of the Middle Gila River canal systems and settlement locations, Woodson (2010:29) concluded that

> water scarcity in the Late Sedentary and Early Classic periods forced a response by Hohokam populations [along the Middle Gila River]. Responses are reflected both in the settlement pattern and canal systems including a decrease in main canal capacities and the lack of new canal system construction in the Classic period. Another key response was the movement of people away from downstream systems, as indicated by steep population declines. Segments of these downstream populations apparently moved to better watered locales either further [sic] upstream along the Gila River or along the lower Salt River.

Differences in the size of public architecture and the number of sites with communally constructed features also suggest that there were substantial differences in population size along the Salt and Gila Rivers in the pre-Classic and Classic periods. There are 28 pre-Classic period ball courts within the study area, including sites with multiple courts, but during the Classic period, only 6 comparatively small platform mounds were built in the same area (Ravesloot and Rice 2004; Rice and Ravesloot 2003) (Figure 66). In contrast, over 40 mounds (including, by far, the 2 largest examples) occur along the lower Salt River, and 26 mounds are present in the Tonto Basin, a location that has far less land that can potentially be irrigated than the Middle Gila River and that also lacks ball courts (Abbott et al. 2003:12; Elson 1998:102; Marshall 2001a).

There is considerable evidence for population growth along the Salt River during the early Classic period—including sites such as Pueblo Grande, which experienced a twofold to threefold increase (Abbott and Foster 2003)—and in the Tonto Basin (Doelle 1995, 2000; Oliver 1997:470). At Pueblo Grande, for example, Abbott and Foster (2003:46) identified a large influx of people at the start of the Classic period, "as entire residential groups newly rooted themselves at the margins of the village." Ingram (2008) found evidence that immigration occurred throughout Canal System 2 along the lower Salt River during the Classic period. Furthermore, reconstructions for the entire lower Salt River Valley have suggested that the overall population of the area increased from the Sedentary period to the Classic period (Doelle 2000; Hill et al. 2004; Meegan 2009).

This population reorganization is expected to have altered economic, political, and ideological relationships within Hohokam society. Existing populations along the Salt River would have been in position to dictate conditions for allowing people from the Gila River or elsewhere to settle near their homes. This is analogous to how the Hopi Bear clan achieved its position at the top of their hierarchy by maintaining access to the best lands and the most "important" (to itself) ceremonies (Levy 1992).

Rather than resulting from the migration of outside ethnic groups, the architectural changes that occurred are consistent with responses to variation in the raw materials available for construction and a shift in performance requirements resulting from changed climatic conditions. pre-Classic period pit houses (Figure 67) were built largely of wood and frequently had multiple support posts, whereas late Classic period adobe structures (Figure 68) used no wood in the walls and commonly only had one main roof-support post each (Haury 1976:46–74; Rice 2003). The down-cutting event destroyed riparian habitats along the Gila and Salt Rivers, eliminating many of the trees in the area (Waters and Ravesloot 2001:292). As the Hohokam concentrated in locations along the Salt River and Tonto Creek, they would have rapidly depleted remaining trees (Kwiatkowski 2003:67). In most areas, house types that used progressively less wood were built over the course of time (Abbott and Foster 2003:26–30; Craig et al. 1992:38–49; Ezell 1961:49; Rice 2003; Sayles 1938:79–80).

Pit houses and surface structures do not have equivalent thermal characteristics, and climatic conditions may also have also played a role in the construction of different house types (Gilman 1987). For example, Craig (1995) identified a tendency for the number of contiguous rooms to increase over time during the Classic period, a pattern also noted by Haury (1976:48). Building structures with shared walls both decreases the construction materials required and reduces the overall thermal-energy loss for individual rooms. This would have facilitated the heating of structures with the limited fuels that were available.

Furthermore, macrobotanical evidence suggests that fewer trees were locally available along the lower Salt River and in the Tonto Basin during the Classic period (Elson et al. 1995:259; Kwiatkowski 2003:57). Faunal data, including patterning in cottontail/jackrabbit ratios, also suggest that less cover existed in lower elevations during the Classic period (Bayham and Hatch 1985; James 2003). The shift from cremation to inhumation that occurred between the pre-Classic and Classic periods is also consistent with a response to constraints imposed by the limited availability of fuels for cremation fires (Loendorf 1998:199–200). Although it is unlikely that the scarcity of cremation fuels, alone, would cause the alteration of mortuary traditions, it is possible that environmental constraints favored the adoption and/or development of beliefs that ameliorated stresses resulting from an inability to complete previous ceremonies.

The disappearance of palettes and censers (Figure 69) also suggests that changes in religious practices occurred at that time, which is reflected by the replacement of Earth Doctor by Elder Brother after the flood. The appearance of Salado polychromes during the Classic period (Figure 70), which Crown (1994) argued were part of a regional cult, also suggests a change in religious practices. Abbott (2000, 2009) argued that pre-Classic period red-on-buff ceramics were largely made along the Middle Gila River instead of

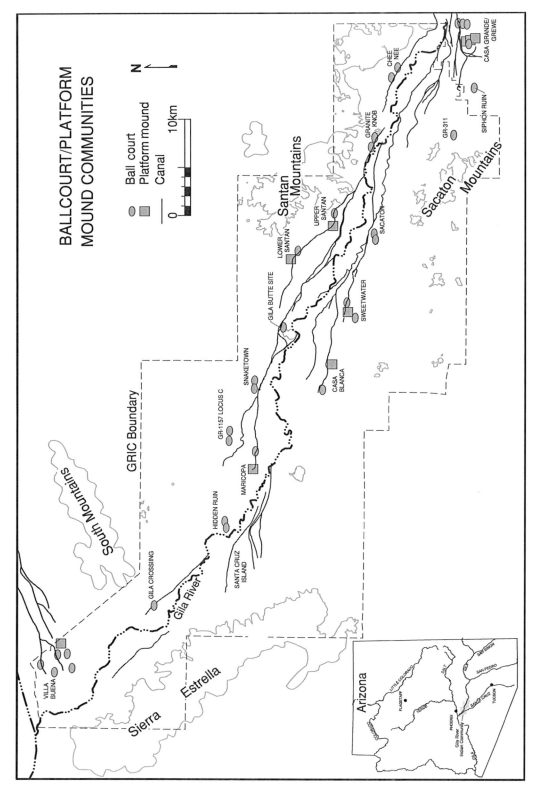

Figure 66. Ball-court and platform-mound locations within the study area (adopted from Ravesloot and Rice [2004]; Rice and Ravesloot [2003]).

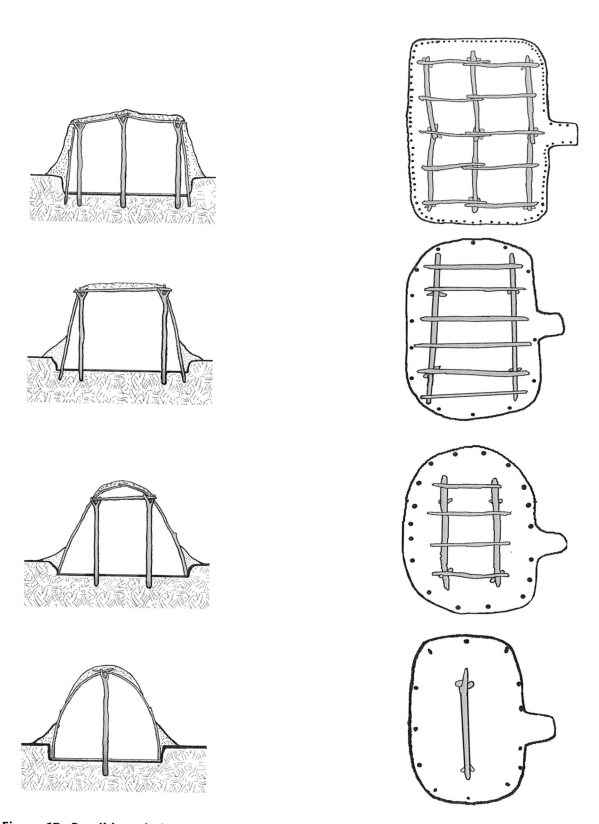

Figure 67. Possible techniques used in the construction of pre-Classic period Hohokam pit houses (not to scale) (adapted from Rice [2003] by Rob Ciaccio).

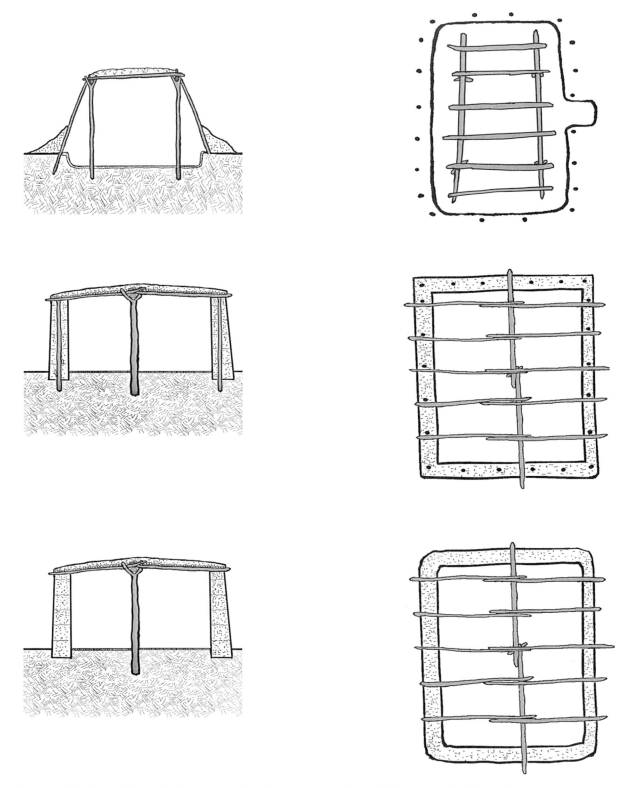

Figure 68. Possible techniques used in the construction of Classic period Hohokam structures (not to scale) (adapted from Rice [2003] by Rob Ciaccio).

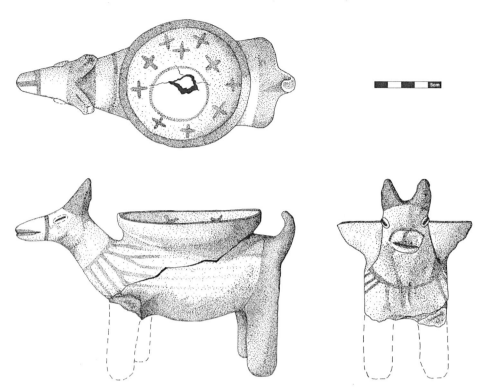

Figure 69. Ceramic red-on-buff effigy censer collected from a pre-Classic period component at GR-522, Locus D, Gila River Indian Community (illustration by Jackie Orcholl).

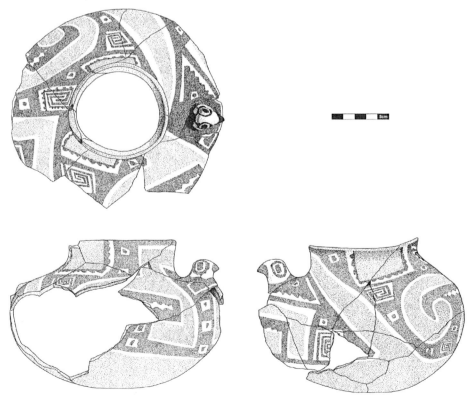

Figure 70. Ceramic Tonto Polychrome effigy jar collected from a Classic period component at GR-522, Locus A, Gila River Indian Community (illustration by John McCool).

the Salt River. The rapid decline of buff ware proportions at Classic period sites is thus also consistent with population loss along the Middle Gila River.

In contrast to the extensive pre-Classic period ceramic-exchange relationships (Abbott 2000, 2009), patterning in Classic period obsidian data suggests that people in the Salt Basin, Middle Gila River, and Casa Grande areas and the Tonto and Salt River portions of the Tonto Basin maintained different exchange relationships. By the late Classic period, little obsidian was transferred between adjacent subregions, suggesting that conflict intensified at that time (see Chapter 6). Variation in projectile point serration data also suggests that the Classic period Hohokam were not a politically integrated entity. The greater incidence of warfare points over time also suggests that conflict intensified, which is reflected by the O'odham story of conquest that resulted in the destruction of the platform-mound villages. The evidence for the movement of highly mobile populations into southern Arizona during the Classic period is consistent with the creation of the Apache after the flood but before the conquest (i.e., during the Classic period), as described in the O'odham traditions.

Pre-Classic and Classic Period Corporate-Network Strategies

A number of observations suggest that pre-Classic period social organization was based on a more corporate strategy and that a shift to a system in which network strategies had greater influence occurred during the early Classic period (Elson 1998:105). pre-Classic period public architecture consisted of facilities, including ball courts (Figure 71) and big rooms designed for community gatherings (Ravesloot and Rice 2004; Rice and Ravesloot 2003). These structures were not associated with specific households, suggesting that they had a more corporate nature: "Some courtyards would be closer to or further [sic] from the public structures, but none were situated in such a way as to indicate a proprietary control of these edifices" (McGuire 1992:157).

During the pre-Classic period, extensive socioeconomic-interaction networks appear to have operated within the Salt Basin and also to have linked it with the Middle Gila River and other areas (Abbott 2000, 2009; Harry 2005). Abbott et al. (2003:5) noted, "In contrast to the clustered

Figure 71. Aerial photograph of the main Pre-Classic period ball court at Snaketown (photograph by Bob Niely).

and patchy spacing of the platform mounds, the ball courts had a continuous distribution, expressing uninterrupted connections among communities across a vast region." This patterning is consistent with the expectations for cooperate organizations. The disruption to existing power relationships within Hohokam society along the Salt and Gila Rivers that resulted from changes in settlement patterns during the Classic period would have created opportunities that some groups may have exploited.

Classic period public architecture, including platform mounds, has more personalized and secluded characteristics (Abbott et al. 2003:12–13; Hegmon et al. 2008:319; McGuire 1992; Wilcox 1991). By the late Classic period, a small segment of the population resided on the mounds (Abbott et al. 2003), suggesting that more-network-orientated strategies had emerged by that time (Figure 72). The named mound leaders in the Akimel O'odham creation story are also consistent with an emphasis on individualized aggrandizement. The socioeconomic interaction networks of the pre-Classic period appear to have broken down, and it appears that there was comparatively little cooperation among sites during the late Classic period (Abbott 2000, 2009; Abbott et al. 2007; Rice et al. 1998; Simon and Gosser 2001).

Patterning in early Classic period burial data suggests that the greatest distinction among community segments occurred in measures of wealth, which is consistent with a more-network-orientated strategy (Loendorf 2001:139). These same burial data suggest that political authority was not highly stratified during the early Classic period (Loendorf 2001:141–142), and it appears that hierarchical ranking may have been greater during the late pre-Classic (i.e., Sedentary) period than in the early Classic period: "During the Colonial and Sedentary periods, the ball-court system became more centralized, with a decrease in the number of courts and an increased regularity in the spacing of courts" (Rice 2000:146).

The amalgamation of social segments into progressively larger units also appears to have occurred over the course of the Classic period. In the Tonto Basin, for example, the numerous, small early Classic period platform mounds were replaced by only two (or possibly three) much larger mounds by the late Classic period (Rice 2000). Thus, by the end of the Classic period, the Hohokam social system may have become more hierarchical than in the early Classic period (Hegmon et al. 2008), and network leadership strategies were more important than they had been in the pre-Classic period.

Figure 72. Aerial photograph of the Cline Terrace platform mound in the Tonto Basin, Roosevelt Platform Mound Study, Arizona State University (photograph by Glen E. Rice).

Classic to Historic Period Transition

When the Spanish arrived in 1694, all or nearly all of the Akimel O'odham within the Hohokam core area were living along the Gila River. The ceramic and projectile data presented in Chapter 6 support this observation. Waters and Ravesloot (2001:292) did not find evidence for a down-cutting episode at that time and suggested that riparian habitats along the Gila River had recovered. No evidence exists that a down-cutting and channel-widening episode occurred at that time along the lower Salt River or in the Tonto Basin (Ravesloot et al. 2009). As a consequence, more wood may have been locally available along those streams and could have been used for construction and other purposes.

Based on stream-flow patterns near the end of the Classic period, Graybill et al. (2006:114–120) argued that conditions for irrigation along the Salt River were substantially worse than along the Gila River and that Gila River communities may have endured longer than those on the Salt River. Graybill et al.(2006:118) suggested, "The collapse of Civano phase Salt River systems undoubtedly resulted in some attrition as well as out-migration, and one interesting possibility is that some portion of the Salt River population may have sought refuge in the Gila during the late 1380s and thereafter."

Regarding that time, in an analysis that employed the concept of a "rigidity trap" from resilience theory, Hegmon et al. (2008:317) argued:

> The end of the Hohokam Classic [period] represents a virtual disappearance of the material culture that archaeologists associate with Hohokam, including pottery, formal architecture, and the irrigation system. Some people did remain in the region, and there are continuities with historic and contemporary populations, but these are difficult to trace archaeologically because of the lack of material continuity.

However, multiple lines of evidence for continuity in projectile point technology between the Classic and Historic periods have been presented in this research. These include strong similarities in projectile point shape and serration data as well as the uninterrupted continuation of trends in obsidian acquisition patterns that began during the Classic period. Furthermore, during that interval, people returned to building structures similar to pre-Classic period pit houses, which require substantially more wood for construction than do adobe houses (Ezell 1963, 1983; Rice 2003:3; Sayles 1938; Seymour 2011:97–138; Whittemore 1898:56–57) (Figure 73). These similarities (Figure 74) led Sayles (1938:83) to conclude, "Indications point strongly to the Pima as being the cultural descendants of the Hohokam. The analogy between the Pima type of single unit dwelling and that of the Hohokam is close." Similarly, Haury (1976:72) wrote that the "Pima house, in my opinion, represents the retention of the old Hohokam architectural idiom, a not insignificant argument in the favor of Hohokam-Pima continuity."

The Akimel O'odham also practiced a dispersed *ranchería* settlement pattern similar to pre-Classic period settlement strategies (Ezell 1961:110–113; Fish 1989:21; Seymour 2011:198–209). They also returned to making red-on-buff pottery, which requires wood for firing (Figure 75) and has close similarities to pre-Classic period ceramics in manufacturing technique, temper, clay, and design (Ezell 1963). The Akimel O'odham were also dependent on irrigation

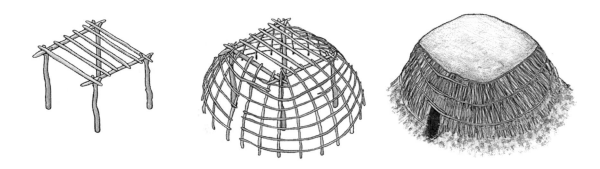

Figure 73. Construction technique for an Akimel O'odham *ke'* (not to scale) (adapted from Nabokov and Easton [1989] by Rob Ciaccio).

Figure 74. Postcard image of an Akimel O'odham *ke'* by the Berryhill Company, Phoenix, Arizona.

Figure 75. Historic period pottery collected by Frank Russell (photograph by De Lancey Gill, Negative 2656 B, National Anthropological Archives, Smithsonian Institution, Washington, D.C.).

Figure 76. Palettes collected by Frank Russell (photograph by De Lancey Gill, BAE GN 2677 B, National Anthropological Archives, Smithsonian Institution, Washington, D.C.).

agriculture, and their canal system shares close correspondences with both Classic and pre-Classic period agricultural strategies and irrigation systems (Ravesloot et al. 2009; Webb 1959:121–126; Woodson 2010:45). After moving to the area, the Pee Posh continued to cremate deceased members of their community (Spier 1933)—by far the most common burial treatment in the pre-Classic period. Russell (1908:112) also collected two palettes from "medicine-men"; one of the palettes had a "horse scratched on one side," which indicates that it is associated with the Historic period (Figure 76). This return of pre-Classic period cultural traditions is similar to the return of people from before the flood that was described in the Akimel O'odham creation story.

Recently, Ravesloot et al. (2009) offered a new model for the Hohokam collapse that supports continuity in cultural traditions within the Hohokam core area. They argued that the Hohokam entered a new adaptive cycle after the Classic period as the result of the declining availability of water in the region. They suggested that the prehistoric population levels could therefore not be maintained and that the Historic period Akimel O'odham represent a reorganized society.

Classic and Historic Period Corporate-Network Strategies

The introduction of epidemic diseases by Europeans would have come at a devastating time for sedentary agriculturalists that had recently experienced population losses and reorganization related to climatic cycles (cf. Ezell 1983:150). Akimel O'odham perceptions of disease are different from western ideas, and there is evidence that the Akimel O'odham believed that diseases were a type of supernatural power that certain individuals could

control (Hrdlička 1908:243–247; Shaw 1994:20). Russell (1908:256–258) described two types of religious specialists, both of them hereditary positions: the "Examining Physicians" treated disease, and "[t]hose who have power over the crops, the weather, and the wars are called Makai, Magicians" (Russell 1908:256). Whittemore (1898:62–64) noted, "They are ambitious, artful, and unscrupulous, and in this vicinity have done more to destroy the efforts of Indian agents." Each village had approximately five of these ceremonial leaders, and they were paid for their services. "These two classes were the true rulers of the tribe, as their influence was much greater than that of the chiefs" (Russell 1908:256).

It is generally argued that these people held little authority, because they were sometimes executed (Bahr 1983:185); however, Russell (1908:262) stated that when the patient of a specialist died, it was generally a rival practitioner who was diagnosed as the cause and killed. This suggests that competition among these specialists was a factor in these executions, and rather than a sign of weakness, the killing of other specialists may have been a mechanism for some individuals to increase their own influence through the elimination of competitors (Grossman 1873:411–412). In any case, these specialists' power was, in part, based upon the perception that they could cause and control disease. This power would have been fundamentally altered by their inability to stop repeated epidemics of European disease, which would have greatly weakened their authority in Akimel O'odham society.

Although these observations suggest that more-network-orientated roles remained, social organization by the late Historic period appears to have returned to a greater emphasis on corporate strategies. Akimel O'odham political leaders could not compel group action, and instead, decision making was based on group consensus (Bahr 1983:185;

Russell 1908:195–196; Whittemore 1898:59; but see Webb 1959:50–51): "The road to authority at nightly council meetings was gift giving. The headman ruled public life only in the sense of being in control of the agenda of the meetings" (Bahr 1983:185). Political leadership positions were not hereditary, although in some cases, sons followed their fathers in office (Russell 1908:196). These leaders were not compensated for their services, and use of their authority for personal economic benefit or favoritism of relatives was discouraged (Bahr 1983:185).

Chapter Summary

Data presented in this document suggest the following conclusions. Climatic oscillations between warmer and colder periods alternately favored conditions for irrigation along the Salt and Gila Rivers. This, in turn, affected ideological, economic, and political relationships within the region. The corporate-network conceptual model provides a basis for understanding the political responses that people developed to ameliorate these constraints.

Pre-Classic period Hohokam social organization was characterized by an emphasis on corporate organizational strategies reflected by the following: communal architecture designed for public gatherings that individual households did not control, socioeconomic networks that linked communities, and little differentiation in wealth among individuals or households. Reorganization in response to a massive down-cutting episode around A.D. 1070 resulted in the emergence of more-network-orientated political strategies with the following properties: increased emphasis on individual aggrandizement, including the association of platform-mound sites with specific leaders; greater wealth accumulation by individuals and social segments; and increased differentiation in residential architecture, with some households exercising control over publicly constructed facilities.

By the late Historic period, the Akimel O'odham and Pee Posh had returned to emphasizing practices that were similar to those of the pre-Classic period. These included the construction of similar architectural styles, the reoccurrence of the most common pre-Classic period burial practice (i.e., cremation), the production of similar ceramic types with shared design elements, and the use of pre-Classic period ritual items, including palettes. At that time, greater importance was again placed on corporate strategies, although vestiges of more-network-focused roles still persisted. The following observations suggest that corporate strategies were important: little differentiation occurred in wealth, no compensation was given to political leaders, specific individuals did not inhabit publicly constructed big rooms (i.e., council *ke'*) (Figure 77), and decision making was based on group consensus.

Figure 77. Photograph of an Akimel O'odham council *ke'* used for community gathering (photograph by Edward Curtis).

CHAPTER 8

Conclusions

Since the inception of historical documentation in the region, episodic alterations in human behavior along the Middle Gila River have been suggested to be associated with the migration of external ethnic groups. Based on architectural differences, eighteenth-century Spanish missionaries who visited the study area thought that the Akimel O'odham must have been recent migrants from elsewhere, and they maintained that the builders of Casa Grande (i.e., the Classic period Hohokam) were ancestors of the Aztecs who abandoned the Middle Gila River and migrated to Mesoamerica (Fewkes 1912:33). Over 200 years later, the Hohokam were still assumed to be migrants, but the direction of travel was reversed, and the people were thought to have moved from Mesoamerica to the Middle Gila River (Haury 1976). Similarly, material-cultural and settlement-pattern changes that occurred during the transition from the pre-Classic period to the Classic period were thought to have resulted from migration, but in this instance, populations were argued to have come from the north (Gladwin and Gladwin 1930).

What the Akimel O'odham, who have lived along the Middle Gila River since the first visit by Spanish missionaries, have said about their past has been almost entirely ignored or misunderstood in this debate. For example, Father Pedro Font's party laughed when they were told the Akimel O'odham creation story in 1775, and Font said that the description was "history and tradition which the Pima of Gila River have preserved from their ancestors concerning said Casa Grande, which all reduces itself to fictions mingled confusedly with some catholic truths" (Fewkes 1912:59). Indeed, the terms "Pima" and "Hohokam," themselves, are a result of misunderstanding (Lewis and Rice 2009). The archaeological term "Hohokam," for example, has been translated and spelled differently from the O'odham word "Huhugam" on which it is based. "Huhugam" more accurately means the spirits of O'odham ancestors (Lewis and Rice 2009; Saxton et al. 1983:25). The term does not refer to a different tribe that is distinct from the modern O'odham, and O'odham become Huhugam when they die.

Close similarities between the prehistoric record and Akimel O'odham social memory are unlikely to have occurred by coincidence (Lewis and Rice 2009; Teague 1993).

This worldview suggests that people are created and that subsequently, they overpopulate, traditional practices break down as a result, and their destruction follows. This pattern then repeats. The O'odham paradigm suggests that the number of people in the study area oscillated dramatically over time, rather than steadily and slowly increasing from incipient populations. The possibility that the prehistoric population fluctuated over time, as suggested by Akimel O'odham traditions, has fundamental implications for the interpretation of archaeological data. Periods of depopulation appear to have disrupted existing socioeconomic- and political-interaction patterns, and material-culture change as well as population movements and reorganization occurred during periodic intervals of low population density.

Research presented here suggests that people from throughout the Hohokam cultural area began immigrating to the Middle Gila River sometime around the end of the Classic period. The Akimel O'odham are therefore the descendants of the prehistoric inhabitants of much of southern Arizona. At the same time, because many of these populations moved from elsewhere in the Hohokam region to the Middle Gila River, they have maintained traditions regarding migration and distinctions among themselves (Webb 1959:22). This process of coalescence resulted in changes to social organization as well as material culture. Because populations from as far away as the Colorado River moved to the GRIC, intermarriage among these groups may also have resulted in genetic differences from the prehistoric populations who lived along the Middle Gila River. All of these people are, however, the direct descendants of the Hohokam inhabitants of southern Arizona.

These conclusions were reached through analyses of projectile point data that previously have received comparatively little attention. Stone points are integral parts of weapon systems, but prior analyses of these data have largely focused on the identification of "styles." Because archaeologists have focused on cultural aspects, discussion of performance characteristics has commonly been directed toward the identification of variables that differ independently from function. Rather than eliminating factors thought to be associated with projectile use, this study has identified and analyzed the tasks that points were designed to perform. Ethnographic research, performance constraints, and archaeological data all indicate that flaked stone points were designed either for hunting large game or for killing people.

The goals of hunting and warfare differ fundamentally in that the former cultural practice is undertaken to obtain food, whereas the primary intent of the latter activity is to kill or wound adversaries. As a result, different performance constraints exist for these two tasks. Because of the considerable effort required to track a wounded animal as well as the increased chance that it will not be recovered for consumption, hunting points were designed to kill as rapidly and consistently as possible. Warfare points, on the other hand, were designed to maximize the probability that injury or death resulted, regardless of how long these might require.

Stone projectile points that were designed for hunting are rare in the surface collection considered here, and unnotched points outnumber side-notched points by a factor of roughly three to one. Hunting-point designs occur in Sedentary and Classic period assemblages, which suggests that big-game hunting was more commonly practiced at those times—an observation that is supported by faunal data. In general, it appears that the incidence of hunting designs decreased over time, whereas the incidence of warfare designs increased. The absence of points with hunting-design features from the Historic period point assemblage is consistent with the observation that big-game hunting only rarely occurred at that time. Rather than reflecting the migration of outside ethnic groups, the disappearance of side-notched points from some Historic period sites resulted from changes in subsistence practices as well as an increase in the intensity of conflict over time.

Projectile points have long been shown to be useful indicators of chronological variation within archaeological assemblages. Indeed, pre–Ceramic cultural traditions (e.g., Clovis) are still defined largely on the basis of stone-point morphology. However, points of identical shapes were made for extended periods of time, and this variable, alone, is a poor predictor of temporal associations. Previous research has concentrated on differences in shape, but the data presented here suggest that projectile point weight is also a good indicator of age. This hypothesis is of particular importance for such regions as the study area, in which some types, such as triangular unnotched, were made during much of the archaeological sequence between roughly 5000 B.C. and A.D. 1880.

Analyses presented here support the suggestion that points generally decreased in size over time within the study area, and in at least some cases, it is possible to identify significant temporal patterning with sufficiently large projectile point assemblages. At the same time, considerable overlap occurs among different contexts, and the weights for individual artifacts cannot be used alone to suggest temporal estimates for sites. The resolution of the size data is limited, and previous researchers have had little success in seriating points from the Ceramic period; there is, consequently, considerable room for improvement. Furthermore, lithic analysts have long used point size to separate atlatl darts from arrow points, and the design theory presented here attempts to more clearly define the underlying performance and technological factors, such as the introduction of the recurved bow, that are associated with that change.

Analyses presented here do not prove that the projectile-point-size hypothesis is correct, but they do suggest that it warrants further testing and may have heuristic value. Although other lines of evidence (e.g., ceramics) are generally used to suggest temporal associations for artifact assemblages from the study area, diagnostic artifacts produced by highly mobile populations (e.g., the Apache) remain poorly understood. Ethnohistorical observations presented in Chapter 6 suggest that these peoples had considerable effects on the Historic period sedentary agriculturalists who lived in the Southwest, and the identification of any temporally diagnostic artifacts they produced is therefore of importance for understanding the past along the Middle Gila River.

Projectile points in the study collection were largely made from nonlocal materials; therefore, analyzing patterning in raw-material source areas provides information regarding socioeconomic interactions. Almost 30 percent of the projectile points considered here were made from obsidian, and it is possible to objectively and precisely define source locations for this material. Further, southwestern sources are generally localized deposits distributed in different directions from the Hohokam heartland. Thus, analyses of temporal and spatial variation in obsidian data compliment aspects of conflict that can be examined through consideration of projectile point design.

Archaeologists have generally focused on the study of diachronic variation in material culture and have paid less attention to long-term traditions that did not change over time. Trends in obsidian acquisition patterns that began during the Classic period and continued into the Historic period suggest that cultural continuity occurred. Close similarities between Classic and Historic period point types also suggest consistency in human behavior. Diachronic patterns in the projectile point blade-margin treatment further suggest continuity between Hohokam practices and those of the Akimel O'odham. Finally, the close parallels between the archaeological record and Akimel O'odham social memory indicate that these people have lived in the Hohokam core area for a considerable period of time.

The study area is located at the junction of the Salt and Gila Rivers. There are major differences in the topography of these two streams and in the elevations of their drainage basins, which create divergent discharge regimes. Data presented here suggest that climatic oscillations between warmer and colder periods alternately favored conditions for irrigation along the Salt and Gila Rivers. This, in turn, affected ideological, economic, and political relationships within the region. Pre-Classic period Hohokam social organization was characterized by an emphasis on corporate organizational strategies. Evidence for the importance of these strategies includes the existence of exchange networks that linked communities, communal architecture designed for public gatherings that individual households did not control, and comparatively little differentiation in wealth.

Economic and social responses as well as changes in settlement patterns caused by a down-cutting episode around roughly A.D. 1070 resulted in the emergence of a more network-orientated political strategy during the Classic period. Evidence for this suggestion is provided by an increased emphasis on individual aggrandizement; the association of named, individual leaders with specific sites; greater wealth accumulation; and increased differentiation in residential architecture, with some households exercising greater control over publicly constructed buildings.

By the late Historic period, the Akimel O'odham and Pee Posh had returned to emphasizing practices that were more similar to those of the pre-Classic period. Conditions for irrigation agriculture along the Middle Gila River had improved, whereas they appear to have deteriorated along the Salt River. At that time, greater emphasis was again placed on corporate strategies, although remnants of more-network-focused roles remained. The importance of corporate strategies is suggested by the observations that little differentiation occurred in wealth, no compensation was given to political leaders, specific individuals did not inhabit publicly constructed architecture, and decision making was based on group consensus.

If the postulated effects of Holocene climatic oscillations on the discharge volumes of the Salt and Gila Rivers in the Hohokam core area are correct, then weather cycles that occurred prior to the Sedentary period are also expected to have affected the settlement patterns of earlier populations who lived along these two streams, and the Akimel O'odham social memory supports that possibility. Although the effects of climatic oscillations are dependent upon a number of different variables, it is possible that population densities along these two streams generally shifted over time, such that periods of high population density along one river corresponded to periods of comparatively low population density along the other.

This study has shown that it is possible to use projectile point data to consider a much wider range of research issues than has traditionally occurred in the study area. This research employed flaked stone point data to analyze synchronic and diachronic variation in settlement patterns, subsistence practices, conflict, and socioeconomic cooperation. By employing projectile point data to identify diachronic patterns in conflict and cooperation, this research has elucidated relationships among Prehistoric and Historic period people who lived along the Middle Gila River and has improved our understanding of the nature and meaning of episodic changes that occurred in the material-cultural traditions of southern Arizona.

REFERENCES CITED

Abbott, David R.
  2000   *Ceramics and Community Organization among the Hohokam.* University of Arizona Press, Tucson.

  2009   Extensive and Long-Term Specialization: Hohokam Ceramic Production in the Phoenix Basin, Arizona. *American Antiquity* 74:531–557.

Abbott, David R. (editor)
  2003   *Centuries of Decline during the Hohokam Classic Period at Pueblo Grande.* University of Arizona Press, Tucson.

Abbott, David R., C. D. Breternitz, and C. K. Robinson
  2003   Challenging Conventional Conceptions. In *Centuries of Decline during the Hohokam Classic Period at Pueblo Grande*, edited by David R. Abbott, pp. 3–23. University of Arizona Press, Tucson.

Abbott, David R., and M. S. Foster
  2003   Site Structure, Chronology, and Population. In *Centuries of Decline during the Hohokam Classic Period*, edited by David R. Abbott, pp. 24–47. University of Arizona Press, Tucson.

Abbott, David R., A. M. Smith, and E. Gallaga
  2007   Ball Courts and Ceramics: The Case for Hohokam Marketplaces in the Arizona Desert. *American Antiquity* 72:461–484.

Adams, C.
  2000   Penetrating the Myths. *North American Hunter* 137:80–81.

Ahler, Stanley A.
  1992   Use-Phase Classifications and Manufacturing Technology in Plains Village Arrowpoints. In *Piecing Together the Past: Applications of Refitting Studies in Archaeology*, edited by Jack L. Hoffman and James G. Enloe, pp. 36–62. BAR International Series 578. Archaeopress, Oxford, England.

Anderson, Kirk
  1992   Lithic Raw Material Sources in Arizona. In *Making and Using Stone Artifacts: Lithic Sites in Arizona*, edited by Mark C. Slaughter, Lee Fratt, Kirk Anderson, and Richard V. N. Ahlstrom, pp. 26–36. Archaeological Report No. 92-5. SWCA, Tucson.

Andrefsky, William A.
  1994   Raw-Material Availability and Technology. *American Antiquity* 59:21–34.

  1998   *Lithics: Macroscopic Approaches to Analysis.* Cambridge University Press, Cambridge, England.

Arizona Silhouettes
  1951   *Rudo Ensayo.* Written by an unknown Jesuit padre. Reprint. Arizona Silhouettes, Tucson. Originally published 1863, Buckingham Smith. Translated by Eusebio Guitéras and published in English in the Records of the American Catholic Historical Society, vol. 5, no. 2, Philadelphia, June 1894.

Bahr, Donald M.
  1975   *Pima and Papago Ritual Oratory: A Study of Three Texts.* Indian Historian Press, San Francisco.

1983 Pima and Papago Social Organization. In *Southwest*, edited by Alfonso Ortiz, pp. 178–192. Handbook of North American Indians, vol. 10, William C. Sturtevant, general editor. Smithsonian Institution, Washington, D.C.

2001 *O'odham Creation and Related Events, as Told to Ruth Benedict in 1927 in Prose, Oratory, and Song by the Pimas William Blackwater, Thomas Vanyiko, Clare Ahiel, William Stevens, Oliver Wellington, & Kisto.* Southwest Center Series. University of Arizona Press, Tucson.

2007 O'odham Traditions about the Hohokam. In *The Hohokam Millennium*, edited by Suzanne K. Fish and Paul R. Fish, pp. 123–140. School for Advanced Research Press, Santa Fe.

Bahr, Donald M., Juan Smith, William Smith Allison, and Julian Hayden
1994 *The Short, Swift Time of Gods on Earth: The Hohokam Chronicles.* University of California Press, Berkeley.

Baker, Betty
1973 *At the Center of the World.* Based on Papago and Pima Myths. Macmillan, New York.

Baker, T.
2001 The Causes of Arrow Speed. In *Primitive Technology II: Ancestral Skills*, edited by David Wescott, pp. 107–114. Society of Primitive Technology. Gibbs Smith, Salt Lake City.

Baldwin, Stuart J.
1997 *Apacheans Bearing Gifts: Prehispanic Influence on the Pueblo Indians.* Arizona Archaeologist No. 29. Arizona Archaeological Society, Phoenix.

Bancroft, Hubert H.
1886 *The Native Races of the Pacific States of North America, Vol. I: Wild Tribes.* Hubert H. Bancroft, San Francisco.

Bartlett, John R.
1854 *Personal Narrative of Explorations and Incidents in Texas, New Mexico, California, Sonora, and Chihuahua connected with the United States and Mexican Boundary Commission, during the Years 1840, '51, '52, and '53.* Wagner-Camp Plains and Rockies Series 234. D. Appleton, New York and London.

Barton, C. Michael
1998 Looking back from the World's End: Paleolithic Settlement and Mobility in Gibraltar. In *Las Culturas del Pleistoceno Superior en Andalucia*, edited by Jose L. Sanchidrian Torti and M. D. Simon Vallego, pp. 13–22. Patronato de la Cueva de Nerja. Cordoba, Spain.

Barton, C. Michael, Joan Bernabeu, J. Emili Aura, and Oreto Garcia
1999 Land-Use Dynamics and Socioeconomic Change: An Example from the Polop Alto Valley. *American Antiquity* 64:609–634.

Basso, Keith H. (editor)
2004 *Western Apache Raiding and Warfare.* From the notes of Grenville Goodwin. University of Arizona Press, Tucson.

Baugh, Dick
2001 A Note on Primitive Bow Making, or The Secrets of Sinew Revealed. In *Primitive Technology II: Ancestral Skills*, edited by David Wescott, pp. 117–118. Society of Primitive Technology. Gibbs Smith, Salt Lake City.

Bayham, Frank E., and Pamela Hatch
1985 Hohokam and Salado Animal Utilization in the Tonto Basin. In *Studies of the Hohokam and Salado of the Tonto Basin*, edited by Glen E. Rice, pp. 191–210. Report No. 63. Office of Cultural Resource Management, Department of Anthropology, Arizona State University, Tempe.

Bayham, Frank E., Donald H. Morris, and M. Steven Shackley
1986 *Prehistoric Hunter-Gatherers of South Central Arizona: Picacho Reservoir Archaic Project.* Anthropological Field Studies No. 13. Department of Anthropology, Arizona State University, Tempe.

Bayman, James M.
1994 Craft Production and Political Economy at the Marana Platform Mound Community. Unpublished Ph.D. dissertation, Department of Anthropology, Arizona State University, Tempe.

1995 Rethinking "Redistribution" in the Archaeological Record: Obsidian Exchange at the Marana Platform Mound. *Journal of Anthropological Research* 51:37–63.

2001   The Hohokam of Southwest North America. *Journal of World Prehistory* 15:257–311.

Bayman, James M., and M. Steven Shackley
1999   Dynamics of Hohokam Obsidian Circulation in the North American Southwest. *Antiquity* 73:836–845.

Bergman, Christopher A., and Edward McEwen
1997   Sinew-Reinforced and Composite Bows: Technology, Function, and Social Implications. In *Projectile Technology*, edited by Heidi Knecht, pp. 143–160. Plenum Press, New York.

Bernard-Shaw, Mary
1988   Chipped Stone Artifacts. In *Material Culture*, edited by David R. Abbott, Kim E. Beckwith, Patricia L. Crown, R. Thomas Euler, David A. Gregory, J. Ronald London, Marilyn B. Saul, Larry A. Schwalbe, and Mary Bernard-Shaw, pp. 273–296. The 1982–1984 Excavations at Las Colinas, vol. 4. Archaeological Series 162. Cultural Resource Management Division, Arizona State Museum, University of Arizona, Tucson.

Berry, Claudia F., and William S. Marmaduke
1982   *The Middle Gila Basin: An Archaeological and Historical Overview.* Northland Research, Phoenix.

Bill, Joseph H.
1862   Notes on Arrow Wounds. *American Journal of the Medical Sciences* 44(88):365–387.

1882   Arrow Wounds. In *International Encyclopedia of Surgery: A Systematic Treatise on the Theory and Practice of Surgery by Authors of Various Nations*, edited by John Ashurst, Jr., pp. 103–118. William Wood, New York.

Binford, Lewis R.
1979   Organization and Formation Processes: Looking at Curated Technologies. *Journal of Anthropological Research* 35:255–272.

Blanton, Richard E., Gary M. Feinman, Stephen A. Kowalewski, and Peter N. Peregrine
1996   A Dual-Processual Theory for the Evolution of Mesoamerican Civilization. *Current Anthropology* 37(1):1–14.

Blyth, P. H.
1980   Ballistic Properties in Ancient Egyptian Arrows. Electronic document, http://margo.student.utwente.nl/sagi/artikel/egyptian/egyptian.html, accessed June 6, 2012.

Bolton, H. E. (editor)
1948   *Kino's Historical Memoir of Pimería Alta: A Contemporary Account of the Beginnings of California, Sonora, and Arizona.* From written accounts by Father Eusebio Francisco Kino, S. J. Pioneer Missionary, Explorer, Cartographer, and Ranchman, 1683–1711. University of California Press, Berkeley.

Bonnichsen, B. Robson, and James D. Keyser
1982   Three Small Points: A Cody Complex Problem. *Plains Anthropologist* 27(96):137–144.

Bourke, John G.
1890   Vesper Hours of the Stone Age. *American Anthropologist* A3(1):55–63.

1891   Arrows and Arrow-Makers: Remarks. *American Anthropology* 4:71–74.

1892   The Medicine-Men of the Apache. In *Ninth Annual Report of the Bureau of American Ethnology to the Secretary of the Smithsonian Institution, 1887–88*, by J. W. Powell, pp. 451–596. Smithsonian Institution, Bureau of American Ethnology, U.S. Government Printing Office, Washington, D.C.

Brantingham, P. J.
2003   A Neutral Model of Stone Raw Material Procurement. *American Antiquity* 68:487–509.

2007   A Unified Evolutionary Model of Archaeological Style and Function Based on the Price Equation. *American Antiquity* 72:395–416.

Brew, Susan A., and Bruce B. Huckell
1987   A Protohistoric Piman Burial and a Consideration of Piman Burial Practices. *The Kiva* 52:163–191.

Bronitsky, Gordon
1985   The Protohistoric Pimans of Southeastern Arizona: A Review of History, Archaeology, and Material Culture. In *Southwestern Culture History: Collected Papers in Honor of Albert H. Schroeder*, edited by Charles H. Lange, pp. 139–151. Papers, vol. 10. Archaeological Society of New Mexico and Ancient City Press, Santa Fe.

Bronitsky, Gordon, and James D. Merritt
  1986   *The Archaeology of Southeast Arizona: A Class 1 Cultural Resource Inventory*. Cultural Resource Series No. 2. U.S. Department of the Interior Bureau of Land Management, Arizona State Office, Phoenix.

Brown, David E. (editor)
  1994   *Biotic Communities: Southwestern United States and Northwestern Mexico*. University of Utah Press, Salt Lake City.

Brown, David E., and Charles H. Lowe
  1980   *Biotic Communities of the Southwest*. General Technical Report RM-78 (map). U.S. Forest Service, Rocky Mountain Forest and Range Experiment Station, Fort Collins, Colorado.

Bubemyre, T., M. Brodbeck, and R. B. Neily
  1998   *A Cultural Resources Survey of the Borderlands Area, Gila River Indian Community, Maricopa County, Arizona*. CRMP Technical Report No. 97-23. Cultural Resource Management Program, Gila River Indian Community, Sacaton, Arizona.

Burch, Monte
  2004   *Making Native American Hunting, Fighting, and Survival Tools*. Lyons, Guilford, Connecticut.

Burns, Mike
  1916   Indian Troubles. In *History of Arizona, Vol. III*, by Thomas E. Farish, pp. 286–355. Thomas E. Farish, Phoenix.

Bustoz, D., Glen E. Rice, and C. M. Thomas
  2009   Special Artifacts, Projectile Points, and Bifaces from Los Cremaciones. In *Las Cremaciones: A Hohokam Ball Court Center in the Phoenix Basin*, edited by Glen E. Rice and John L. Czarzasty, pp. 85–122. Occasional Papers No. 6. Pueblo Grande Museum, Phoenix.

Cable, J. S., and David E. Doyel
  1987   Pioneer Period Village Structure and Settlement Pattern in the Phoenix Basin. In *Hohokam Village: Site Structure and Organization*, edited by David E. Doyel, pp. 21–70. Publication No. 87-15. American Association of Science, Southwestern and Rocky Mountain Division, Glenwood Springs, Colorado.

Camp, P.
  1986   *Soil Survey of the Gila River Indian Reservation, Arizona, Parts of Maricopa and Pinal Counties*. Draft. On file, Soil Conservation Service Office, Chandler, Arizona.

Canouts, Veletta, Edward Germeshausen, and Robert Larken
  1972   *Archaeological Survey of the Santa Rosa Wash Project*. Archaeological Series No. 18. Arizona State Museum, University of Arizona, Tucson.

Carr, Christopher
  1995   A Unified Middle-Range Theory of Artifact Design. In *Style, Society, and Person: Archeological and Ethnological Perspectives*, edited by Christopher Carr and Jill Neitzel, pp. 171–258. Plenum Press, New York.

Catlin, George
  1975   *Letter and Notes on the North American Indians*. Gramercy, New York.

Cheshier, Joseph, and Robert L. Kelly
  2006   Projectile Point Shape and Durability: The Effect of Thickness:Length. *American Antiquity* 71:353–363.

Christenson, Andrew L.
  1997   Side-Notched and Unnotched Arrowpoints: Assessing Functional Differences. In *Projectile Technology*, edited by Heidi Knecht, pp. 131–142. Plenum Press, New York.

Ciolek-Torrello, Richard
  1995   The Houghton Road Site, the Agua Caliente Phase, and the Early Formative Period in the Tucson Basin. *Kiva* 60:531–574.

Clark, G. A.
  1989   Romancing the Stones: Biases, Style and Lithics at La Rivera. In *Alternative Approaches to Lithic Analysis*, edited by Donald O. Henry and George H. Odell, pp. 27–50. Archaeological Papers No. 1. American Anthropological Association, Arlington, Virginia.

Clark, Jeffrey J.
  2001   *Tracking Prehistoric Migrations: Pueblo Settlers among the Tonto Basin Hohokam*. Anthropological Papers No. 66. University of Arizona Press, Tucson.

Clark, Jeffrey J., Patrick D. Lyons, J. Brett Hill, Anna A. Neuzil, and William H. Doelle
2008 Immigrants and Population Collapse in the Southern Southwest. In *Archaeology Southwest* 22(2):1–15.

Clark, Tiffany C.
2007 Faunal Remains. In *Results of Testing and Data Recovery, SFPP, LP, East Line Expansion Project, Arizona Portion: Cochise, Pima, Pinal, and Maricopa Counties, Arizona, Final Report, Vol. 2, Chapters 10–22*, edited by John C. Ravesloot, M. Kyle Woodson, and Michael J. Boley, pp. 18.1–18.32. Technical Report No. 2007-04. Draft. William Self Associates, Tucson.

Cottrell, Brian, and Johan Kamminga
1987 The Formation of Flakes. *American Antiquity* 52:675–708.

1992 *Mechanics of Pre-Industrial Technology*. Cambridge University Press, New York.

Coues, Elliott
1866 Some Notes on Arrow Wounds. *Chicago Medical Examiner* 7(1):350–357.

Cozzens, Samuel W.
1874 *The Marvelous Country: Three Years in Arizona and New Mexico, the Apaches' Home*. Sampson Low, Marston, Searle and Rivington, London, England.

Crabtree, D. E.
1973 Experiments in Replications: Hohokam Points. *Tebiwa* 16(1):10–45.

Craig, Douglas B.
1992 Chipped Stone Artifacts. In *Artifacts and Special Analyses*, edited by Mark D. Elson and Douglas B. Craig, pp. 215–248. The Rye Creek Project: Archaeology in the Upper Tonto Basin, vol. 2. Anthropological Papers No. 11. Center for Desert Archaeology, Tucson.

1995 The Timing and Tempo of Architectural Change during the Hohokam Classic Period. In *Canal and Synthetic Studies,* edited by Mark R. Hackbarth, T. Kathleen Henderson, and Douglas B. Craig, pp. 155–172. Archaeology at the Head of the Scottsdale Canal System, vol. 3. Anthropological papers No. 95-1. Northland Research, Tempe.

2004 Beyond Snaketown: Household Inequality and Political Power in Early Hohokam Society. Unpublished Ph.D. dissertation, University of Arizona, Tucson.

Craig, Douglas B., Mark D. Elson, and D. Jacobs
1992 Architectural Variability in the Tonto Basin: A Roosevelt Perspective. In *Proceedings of the Second Salado Conference, Globe, AZ, 1992*, edited by Richard C. Lange and Stephen Germick, pp. 38–49. Occasional Paper. Arizona Archaeological Society, Phoenix.

Cremony, John C.
1868 *Life among the Apaches*. A. Roman, San Francisco.

Crown, Patricia L.
1991 The Hohokam: Current Views of Prehistory and the Regional System. In *Chaco and Hohokam: Prehistoric Regional Systems in the American Southwest*, edited by Patricia L. Crown and W. James Judge, pp. 135–157. School of American Research Press, Santa Fe.

1994 *Ceramics and Ideology: Salado Polychrome Pottery*. University of New Mexico Press, Albuquerque.

Crown, Patricia L., and W. James Judge (editors)
1991 *Chaco and Hohokam: Prehistoric Regional Systems in the American Southwest*. School of American Research Press, Santa Fe.

Curtis, E. S.
1909 Village Tribes of the Desert Lands. *Scribner's Magazine* 45(1).

Cushing, Frank H.
1895 The Arrow. *American Anthropologist* 8(4):307–349.

Darling, J. Andrew
2000 *Obsidian Sourcing Studies, Research Design and Analysis Plan*. P-MIP Technical Report No. 2000-08. Gila River Indian Community, Cultural Resource Management Program, Sacaton, Arizona.

2009 O'odham Trails and the Archaeology of Space. In *Landscapes of Movement: Trails, Paths, and Roads in Anthropological Perspective*, edited by James E. Snead, Clark L. Eickson, and J. Andrew Darling, pp. 61–83. University of Pennsylvania Press, Philadelphia.

2011   S-cuk Kavick: Thoughts on Migratory Processes and the Archaeology of O'odham Migration. In *Rethinking Anthropological Perspectives on Migration*, edited by Graciela S. Cabana and Jeffrey J. Clark, pp. 68–83. University Press of Florida, Gainesville.

Darling, J. Andrew, John C. Ravesloot, and Michael R. Waters.
2004   Village Drift and Riverine Settlement: Modeling Akimel O'odham Land Use. *American Anthropologist* 106(2):282–295.

Dean, Jeffrey S.
1991   Thoughts on Hohokam Chronology. In *Exploring the Hohokam: Prehistoric Desert Peoples of the American Southwest*, edited by George J. Gumerman, pp. 61–149. University of New Mexico Press, Albuquerque.

2000   Complexity Theory and Sociocultural Change in the American Southwest. In *The Way the Wind Blows: Climate, History, and Human Action*, edited by Roderick J. McIntosh, Joseph A. Tainter, and Susan K. McIntosh, pp. 89–118. Columbia University Press, New York.

Dean, Rebecca M.
2003   People, Pests, and Prey: The Emergence of Agricultural Economies in the Desert Southwest. Unpublished Ph.D. dissertation, University of Arizona, Tucson.

2005   Site-Use Intensity, Cultural Modification of the Environment, and the Development of Agricultural Communities in Southern Arizona. *American Antiquity* 70:403–431.

DeJong, David H.
2009   *Stealing the Gila: The Pima Agricultural Economy and Water Deprivation, 1848–1921*. University of Arizona Press, Tucson.

Densmore, Frances
1929   *Papago Music*. Bulletin No. 90. Smithsonian Institution, Bureau of American Ethnology, U.S. Government Printing Office, Washington, D.C.

Dewitt, Calvin
1871   Report of an Arrow-Wound of the Back and Kidney. In *A Report of Surgical Cases Treated in the Army of the United States from 1865 to 1871*, by George A. Otis, p. 154. Circular No. 3. U.S. Surgeon General, U.S. Government Printing Office, Washington, D.C.

Diehl, Michael W.
2003   *The Organization of Resource Use in a Desert Landscape: The Early Agricultural Period in Southern Arizona*. Anthropological Papers No. 34. Center for Desert Archaeology, Tucson.

Di Peso, Charles C.
1951   *The Babocomari Village Site on the Babocomari River, Southeastern Arizona*. Publication No. 5. Amerind Foundation, Dragoon, Arizona.

1953   *The Sobaipuri Indians of the Upper San Pedro River Valley*. Publication No. 6. Amerind Foundation, Dragoon, Arizona.

1974   *The Medio Period*. Casas Grandes, a Fallen Trading Center of the Gran Chichimeca, vol. 2. Series 9. Amerind Foundation, Dragoon, Arizona.

Dobyns, Henry F.
1989   *The Pima-Maricopa*. Chelsea House, New York.

Doelle, William H.
1981   The Gila Pima in the Seventeenth Century. In *The Protohistoric Period in the North American Southwest, A.D. 1450–1700*, edited by David R. Wilcox and W. Bruce Masse, pp. 57–70. Anthropological Research Papers No. 24. Arizona State University, Tempe.

1984   The Tucson Basin during the Protohistoric Period. *The Kiva* 49:195–211.

1995   Tonto Basin Demography in a Regional Perspective. In *The Roosevelt Community Development Study*, edited by Mark D. Elson, Miriam T. Stark, and David A. Gregory, pp. 201–226. Anthropological Papers No. 15. Center for Desert Archaeology, Tucson.

2000   Tonto Basin Demography in a Regional Perspective. In *Salado,* edited by Jeffrey S. Dean, pp. 81–105. New World Studies Series 4. Amerind Foundation, Dragoon, Arizona. University of New Mexico Press, Albuquerque.

Doyel, David E.

1977 *Excavations in the Middle Santa Cruz River Valley, Southeastern Arizona.* Contributions to Highway Salvage Archaeology in Arizona No. 44. Arizona State Museum, University of Arizona, Tucson.

1978 *The Miami Wash Project: Hohokam and Salado in the Globe-Miami Area, Central Arizona.* Contributions to Highway Salvage Archaeology in Arizona No. 52. Arizona State Museum, University of Arizona, Tucson.

1980 Hohokam Social Organization and the Sedentary to Classic Tradition. In *Current Issues in Hohokam Prehistory*, edited by David E. Doyel and Fred Plog, pp. 23–40. Anthropological Research Papers No. 23. Arizona State University, Tempe.

1991 Hohokam Cultural Evolution in the Phoenix Basin. In *Exploring the Hohokam: Prehistoric Desert People of the American Southwest*, edited by George J. Gumerman, pp. 231–278. University of New Mexico Press, Albuquerque.

1993 Interpreting Prehistoric Cultural Diversity in the Arizona Desert. In *Culture and Contact: Charles C. Di Peso's Gran Chichimeca*, edited by Anne I. Woosley and John C. Ravesloot, pp. 39–63. New World Studies Series No. 2. Amerind Foundation, Dragoon, Arizona. University of New Mexico Press, Albuquerque.

Doyel, David E., Suzanne K. Fish, and Paul R. Fish

2000 *The Hohokam Village Revisited.* American Association for Advancement of Science, Southwestern and Rocky Mountain Division, Fort Collins, Colorado.

Eiselt, B. Sunday

2002 *Historic Vernacular Dwellings on the Gila River Indian Community, Arizona.* P-MIP Technical Report No. 2002-11. Gila River Indian Community, Cultural Resource Management Program, Sacaton, Arizona.

Ellis, C. J.

1997 Factors Influencing the Use of Stone Projectile Tips: An Ethnographic Perspective. In *Projectile Technology*, edited by Heidi Knecht, pp. 37–74. Plenum Press, New York.

Elson, Mark D.

1998 *Expanding the View of Hohokam Platform Mounds: An Ethnographic Perspective.* Anthropological Papers No. 63. University of Arizona Press, Tucson.

Elson, Mark D., Suzanne K. Fish, Steven R. James, and Charles H. Miksicek

1995 Prehistoric Subsistence in the Roosevelt Community Development Study Area. In *Paleobotanical and Osteological Analyses*, edited by Mark D. Elson and Jeffrey J. Clark, pp. 217–260. The Roosevelt Community Development Study, vol. 3. Anthropological Papers No. 14. Center for Desert Archaeology, Tucson.

Emory, William H.

1848 *Notes of a Military Reconnaissance from Fort Leavenworth, in Missouri, to San Diego, in California, Including Parts of the Arkansas Del Norte, and Gila Rivers.* 30th U.S. Congress, 1st Session, Senate Executive Document No. 7 (Serial No. 505). Wendell and Van Benthuysen, Washington, D.C.

Ezell, Paul H.

1961 *American Anthropologist: The Hispanic Acculturation of the Gila River Pimas.* Memoir 90. American Anthropological Association, Menasha, Wisconsin.

1963 Is there a Hohokam-Pima Culture Continuum? *American Antiquity* 29:61–66.

1983 History of the Pima. In *Southwest*, edited by Alfonso Ortiz, pp. 149–160. Handbook of North American Indians, vol. 10, William C. Sturtevant, general editor. Smithsonian Institution, Washington, D.C.

1994 Plants without Water: The Pima-Maricopa Experience. *Journal of the Southwest* 36(4):315–392.

Farish, Thomas E.

1916 *History of Arizona, Vol. III.* Thomas E. Farish, Phoenix.

Feinman, Gary M., Kent G. Lightfoot, and Steadman Upham

2000 Political Hierarchies and Organizational Strategies in the Puebloan Southwest. *American Antiquity* 65:449–470.

Ferg, Alan, and Norm Tessman
1997 Two Archival Case Studies in Western Apache and Yavapai Archaeology. In *Overview, Synthesis, and Conclusions*, edited by Stephanie M. Whittlesey, Richard Ciolek-Torrello, and Jeffrey H. Altschul, pp. 215–279. Vanishing River: Landscapes and Lives of the Lower Verde Valley: The Lower Verde Archaeological Project. SRI Press, Tucson.

Fertelmes, Craig M.
2010 *Archaeological Testing and Data Recovery at GR-69, GR-140, and GR-189 for the District One Roads Improvement Project.* CRMP Technical Report No. 2008-07. Cultural Resource Management Program, Gila River Indian Community, Sacaton, Arizona.

Fewkes, Jesse W.
1912 Casa Grande, Arizona. In *Twenty-Eighth Annual Report of the Bureau of American Ethnology to the Secretary of the Smithsonian Institution*, by William H. Holmes, pp. 25–180. Smithsonian Institution, Bureau of American Ethnology, Washington, D.C.

Fish, Paul R.
1989 The Hohokam: 1,000 Years of Prehistory in the Sonoran Desert. In *Dynamics of Southwest Prehistory*, edited by Linda S. Cordell and George J. Gumerman, pp. 19–63. Series in Archaeological Inquiry. Smithsonian Institution Press, Washington, D.C.

Fish, Suzanne K., and Paul R. Fish
1993 *Arizona State Museum Archaeological Site Recording Manual.* Arizona State Museum, University of Arizona, Tucson.

1994 Multisite Communities as Measures of Hohokam Aggregation. In *The Ancient Southwestern Community: Models and Methods for the Study of Prehistoric Social Organization*, edited by Wirt H. Wills and Robert D. Leonard, pp. 119–129. University of New Mexico Press, Albuquerque.

2007 The Hohokam Millennium. In *The Hohokam Millennium*, edited by Suzanne K. Fish and Paul R. Fish, pp. 1–12. School for Advanced Research Press, Santa Fe.

Flenniken, J. Jeffrey, and Anan W. Raymond
1986 Morphological Projectile Point Typology: Replication Experimentation and Technological Analysis. *American Antiquity* 51:603–614.

Fontana, Bernard L.
1975 Introduction to the Re-Edition. In *The Pima Indians,* by Frank Russell, pp. ix–xv. University of Arizona Press, Tucson.

Geneste, Jean-Michele, and Serge Maury
1997 Contributions of Multidisciplinary Experimentation to the Study of Upper Paleolithic Projectile Points. In *Projectile Technology*, edited by Heidi Knecht, pp. 165–189. Plenum Press, New York.

Gifford, Edward W.
1936 *Northeastern and Western Yavapai.* American Archaeology and Ethnology, vol. 34, no. 4. University of California Press, Berkeley.

Gilman, Patricia A.
1987 Architecture as Artifact: Pit Structures and Pueblos in the American Southwest. *American Antiquity* 52:538–564.

Gilpin, Dennis, and David A. Phillips
1998 *The Prehistoric to Historic Transition Period in Arizona, circa A.D. 1519 to 1692: A Component of the Arizona Historic Preservation Plan.* SWCA, Phoenix. Submitted to the Arizona State Historic Preservation Office, Arizona State Parks Board, Phoenix.

Gladwin, Winifred J., and Harold S. Gladwin
1930 *Some Southwestern Pottery Types, Series I.* Medallion Papers No. 8. Gila Pueblo, Globe, Arizona.

Gladwin, Harold S., Emil W. Haury, Edwin B. Sayles, and Nora Gladwin
1937 *Excavations at Snaketown: Material Culture.* Medallion Papers 25. Gila Pueblo, Globe, Arizona.

Goodwin, Grenville
1942 *The Social Organization of the Western Apache.* University of Chicago Press, Chicago.

Goodyear, Albert C.
1989 A Hypothesis for the Use of Cryptocrystalline Raw Materials among Paleoindian Groups of North America. In *Eastern Paleoindian Lithic Resource Use*, edited by Christopher J. Ellis and Jonathan C. Lothrop, pp. 1–9. Westview Press, Boulder.

Govindaraju, K.
1994   1994 Compilation of Working Values and Sample Description for 383 Geostandards. *Geostandards Newsletter* 18 (special issue).

Graybill, Donald A.
1989   Reconstruction of Prehistoric Salt River Streamflow. In *Environment and Subsistence*, edited by Charles H. Miksicek, Donald A. Graybill, Christine R. Szuter, Robert E. Gasser, David A. Gregory, Fred L. Nials, and Suzanne K. Fish, and pp. 25–38. The 1982–1984 Excavations at Las Colinas, vol. 5. Archaeological Series 162. Cultural Resource Management Division, Arizona State Museum, University of Arizona, Tucson.

Graybill, Donald A., David A. Gregory, Gary S. Funkhouser, and Fred L. Nials
2006   Long-Term Streamflow Reconstructions, River Channel Morphology, and Aboriginal Irrigation Systems along the Salt and Gila Rivers. In *Environmental Change and Human Adaptation in the Ancient Southwest*, edited by David E. Doyel and Jeffrey S. Dean, pp. 69–123. University of Utah Press, Salt Lake City.

Grebinger, Paul
1976   Salado: Perspectives from the Middle Santa Cruz Valley. *The Kiva* 42:39–46.

Greenspan, Ruth L.
2001   *Zooarchaeological Studies on the Gila River Indian Community, Arizona*. P-MIP Technical Report No. 2003-01. Cultural Resource Management Program, Gila River Indian Community, Sacaton, Arizona.

Gregory, David A., and Gary Huckleberry
1994   *The History of Human Settlement in the Blackwater Area*. An Archaeological Survey of the Blackwater Area, vol. 1. Cultural Resources Report No. 86. Archaeological Consulting Services, Tempe.

Griffen, William B.
1969   *Culture Change and Shifting Populations in Central Northern Mexico*. Anthropological Papers No. 13. University of Arizona Press, Tucson.

Grossman, F. E.
1873   The Pima Indians of Arizona. In *Annual Report of the Board of Regents of the Smithsonian Institution Showing the Operations, Expenditures, and Condition of the Institution for the Year 1871*, pp. 407–419. Smithsonian Institution Board of Regents, U.S. Government Printing Office, Washington, D.C.

Gumerman, George J. (editor)
1991   *Exploring the Hohokam: Prehistoric Desert Peoples of the American Southwest*. New World Studies Series No. 1. Amerind Foundation, Dragoon, Arizona; U.S. Department of the Interior Bureau of Reclamation; and University of New Mexico Press, Albuquerque.

Hackenberg, Robert A.
1974   *Aboriginal Land Use and Occupancy of the Pima-Maricopa Indians, Vol. II*. American Indian Ethnohistory: Indians of the Southwest. Garland, New York.

1983   Pima and Papago Ecological Adaptations. In *Southwest*, edited by Alfonso Ortiz, pp. 161–177. Handbook of North American Indians, vol. 10, William C. Sturtevant, general editor. Smithsonian Institution, Washington, D.C.

Hall, Sharlot M.
1907   The Story of a Pima Record Rod. In *Out West: A Magazine of the Old Pacific and the New (Formerly the Land of Sunshine)*, edited by Charles F. Lummis and Charles Amadon Moody, pp. 413–423. Out West Magazine Company, Los Angeles.

Hallenbeck, Cleve
1940   *Álvar Núñez Cabeza de Vaca: The Journey and Route of the First European to Cross the Continent of North America, 1534–1536*. Arthur H. Clark, New York.

Hamm, Jim
1991   *Bows and Arrows of the Native Americans: A Complete Step-by-Step Guide to Wooden Bows, Sinew-Backed Bows, Composite Bows, Strings, Arrows & Quivers*. Lyons and Burford, New York.

Harlan, Mark
2009   Protohistoric Arrow Head Variability in the Greater Southwest. Electronic document, http://www.seymourharlan.com/My_Homepage_Files/Page47.html, accessed June 6, 2012.

Harry, Karen G.
    2005   Ceramic Specialization and Agricultural Marginality: Do Ethnographic Models Explain the Development of Specialized Pottery Production in the Prehistoric American Southwest? *American Antiquity* 70:295–319.

Haury, Emil W.
    1950   *The Stratigraphy and Archaeology of Ventana Cave.* University of Arizona Press, Tucson.

    1976   *The Hohokam: Desert Farmers and Craftsmen—Excavations at Snaketown.* University of Arizona Press, Tucson.

Hayes, Benjamin I.
    1976   *Pioneer Notes from the Diaries of Judge Benjamin Hayes, 1849–1875.* Reprint. Arno Press, New York. Originally published 1929, Marjorie T. Wolcott, Los Angeles.

Heath, Hari
    2001   Wood under Stress. In *Primitive Technology II: Ancestral Skills,* edited by David Wescott, pp. 104–106. Society of Primitive Technology. Gibbs Smith, Salt Lake City.

Hegmon, Michelle, Matthew A. Peeples, Ann P. Kinzig, Stephanie Kulow, Cathryn M. Meegan, and Margaret C. Nelson
    2008   Social Transformation and Its Human Costs in the Prehispanic U.S. Southwest. *American Anthropologist* 110(3):313–324.

Hendricks, David M.
    1985   *Arizona Soils.* College of Agriculture, University of Arizona, Tucson.

Herr, Sarah, Chris North, and J. Scott Wood
    2009   Scouting for Apache Archaeology in the Sub-Mogollon Rim Region. *Kiva* 75:35–62.

Hill, J. Brett, Jeffrey J. Clark, William H. Doelle, and Patrick D. Lyons
    2004   Prehistoric Demography in the Southwest: Migration, Coalescence, and Hohokam Population Decline. *American Antiquity* 69:689–716.

Hodder, Ian
    1982   *Symbols in Action: Ethnoarchaeological Studies of Material Culture.* Cambridge University Press, Cambridge, England.

Hodge, Frederick W.
    1895   The Early Navaho and Apache. *American Anthropologist* 8(14):223–240.

    1910   *Handbook of American Indians North of Mexico, Part 2.* Bulletin 30. Smithsonian Institution, Bureau of American Ethnology, U.S. Government Printing Office, Washington, D.C.

Hoffman, Charles M.
    1985   Projectile Point Maintenance and Typology: Assessment with Factor Analysis and Canonical Correlation. In *For Concordance in Archaeological Analysis: Bridging Data Structure, Quantitative Technique, and Theory,* edited by Christopher Carr, pp. 566–612. Waveland Press, Prospect Heights, Illinois.

    1988   Lithic Technology and Lithic Tool Production at Casa Buena. In *Excavations at Casa Buena: Changing Hohokam Land Use along the Squaw Peak Parkway, Vol. 1,* edited by J. B. Howard, pp. 359–458. Publications in Archaeology No. 11. Soil Systems, Phoenix.

    1997   Alliance Formation and Social Interaction during the Sedentary Period: A Stylistic Analysis of Hohokam Arrowpoints. Unpublished Ph.D. dissertation, Arizona State University, Tempe.

Hoffman, Teresa L., and David E. Doyel
    1985   Ground Stone Tool Production in the New River Basin. In *Hohokam Settlement and Economic Systems in the Central New River Drainage, Arizona, Vol. 2,* edited by David E. Doyel and Mark D. Elson, pp. 521–564. Publications in Archaeology No. 4. Soil Systems, Phoenix.

Hoffman, Walter J.
    1878   Miscellaneous Ethnographic Observation on Indians Inhabiting Nevada, California, and Arizona. In *Tenth Annual Report of the United States Geological and Geographical Survey of the Territories Embracing Colorado and Parts of Adjacent Territories, Being a Report of Progress of the Exploration for the Year 1876,* by F. V. Hayden, pp. 461–479. U.S. Government Printing Office, Washington, D.C.

Holmer, Richard N.
1986   Common Projectile Points of the Intermountain West. In *Anthropology of the Desert West: Essays in Honor of Jesse D. Jennings,* edited by Carol J. Condie and Don D. Fowler, pp. 89–115. Anthropological Papers No. 110. University of Utah, Salt Lake City.

Howard, Jerry B.
2000   Quantitative Approaches to Spatial Patterning in the Hohokam Village: Testing the Village Segment Model. In *The Hohokam Village Revisited,* edited by David E. Doyel, Suzanne K. Fish, and Paul R. Fish, pp. 167–196. American Association for Advancement of Science, Southwestern and Rocky Mountain Division, Fort Collins, Colorado.

2006   Hohokam Irrigation Communities: A Study of Internal Structure, External Relationships, and Sociopolitical Complexity. Unpublished Ph.D. dissertation, Arizona State University, Tempe.

Hrdlička, Aleš
1908   *Physiological and Medical Observations among the Indians of Southwestern United States and Northern Mexico.* Bulletin 34. Smithsonian Institution, Bureau of American Ethnology, U.S. Government Printing Office, Washington, D.C.

Huckell, Bruce B.
1984a   *The Archaic Occupation of the Rosemont Area, Northern Santa Rita Mountains, Southeastern Arizona.* Archaeological Series No. 147. Cultural Resource Management Division, Arizona State Museum, University of Arizona, Tucson.

1984b   The Paleo-Indian and Archaic Occupation of the Tucson Basin: An Overview. *The Kiva* 49:133–145.

1995   *Of Marshes and Maize: Preceramic Agricultural Settlements in the Cienega Valley, Southeastern Arizona.* Anthropological Papers No. 59. University of Arizona Press, Tucson.

Ingram, Scott E.
2008   Streamflow and Population Change in the Lower Salt River Valley of Central Arizona, ca. 775–1450. *American Antiquity* 73:136–165.

2010   Human Vulnerability to Climatic Dry Periods in the Prehistoric U.S. Southwest. Unpublished Ph.D. dissertation, Arizona State University, Tempe.

Jacoby, Karl
2008   *Shadows at Dawn: A Borderlands Massacre and the Violence of History.* Penguin, New York.

James, Steven R.
2003   Hunting and Fishing Patterns Leading to Resource Depletion. In *Centuries of Decline during the Hohokam Classic Period at Pueblo Grande,* edited by David R. Abbott, pp. 70–81. University of Arizona Press, Tucson.

Johnson, Gregory A.
1989   Dynamics of Southwestern Prehistory: Far Outside—Looking In. In *Dynamics of Southwest Prehistory,* edited by Linda S. Cordell and George J. Gumerman, pp. 371–389. Series in Archaeological Inquiry. Smithsonian Institution Press, Washington, D.C.

Justice, Noel D.
2002   *Stone Age Spear and Arrow Points of the Southwestern United States.* Indiana University Press, Bloomington.

Keeley, Lawrence H.
1996   *War before Civilization: The Myth of the Peaceful Savage.* Oxford University Press, New York.

Khera, Sigrid, and Patricia S. Mariella
1983   Yavapai. In *Southwest,* edited by Alfonzo Ortiz, pp. 38–54. Handbook of North American Indians, vol. 10, William C. Sturtevant, general editor. Smithsonian Institution, Washington, D.C.

Kintigh, Keith W.
1998   Leadership Strategies in Protohistoric Zuni Towns. Paper presented at the 63rd Annual Meeting of the Society for American Archaeology, Seattle.

Klopsteg, Paul E.
1993   The Physics of Bows and Arrows. In *Physics of Sports,* edited by Angelo Armenti, pp. 9–28. American Institute of Physics, New York.

Knecht, Heidi
1997   Projectile Points of Bone, Antler, and Stone: Experimental Explorations of Manufacture and Use. In *Projectile Technology*, edited by Heidi Knecht, pp. 191–212. Plenum Press, New York.

Kooi, Bote W.
1983   On the Mechanics of the Bow and Arrow. Unpublished Ph.D. dissertation, Mathematisch Instituut, Rijksuniversiteit Groningen, The Netherlands.

Kooyman, Brian P
2000   *Understanding Stone Tools and Archaeological Sites*. University of Calgary Press, Alberta, Canada.

Kozak, David L., and David I. Lopez
1999   *Devil Sickness and Devil Songs*. Smithsonian Institution Press, Washington, D.C.

Kroeber, Clifton B., and Bernard L. Fontana
1986   *Massacre on the Gila—An Account of the Last Major Battle between American Indians, with Reflections on the Origin of War*. University of Arizona Press, Tucson.

Kwiatkowski, Scott M.
2003   Evidence for Subsistence Problems. In *Centuries of Decline during the Hohokam Classic Period at Pueblo Grande*, edited by David R. Abbott, pp. 48–69. University of Arizona Press, Tucson.

Lambert, Marjorie, and J. Richard Ambler
1965   *A Survey and Excavation of Caves in Hidalgo County, New Mexico, 1961*. Monograph 25. School for American Research Press, Santa Fe.

Laubin, Reginald, and Gladys Laubin
1980   *American Indian Archery*. University of Oklahoma Press, Norman.

LeBlanc, Steven A.
1999   *Prehistoric Warfare in the American Southwest*. University of Utah Press, Salt Lake.

2003   *Constant Battles: The Myth of the Peaceful, Noble Savage*. St. Martin's Press, New York.

2006   Warfare and the Development of Social Complexity: Some Demographic and Environmental Factors. In *The Archaeology of Warfare: Prehistories of Raiding and Conquest*, edited by Elizabeth N. Arkush and Mark W. Allen, pp. 437–468. University Press of Florida, Gainesville.

Lekson, Stephen H.
2002   War in the Southwest, War in the World. *American Antiquity* 67:607–624.

Levy, Jerrold E.
1992   *Orayvi Revisited: Social Stratification in an "Egalitarian" Society*. School of American Research Press, Santa Fe.

Lewis, Barnaby V., and Glen E. Rice
2009   On the Terms *Huhugam* and *Hohokam*. In *Las Cremaciones: A Hohokam Ball Court Center in the Phoenix Basin*, edited by Glen E. Rice and John L. Czarzasty, pp. xvii–xix. Occasional Papers No. 6. Pueblo Grande Museum, Phoenix.

Lloyd, J. William
1911   *Aw-Aw-Tam Indian Nights: The Myths and Legends of the Pimas of Arizona*. As Received from Comalk-Hawk-Kih (Thin Buckskin) through the Interpretation of Edward Hubert Wood. Lloyd Group, Westfield, New Jersey.

Loendorf, Chris R.
1996   Burial Practices at the Cline Mesa Sites. In *Salado Residential Settlements on Tonto Creek, Roosevelt Platform Mound Study, Part 2*, by David Jacobs and Ted Oliver, pp. 769–814. Roosevelt Monograph Series 9, Anthropological Field Studies 38. Office of Cultural Resource Management, Department of Anthropology, Arizona State University, Tempe.

1998   Salado Burial Practices and Social Organization. In *A Synthesis of Tonto Basin Prehistory: The Roosevelt Archaeology Studies, 1989 to 1998*, edited by Glen E. Rice, pp. 193–230. Roosevelt Monograph Series 12, Anthropological Field Studies 41. Arizona State University, Tempe.

2001   Salado Burial Practices. In *Ancient Burial Practices in the American Southwest: Archaeology, Physical Anthropology, and Native American Perspectives*, edited by Douglas R. Mitchell and Judy L. Brunson-Hadley, pp. 123–148. University of New Mexico Press, Albuquerque.

2007 Lithics. In *Results of Testing and Data Recovery, SFPP, LP, East Line Expansion Project, Arizona Portion: Cochise, Pima, Pinal, and Maricopa Counties, Vol. 2*, edited by John C. Ravesloot, M. Kyle Woodson, and Michael J. Boley, pp. 12.1–12.35. Technical Report No. 2007-04. Draft. William Self Associates, Tucson.

2008 *Archaeological Testing at Four Proposed Home Sites on Allotted Lands, Gila River Indian Community, Pinal and Maricopa Counties, Arizona: Quarterly Report, October 1, 2006–December 31, 2006.* CRMP Technical Report No. 2008-05. Cultural Resource Management Program, Gila River Indian Community, Sacaton, Arizona.

2010 Regional and Temporal Variation in Obsidian Use within the Hohokam Region. *Journal of Arizona Archaeology* 1(1):47–59.

Loendorf, Chris R., J. Andrew Darling, and M. Steven Shackley
2004 Hohokam Obsidian Procurement and Distribution in the Middle Gila River Valley: A Regional Approach. Paper presented at the Inaugural Symposium of the Archaeological Sciences of the Americas, Tucson.

Loendorf, Chris R., and Glen E. Rice
2004 *Projectile Point Typology, Gila River Indian Community, Arizona.* Anthropological Research Papers No. 2. Cultural Resource Management Program, Gila River Indian Community, Sacaton, Arizona.

Lumholtz, Carl
1912 *New Trails in Mexico: An Account of One Year's Exploration in North-Western Sonora, Mexico, and South-Western Arizona, 1909–1910.* Charles Scribner's Sons, New York.

Mabry, Jonathan B.
1998 *Paleoindian and Archaic Sites in Arizona.* Technical Report No. 97-7. Center for Desert Archaeology, Tucson.

Mails, Thomas E.
1995 *The Mystic Warriors of the Plains: The Culture, Arts, Crafts and Religion of the Plains Indians, Profusely Illustrated.* Marlowe, New York.

Marshall, John T.
2001a Ballcourt. In *Material Culture, Part II: Stone, Shell, and Bone Artifacts and Biological Remains*, edited by Douglas B. Craig, pp. 463–518. The Grewe Archaeological Research Project, vol. 2. Anthropological Papers No. 99-1. Northland Research, Tempe.

2001b Flaked Stone Artifacts. In *Project Background and Feature Descriptions*, edited by Douglas B. Craig. pp. 109–124. The Grewe Archaeological Research Project, vol. 1. Anthropological Papers No. 99-1. Northland Research, Tempe.

2002 Obsidian and the Northern Periphery: Tool Manufacture, Source Distribution, and Patterns of Interaction. In *Phoenix Basin to Perry Mesa: Rethinking the "Northern Periphery,"* edited by Mark R. Hackbarth, Kelly Hays-Gilpin, and Lynn Neal. Arizona Archaeologist No. 34. Arizona Archaeological Society, Phoenix.

Mason, Otis T.
1894 *North American Bows, Arrows, and Quivers.* U.S. Government Printing Office, Washington, D.C.

Masse, W. Bruce
1981 A Reappraisal of Protohistoric Sobaipuri Indians of Southeastern Arizona. In *The Protohistoric Period in the North American Southwest, A.D. 1450–1700*, edited by David R. Wilcox and W. Bruce Masse, pp. 28–56. Department of Anthropology, Arizona State University, Tempe.

Matson, Richard G.
1991 *Origins of Southwestern Agriculture.* University of Arizona Press, Tucson.

Mayewskia, P.A., E. E. Rohlingb, J. C. Stagerc, W. Karle, K. A. Maascha, L. D. Meekere, E. A. Meyersona, F. Gassef, S. van Kreveldg, K. Holmgrend, J. Lee-Thorph, G. Rosqvistd, F. Racki, M. Staubwasserj, R. R. Schneiderk, and E. J. Steigl
2004 Holocene Climate Variability. *Quaternary Research* 62(2004):243–255.

McGee, William J.
1898 Piratical Acculturation. *American Anthropologist* 11(8):243–249.

McGuire, Randall H.
1980 The Mesoamerican Connection in the Southwest. *The Kiva* 49:3–39.

1992   *Death, Society, and Ideology in a Hohokam Community.* Westview Press, Boulder.

McIntosh, Roderick J.
2000   Social Memory in Mande. In *The Way the Wind Blows: Climate, History, and Human Action*, edited by Roderick J. McIntosh, Joseph A. Tainter, and Susan K. McIntosh, pp. 141–180. Columbia University Press, New York.

Meegan, Cathryn M.
2009   Nutritional Stress and the Depopulation of the Lower Salt River Valley Hohokam. Unpublished Ph.D. dissertation, Arizona State University, Tempe.

Mesoudi, Alex, and Michael J. O'Brien
2008   The Cultural Transmission of Great Basin Projectile Point Technology I: An Experimental Simulation. *American Antiquity* 73:3–28.

Mindeleff, Cosmos
1897   Casa Grande: Hohokam Indian Ruins, Arizona. *New England Magazine.* J. N. McClinctock, Boston. Facsimile.

Mitchell, Douglas R., and M. Steven Shackley
1995   Classic Period Hohokam Obsidian Studies in Southern Arizona. *Journal of Field Archaeology* 22(3):291–304.

Montero, L. G.
1993   Chipped Stone. In *Classic Period Occupation on the Santa Cruz Flats: The Santa Cruz Archaeological Project, Part 2*, edited by T. Kathleen Henderson and Richard J. Martynec, pp. 313–362. Northland Research, Flagstaff.

Nabokov, Peter, and Robert Easton
1989   *Native American Architecture.* Oxford University Press, New York.

Neily, R. B., M. Brodbeck, and C. M. Peterson
1999   *A Cultural Resource Survey of the Borderlands-West Area, District 6, Gila River Indian Community, Maricopa County, Arizona.* CRMP Technical Report No. 98-10. Cultural Resource Management Program, Gila River Indian Community, Sacaton, Arizona.

Nelson, Ben A.
1995   Complexity, Hierarchy, and Scale: A Controlled Comparison between Chaco Canyon, New Mexico, and La Quemada, Zacatecas. *American Antiquity* 60:597–618.

Nelson, Margaret C.
1997   Projectile Points: Form, Function, and Design. In *Projectile Technology*, edited by Heidi Knecht, pp. 371–382. Plenum Press, New York.

Noble, David G. (editor)
1991   *The Hohokam: Ancient People of the Desert.* School of American Research Press, Santa Fe.

Odell, George H.
2003   *Lithic Analysis.* Manuals in Archaeological Method, Theory and Technique. Springer, New York.

Oliver, Theodore J.
1997   *Classic Period Settlement in the Uplands of Tonto Basin, Roosevelt Platform Mound Study: Report of the Uplands Complex.* Roosevelt Monograph Series 5, Anthropological Field Studies 34. Office of Cultural Resource Management, Department of Anthropology, Arizona State University, Tempe.

Owens, Mark, Chris R. Loendorf, Vincent Schiavitti, and Lawrence L. Loendorf
2000   *Archaeological Sites Inventory in the Black Hills of the Pinon Canyon Maneuver Site, Las Animas County, Colorado.* Cultural Resource Management Series Contribution No. 4. Directorate of Environmental Management and Compliance, Department of the Army, Fort Carson, Colorado.

Parker, William T.
1912   *Personal Experiences among Our North American Indians from 1867 to 1885.* Northampton, Massachusetts.

Parry, William J., and Robert L. Kelly
1997   Expedient Core Technology and Sedentism. In *The Organization of Core Technology*, edited by Jay K. Johnson and Carol A. Morrow, pp. 285–304. Westview Press, Boulder.

Patterson, Leland W.
1985   Distinguishing between Arrow and Spear Points on the Upper Texas Coast. *Lithic Technology* 14:81–89.

Peterson, Jane, Douglas R. Mitchell, and M. Steven Shackley
1997   The Social and Economic Contexts of Lithic Procurement: Obsidian from Classic-Period Hohokam Sites. *American Antiquity* 62:231–259.

Peterson, Jane D.
1994   Chipped Stone. In *The Pueblo Grande Project: Material Culture*, edited by Michael S. Foster, pp. 49–118. Publications in Archaeology, vol. 4, no. 20. Soil Systems, Phoenix.

Pfaff, Christine
1994   *The San Carlos Irrigation Project: An Historic Overview and Evaluation of Significance, Pinal County, AZ*. U.S. Department of the Interior Bureau of Reclamation, Technical Services Center, Denver.

1996   *The San Carlos Irrigation Project—Photographs: Written Historical and Descriptive Data*. Historic American Engineering Record No. AZ-50. U.S. Department of the Interior National Park Service, Western Region, San Francisco.

Pfefferkorn, Ignaz
1989   *Sonora: A Description of the Province*. Translated and annotated by Theodore E. Treitlein. University of Arizona Press, Tucson.

Pierce, H. Wesley
1985   Introduction—Geologic Framework of Arizona. In *Arizona Soils*, edited by David M. Hendricks, pp. 12–32. College of Agriculture, University of Arizona, Tucson.

Pinter, Teresa L., and Robert J. Stokes
2009   *Settlement History along SR 88/188 from the Globe Highlands to Tonto National Monument, Arizona, Part 1*. Cultural Resources Report No. 141. Archaeological Consulting Services, Tempe.

Pope, Saxton T.
2000   *Hunting with the Bow and Arrow*. Reprint. Joe St. Charles. Originally published 1923, Sylvan Toxophilite Classics.

Preston, Beth
2000   The Functions of Things: A Philosophical Perspective on Material Culture. In *Matter, Materiality and Modern Culture*, edited by Paul M. Graves-Brown, pp. 22–49. Routledge, London.

Randolph, B. G., J. Andrew Darling, Chris R. Loendorf, and B. Rockette
2002   Historic Piman Structure and the Evolution of the Sacate Site (GR-909), Gila River Indian Community. In *Visible Archaeology on the Gila River Indian Reservation*, edited by John C. Ravesloot. P-MIP Report No. 21. Cultural Resource Management Program, Gila River Indian Community, Sacaton, Arizona.

Ratzat, Craig
1999   Atlatls: Throwing for Distance. In *Primitive Technology: A Book of Earth Skills*, edited by David Wescott, pp. 200–201. Society of Primitive Technology. Gibbs Smith, Layton, Utah.

Ravesloot, John C.
2007   Changing Views of Snaketown in a Larger Landscape. In *The Hohokam Millennium*, edited by Suzanne K. Fish and Paul R. Fish, pp. 91–98. School for Advanced Research Press, Santa Fe.

Ravesloot, John C., J. Andrew Darling, and Michael R. Waters
2009   Hohokam and Pima-Maricopa Irrigation Agriculturalists: Maladaptive or Resilient Societies? In *The Archaeology of Environmental Change*, edited by Christopher T. Fisher, J. Brett Hill, and Gary M. Feinman, pp. 232–245. University of Arizona Press, Tucson.

Ravesloot, John C., and Glen E. Rice
2004   The Growth and Consolidation of Settlement Complexes and Irrigation Communities on the Middle Gila. Paper presented for Hohokam Trajectories in World Perspective: An Advanced Seminar, January 27–31, Amerind Foundation, Dragoon, Arizona.

Ravesloot, John C., and Michael R. Waters
2004   Geoarchaeology and Archaeological Sites Patterning on the Middle Gila River, Arizona. *Journal of Field Archaeology* 29(1–2):203–214.

Ravesloot, John C., and Stephanie M. Whittlesey
1987   Inferring the Protohistoric Period in Southern Arizona. In *The Archaeology of the San Xavier Bridge Site (AZ BB:13:14), Tucson Basin, Southern Arizona*, edited by John C. Ravesloot, pp. 81–98. Archaeological Series No. 171. Arizona State Museum, University of Arizona, Tucson.

Rea, Amadeo M.
1998   *Folk Mammalogy of the Northern Pimas*. University of Arizona Press, Tucson.

2007a   The Poorwill in Pima Oral Tradition. *Archaeology Southwest* 21(1):7.

2007b   *Wings in the Desert: A Folk Ornithology of the Northern Pimans*. University of Arizona Press, Tucson.

Redding, B. B.
1879   How Our Ancestors in the Stone Age Made Their Implements. *American Naturalist* 13:667–674.

Redman, Charles L.
1999   *Human Impacts on Ancient Environments*. University of Arizona Press, Tucson.

Redman, Charles L., and Patty Jo Watson
1970   Systematic, Intensive Surface Collection. *American Antiquity* 35:279–291.

Reid, J. Jefferson, and Stephanie M. Whittlesey
1997   *The Archaeology of Ancient Arizona*. University of Arizona Press, Tucson.

Renfrew, Colin
1977   Alternative Models for Exchange and Spatial Distribution. In *Exchange Systems in Prehistory*, edited by Timothy K. Earle and Jonathon E. Ericson, pp. 71–90. Academic Press, New York.

Reynolds, Stephen J.
1985   *Geology of the South Mountains, Central Arizona*. Bulletin No. 195. Arizona Bureau of Geology and Mineral Technology, Geological Survey Branch, University of Arizona, Tucson.

Rice, Glen E.
1998a   Organization of Trade and Craft Production in a Gila Phase Platform Mound Complex. In *A Synthesis of Tonto Basin Prehistory: The Roosevelt Archaeology Studies, 1989 to 1998*, edited by Glen E. Rice, pp. 131–152. Roosevelt Monograph Series 12, Anthropological Field Studies 41. Arizona State University, Tempe.

1998b   War and Water: An Ecological Perspective on Hohokam Irrigation. *Kiva* 63:263–301.

2000   Hohokam and Salado Segmentary Organization: The Evidence from the Roosevelt Platform Mound Study. In *Salado*, edited by Jeffrey S. Dean, pp. 143–166. New World Studies Series 4. Amerind Foundation, Dragoon, Arizona. University of New Mexico Press, Albuquerque.

2003   *A Research Design for the Study of Hohokam Houses and Households*. P-MIP Technical Report No. 2003-05. Cultural Resource Management Program, Gila River Indian Community, Sacaton, Arizona.

Rice, Glen E., and John C. Ravesloot
2003   *The Archaeology of Public Architecture and Settlement Complexes in the Middle Gila Valley*. P-MIP Technical Report 2003-13. Cultural Resource Management Program, Gila River Indian Community, Sacaton, Arizona.

Rice, Glen E., and Arleyn W. Simon
1994   Flaked- and Carved-Stone Artifacts from the Schoolhouse Point Mound, U:8:23/13a. In *The Place of the Storehouses, Roosevelt Platform Mound Study: Report on the Schoolhouse Point Mound, Pinot Creek Complex, Part 2*, edited by Owen Lindauer, pp. 521–548. Roosevelt Monograph Series 6, Anthropological Field Studies 35. Arizona State University, Tempe.

Rice, Glen E., Arleyn W. Simon, and Chris R. Loendorf
1998   Production and Exchange of Economic Goods. In *A Synthesis of Tonto Basin Prehistory: The Roosevelt Archaeology Studies, 1989 to 1998*, edited by Glen E. Rice, pp. 105–130. Roosevelt Monograph Series 12, Anthropological Field Studies 41. Arizona State University, Tempe.

Riel-Salvatore, Julien, and C. Michael Barton
2004   Late Pleistocene Technology, Economic Behavior, and Land-Use Dynamics in Southern Italy. *American Antiquity* 69:257–274.

Roffler, Joshua
2006   Frank Russell at Gila River: Constructing an Ethnographic Description. *Kiva* 71:373–396.

Rosenthal, E. Jane, Douglas R. Brown, Marc Severson, and John B. Clonts
1978   *The Quijotoa Valley Project*. U.S. Department of the Interior National Park Service, Cultural Resources Management Division, Western Archaeological Center, Tucson.

Rozen, Kenneth C.
  1984   Flaked Stone. In *Hohokam Habitation Sites in the Northern Santa Rita Mountains, Vol. 1, Part 1,* by Alan Ferg, Kenneth C. Rozen, William L. Deaver, Martyn D. Tagg, David A. Phillips, Jr., and David A. Gregory, pp. 421–604. Archaeological Series No. 147. Cultural Resource Management Division, Arizona State Museum, University of Arizona, Tucson.

Russell, Frank
  1908   *The Pima Indians.* Twenty-Sixth Annual Report of the Bureau of American Ethnology to the Secretary of the Smithsonian Institution, 1904–1905, pp. 3–389. Smithsonian Institution, Bureau of American Ethnology, U.S. Government Printing Office, Washington, D.C.

Sackett, James R.
  1982   Approaches to Style in Lithic Archaeology. *Journal of Anthropological Archaeology* 1:59–112.

  1985   Style and Ethnicity in the Kalahari: A Reply to Wiessner. *American Antiquity* 50:154–159.

  1986   Style, Function, and Assemblage Variability: A Reply to Binford. *American Antiquity* 51:628–634.

  1990   Style and Ethnicity in Archaeology: The Case for Isochrestism. In *The Uses of Style in Archaeology,* edited by Margaret W. Conkey and Christine A. Hastorf, pp. 32–43. Cambridge University Press, Cambridge, England.

Saxton, Dean, Lucille Saxton, and Susie Enos
  1983   *Dictionary: Tohono O'odham/Pima to English, English to Tohono O'odham.* University of Arizona Press, Tucson.

Sayles, Edwin B.
  1938   Houses. In *Excavations at Snaketown: Material Culture,* by Harold S. Gladwin, Emil W. Haury, Edwin B. Sayles, and Nora Gladwin, pp. 59–92. Medallion Papers No. 25. Gila Pueblo, Globe, Arizona.

Schaafsma, Polly
  2000   *Warrior, Shield, and Star: Imagery and Ideology of Pueblo Warfare.* Western Edge Press, Santa Fe.

Sellers, William D., and Richard H. Hill (editors)
  1974   *Arizona Climate.* University of Arizona Press, Tucson.

Sellers, William D., Richard H. Hill, and Margaret Sanderson-Rae (editors)
  1985   *Arizona Climate: The First Hundred Years.* University of Arizona Press, Tucson.

Seymour, Deni J.
  1993   In Search of the Sobaipuri Pima: Archaeology of the Plain and Subtle. *Archaeology in Tucson* 7(1):1–4.

  2009   Evidence of Protohistoric Mobile Occupants in the Southern Southwest. *Kiva* 74:421–446.

  2011   *Where the Earth and Sky are Sewn Together: Sobaipuri-O'odham Contexts of Contact and Colonialism.* University of Utah Press, Salt Lake City.

Shackley, M. Steven
  1988   Sources of Archaeological Obsidian in the Southwest: An Archaeological, Petrological, and Geochemical Study. *American Antiquity* 53:752–772.

  1990   Early Hunter-Gatherer Procurement Ranges in the Southwest: Evidence from Obsidian Geochemistry and Lithic Technology. Unpublished Ph.D. dissertation, Department of Anthropology, Arizona State University, Tempe.

  1992   The Upper Gila River Gravels as an Archaeological Obsidian Source Region: Implications for Models of Exchange and Interaction. *Geoarchaeology* 7(4):315–326.

  1995   Sources of Archaeological Obsidian in the Greater American Southwest: An Update and Quantitative Analysis. *American Antiquity* 60:531–551.

  2005   *Obsidian: Geology and Archaeology in the North American Southwest.* University of Arizona Press, Tucson.

Shackley, M. Steven, and James M. Bayman
  2001   Obsidian Source Provenance, Projectile Point Morphology and Sacaton Phase Hohokam Cultural Identity. Paper presented in the symposium, A Snaketown Retrospective, 66th Annual Meeting of the Society for American Archaeology, New Orleans.

Shackley, M. Steven, and J. Daehnke
2004   Source Provenance of Obsidian Artifacts from Various Contexts on the Gila River Indian Community Land, Central Arizona. Unpublished report available from Berkeley Archaeological XRF Laboratory, University of California, Berkeley.

Shackley, M. Steven, and David B. Tucker
2001   Limited Prehistoric Procurement of Sand Tank Obsidian. *Kiva* 66:345–374.

Shaul, David L., and Jane H. Hill
1998   Tepimans, Yumans, and Other Hohokam. *American Antiquity* 63:375–396.

Shaw, Anna M.
1994   *A Pima Past*. University of Arizona Press, Tucson.

1995   *Pima Indian Legends*. University of Arizona Press, Tucson.

Shennan, Stephen J.
1990   *Quantifying Archaeology*. Academic Press, San Diego.

Shott, Michael J.
1996   Innovation and Selection in Prehistory: A Case Study from the American Bottom. In *Stone Tools, Theoretical Insights into Human Prehistory*, edited by George H. Odell, pp. 279–309. Plenum Press, New York.

Simon, Arleyn W.
2003   *Ceramic Research Design for the Pima-Maricopa Irrigation Project (P-MIP)*. P-MIP Technical Report No. 2003-15. Cultural Resource Management Program, Gila River Indian Community, Sacaton, Arizona.

Simon, Arleyn W., James H. Burton, and David R. Abbott
1998   Intraregional Connections in the Development and Distribution of Salado Polychromes in Central Arizona. *Journal of Anthropological Research* 54(4):521–550.

Simon, Arleyn W., and Dennis C. Gosser
2001   Conflict and Exchange among the Salado of Tonto Basin: Warfare Motivation or Alleviation? In *Deadly Landscapes: Case Studies in Prehistoric Warfare*, edited by Glen E. Rice and Steven A. LeBlanc, pp. 219–238. University of Utah Press, Salt Lake City.

Sliva, R. Jane
1997   *An Introduction to the Study and Analysis of Flaked Stone Artifacts and Lithic Technology*. Center for Desert Archaeology, Tucson.

1999   Cienega Points and Late Archaic Period Chronology in the Southern Southwest. *Kiva* 64:339–367.

2003   *The Early Agricultural Period in Southern Arizona: Material Culture*. Anthropological Papers No. 35. Center for Desert Archaeology, Tucson.

2006   Projectile Points in Regional Perspective. In *Sunset Crater Archaeology: The History of a Volcanic Landscape: Stone, Shell, Bone, and Mortuary Analyses*, edited by Mark D. Elson, pp. 31–63. Anthropological Papers No. 31. Center for Desert Archaeology, Tucson.

2010   Virtuoso Hohokam Flintknapping in the Gila Bend Region. *Journal of the Southwest* 52:237–253.

Spicer, Edward H.
1962   *The Cycles of Conquest: The Impact of Spain, Mexico, and the United States on the Indians of the Southwest, 1533–1960*. University of Arizona Press, Tucson.

Spier, Leslie
1933   *The Yuman Tribes of the Gila River*. University of Chicago Press, Chicago.

Spotted Eagle, Douglas
1988   *Making Indian Bows and Arrows the Old Way*. Eagle's View, Liberty, Utah.

Stevens, Edward T.
1870   *Flint Chips. A Guide to Pre-Historic Archaeology, as Illustrated by the Collection in the Blackmore Museum, Salisbury*. Bell and Daldy, London.

Szuter, Christine R.
1991   *Hunting by Prehistoric Horticulturists in the American Southwest*. Garland, New York.

Tainter, Joseph A.
1988   *The Collapse of Complex Societies*. Cambridge University Press, Cambridge, England.

Teague, Lynn S.
1984   Role and Ritual in Hohokam Society. In *Synthesis and Conclusions*, edited by Lynn S. Teague and Patricia L. Crown, pp. 155–185. Hohokam Archaeology along the Salt-Gila Aqueduct, Central Arizona Project, vol. 9. Archaeological Series No. 150. Cultural Resource Management Division, Arizona State Museum, University of Arizona, Tucson.

1993   Prehistory and the Traditions of the O'odham and Hopi. *Kiva* 58:435–454.

Thomas, Daniel
1917   Yesterday and Today with the Pimas. *The Southern Workman* 45:503–507.

Thomas, David H.
1978   Arrowheads and Atlatl Darts: How the Stones Got the Shaft. *American Antiquity* 43:461–472.

Upham, Steadman
1983   Aspects of Gila Pima Acculturation. In *Alicia, the History of a Piman Homestead*, edited by Glen E. Rice, Steadman Upham, and Linda Nicholas, pp. 37–59. Anthropological Field Studies No. 4. Office of Cultural Resource Management, Department of Anthropology, Arizona State University, Tempe.

1988   Archaeological Visibility and the Underclass of Southwestern Prehistory. *American Antiquity* 53:245–261.

VanPool, Todd L.
2003   Explaining Changes in Projectile Point Morphology: A Case Study from Ventana Cave. Unpublished Ph.D. dissertation, University of New Mexico, Albuquerque.

Vint, James M.
2005   *An Instance of Violence along Cienega Creek: The Cienega Creek Burials (AZ EE:2:480 [ASM]) and a Study of Protohistoric Projectile Technology in Southeastern Arizona.* Technical Report No. 2005-101. Center for Desert Archaeology, Tucson.

Wallace, Henry D.
1997   Presence of Parlance? The Meaning of "Hohokam" and Concepts of Culture, A.D. 800 to 1050 in Southeastern Arizona. Paper presented at the symposium, The Archaeology of a Land Between: Regional Dynamics in the Prehistory and History of Southeastern Arizona. Amerind Foundation, Dragoon, Arizona.

Wallace, Henry D., James M. Heidke, and William H. Doelle
1995   Hohokam Origins. *Kiva* 60:575–618.

Wasley, W. W., and Alfred E. Johnson
1965   *Salvage Archaeology in the Painted Rocks Reservoir, Western Arizona.* Anthropological Papers No. 9. University of Arizona Press, Tucson.

Waters, Frank
1963   *Book of the Hopi: The First Revelation of the Hopi's Historical and Religious Worldview of Life.* Penguin, New York.

Waters, Michael R.
1996   *Surficial Geologic Map of the Gila River Indian Community.* P-MIP Technical Report No. 96-1. Cultural Resource Management Program, Gila River Indian Community, Sacaton, Arizona.

Waters, Michael R., and John C. Ravesloot
2000   Late Quaternary Geology of the Middle Gila River, Gila River Indian Reservation, Arizona. *Quaternary Research* 45:49–57.

2001   Landscape Change and the Cultural Evolution of the Hohokam along the Middle Gila River and Other River Valleys in South-Central Arizona. *American Antiquity* 66:285–299.

2003   Disaster or Catastrophe: Human Adaptation to High- and Low-Frequency Landscape Processes. *American Antiquity* 68:400–405.

Weaver, Donald E.
1972   A Cultural-Ecological Model for the Classic Hohokam Period in the Lower Salt River Valley, Arizona. *The Kiva* 38:43–52.

Webb, George
1959   *A Pima Remembers*. University of Arizona Press, Tucson.

Wells, E. Christian

2006   *From Hohokam to O'odham: The Protohistoric Occupation of the Middle Gila River Valley, Central Arizona.* Anthropological Research Papers No. 3. Cultural Resource Management Program, Gila River Indian Community, Sacaton, Arizona.

Wells, E. Christian, Chris R. Loendorf, and M. Kyle Woodson

2004   From Hohokam to O'odham: Quantitative Measures for Identifying Protohistoric Ceramic Assemblages in the Middle Gila Valley, Central Arizona. Invited paper prepared for the Arizona Archaeological Council Conference, Faint Traces of Past Places: The Archaeology of High Mobility Groups in Arizona, University of Arizona and the Center for Desert Archaeology, Tucson, October 22–23.

Wells, E. Christian, Glen E. Rice, and John C. Ravesloot

2004   Peopling Landscapes between Villages in the Middle Gila River Valley of Central Arizona. *American Antiquity* 69:627–652.

Whittaker, John C.

1984   *Arrowheads and Artisans: Stone Tool Manufacture and Individual Variation at Grasshopper Pueblo.* Ph.D. dissertation, University of Arizona, Tucson. University Microfilms International, Ann Arbor, Michigan.

1987   Individual Variation as an Approach to Economic Organization: Projectile Points at Grasshopper Pueblo, Arizona. *Journal of Field Archaeology* 14:465–479.

1994   *Flintknapping: Making and Understanding Stone Tools.* University of Texas Press, Austin.

Whittemore, Isaac T.

1898   The Pima Indians, Their Manners and Customs. In *Among the Pimas or the Mission to the Pima and Maricopa Indians,* by Charles H. Cook and Isaac T. Whittemore, pp. 51–136. Ladies Union Social Association, Albany, New York.

Whittlesey, Stephanie M.

1995   Mogollon, Hohokam, and O'otam: Rethinking the Early Formative Period in Southern Arizona. *Kiva* 60:465–480.

Whittlesey, Stephanie M., and Richard Ciolek-Torrello

1996   The Archaic–Formative Transition in the Tucson Basin. In *Early Formative Adaptations in the Southern Southwest*, edited by Barbara J. Roth, pp. 49–64. Monographs in World Archaeology No. 25. Prehistory Press, Madison, Wisconsin.

Whittlesey, Stephanie M., William L. Deaver, and J. Jefferson Reid

1997   Yavapai and Western Apache Archaeology of Central Arizona. In *Overview, Synthesis, and Conclusions,* edited by Stephanie M. Whittlesey, Richard Ciolek-Torrello, and Jeffrey H. Altschul, pp. 185–214. Vanishing River: Landscapes and Lives of the Lower Verde Valley: The Lower Verde Archaeological Project. SRI Press, Tucson.

Wiessner, Polly

1983   Style and Social Information in Kalahari San Projectile Points. *American Antiquity* 48:253–276.

1985   Style or Isochrestic Variation? A Reply to Sackett. *American Antiquity* 50:160–166.

1990   Is There a Unity to Style? In *The Uses of Style in Archaeology,* edited by Margaret W. Conkey and Christine A. Hastorf, pp. 105–112. Cambridge University Press, Cambridge, England.

Wilcox, David R.

1979   The Hohokam Regional System. In *An Archaeological Test of the Sites in the Gila Butte–Santan Region, South-Central Arizona,* edited by Glen E. Rice, David R. Wilcox, Kevin Rafferty, and James Schoenwetter, pp. 77–116. Anthropological Research Papers No. 18. Arizona State University, Tempe.

1991   Hohokam Social Complexity. In *Chaco and Hohokam: Prehistoric Regional Systems in the American Southwest,* edited by Patricia L. Crown and W. James Judge, pp. 253–276. School of American Research Press, Santa Fe.

Wilcox, David R., Thomas R. McGuire, and Charles Sternberg

1981   *Snaketown Revisited: A Partial Cultural Resource Survey, Analysis of Site Structure, and an Ethnohistoric Study of the Proposed Hohokam-Pima National Monument.* Archaeological Series No. 155. Arizona State Museum, University of Arizona, Tucson.

Wilcox, David R., and Charles Sternberg
  1983 *Hohokam Ball Courts and Their Interpretation.* Archaeology Series No. 160. Cultural Resource Management Division, Arizona State Museum, University of Arizona, Tucson.

Wilson, Eldred D.
  1969 *Mineral Deposits of the Gila River Indian Reservation, Arizona.* Bulletin 179. Arizona Bureau of Mines, University of Arizona, Tucson.

Wilson, Eldred D., Richard T. Moore, and John R. Cooper
  1969 *Geological Map of Arizona.* Arizona Bureau of Mines, Tucson, and U.S. Geological Survey, Reston, Virginia.

Wilson, John P.
  forthcoming *Peoples of the Middle Gila: A Documentary History of the Pimas and Maricopas, 1500s–1945.* On file, Cultural Resource Management Program, Gila River Indian Community, Sacaton, Arizona.

Wilson, Thomas
  1899 *Arrowheads, Spearheads, and Knives of Prehistoric Times.* U.S. Government Printing Office, Washington, D.C.

Winship, George
  1896 The Coronado Expedition, 1540–1542. In *U.S. Bureau of American Ethnology Annual Report, 1892–1893,* No. 14, Part 1, pp. 329–615. U.S. Government Printing Office, Washington, D.C.

Winter, Joseph C.
  1973 Cultural Modifications of the Gila Pima: A.D. 1697–A.D. 1846. *Ethnohistory* 20(1):67–77.

Wobst, H. Martin
  1977 Stylistic Behavior and Information Exchange. In *For the Director: Research Essays in Honor of James B. Griffin,* edited by Charles E. Cleland, pp. 317–342. Anthropological Papers No. 61. Museum of Anthropology, University of Michigan, Ann Arbor.

Woodson, M. Kyle
  2010 The Social Organization of Hohokam Irrigation in the Middle Gila River Valley, Arizona. Unpublished Ph.D. dissertation, Arizona State University, Tempe.

Woodson, M. Kyle (editor)
  2003 *Archaeological Investigations at the Sweetwater Site along State Route 587 on the Gila River Indian Community.* P-MIP Technical Report No. 2002-14. Cultural Resource Management Program, Gila River Indian Community, Sacaton, Arizona.

Woodson, M. Kyle, and E. Davis
  2001 *A Cultural Resources Assessment of the Western Half of the Blackwater Management Area, Pima-Maricopa Irrigation Project (P-MIP), Gila River Indian Community, Arizona.* P-MIP Report No. 14. Cultural Resource Management Program, Gila River Indian Community, Sacaton, Arizona.